THE ADVANCE OF DEMOCRACY

THE INTERPRETATIONS OF AMERICAN HISTORY

★ ★ ★ JOHN HIGHAM AND BRADFORD PERKINS, EDITORS

Joseph C. Ellis

THE ADVANCE OF DEMOCRACY

EDITED BY
J. R. POLE

*Reader in American History and Government
in the University of Cambridge and
Fellow of Churchill College*

HARPER & ROW, PUBLISHERS
NEW YORK, EVANSTON, AND LONDON

THE ADVANCE OF DEMOCRACY
Copyright © 1967 by J. R. Pole
Printed in the United States of America. All rights reserved. No part of this book
may be used or reproduced in any manner whatsoever without written permission
except in the case of brief quotations embodied in critical articles and reviews. For
information address Harper & Row, Publishers, Incorporated, 49 East 33rd Street,
New York, N.Y. 10016.

Library of Congress Catalog Card Number: 67-21576

CONTENTS

EDITORS' INTRODUCTION

This volume—and companions in the series, "Interpretations of American History"—makes a special effort to cope with one of the basic dilemmas confronting every student of history. On the one hand, historical knowledge shares a characteristic common to all appraisals of human affairs. It is partial and selective. It picks out some features and facts of a situation while ignoring others that may be equally pertinent. The more selective an interpretation is, the more memorable and widely applicable it can be. On the other hand, history has to provide what nothing else does: a total estimate, a multifaceted synthesis, of man's experience in particular times and places. To study history, therefore, is to strive simultaneously for a clear, selective focus and for an integrated, overall view.

In that spirit, each book of the series aims to resolve the varied literature on a major topic or event into a meaningful whole. One interpretation, we believe, does not deserve as much of a student's attention as another simply because they are in conflict. Instead of contriving a balance between opposing views, or choosing polemical material simply to create an appearance of controversy, Mr. Pole has exercised his own judgment on the relative importance of different aspects or interpretations of a problem. We have asked him to select some of what he considers the best, most persuasive writings bearing on the advance of democracy, indicating in the introductory essay and headnotes his reasons for considering these accounts convincing or significant. When appropriate, he has also brought out the relation between older and more recent approaches to the subject. The editor's own competence and experience in the field enable him to provide a sense of order and to indicate the evolution and complexity of interpretations. He is, then, like other editors in this series, an informed participant rather than a mere observer, a student sharing with other students the results of his own investigations of the literature on a crucial phase of American development.

JOHN HIGHAM
BRADFORD PERKINS

vii

INTRODUCTION:
AMERICAN HISTORIANS
AND THE DEMOCRATIC PROCESS

After the election of Andrew Jackson in 1828, it was easy to see the advance of democracy in the United States as the inevitable consequence of all previous American history. Within a few years of that election, politics developed certain procedures and characteristics which run directly into modern times. The most influential of these was the formation of parties which maintained a permanent and a partly professional organization, which held nominating conventions increasingly on a national basis, and which made claims on the emotional loyalties of a far wider range of people than they could hope to reward from the spoils of power. These spoils were a further recognized attribute of the arrival of a permanent system of party politics. Jackson did not initiate the practice of appointing his followers to public office, but his followers did much to establish it on a systematic basis and to give it the benefits of doctrinal support. All of these developments had precedents, and all had roots, both in federal and in state politics going back thirty years or more; yet in Jackson's time they gained so much that was new, both in moral force and in institutional form, that people believed they lived in the presence of a revolution.

Looking back and trying to explain these events, we are bound to see them as representing the outcome of forces that had long been pushing

I

their way up in American life, some already present during the American Revolution. Yet hardly any of the men of that earlier era could have anticipated the features of Jacksonian politics, and very few would have approved of them if they had. The problem confronting historians has, therefore, not been that of tracing a simple continuity of events to their inevitable—and inevitably happy—outcome in the flowering of pure democracy; it has been very much more complicated, and has never received a completely satisfactory synthetic treatment.

The organization of American historical writing has not tended to elucidate the problem. Specialists generally write about their own periods, and pick up from other specialists the threads of continuity they need to begin with; historians of the nineteenth century have not usually concerned themselves with a detailed examination of the social structure or political beliefs of the revolutionary era. Yet the leaders of the North American colonies represented a profoundly different society from that of their successors half a century later, a society that did not regard itself as democratic and showed comparatively little interest in or respect for what would later be regarded as normal democratic principles. Since George Bancroft, himself a dedicated Jacksonian Democrat, composed his lengthy (and still highly readable) *History of the United States* (1879), American historians have tended to take the development of democracy as the fulfilment of an original national purpose; and this purpose is seen to have been inherent in the American Revolution. According to the line of historiography that concerned itself chiefly with the growth of institutions, and which is almost as powerful today as it was at the beginning of this century, American history seems to emerge as an advanced case of Whig history.

But what is "Whig" history? The Whig interpretation[1] had been developed in England to explain, but also to justify, the overthrow of the Stuart monarchy. It was history told from the point of view of Parliament against the king—or, more fully, against Charles I and James II—in which one side was right and the other side was wrong. Thus Whig history was English history. But it gained enormous strength when it was extended to America, because the explanation that it offered for the American Revolution agreed with the reasons given by the colonial leaders themselves, and was endorsed by influential British historians. The main application of this view was to explain the American Revolution as a revolt against the systematic program implemented, on the instigation of King George III, for the purpose of bringing the American

[1] For an acute critique, see Herbert Butterfield, *The Whig Interpretation of History* (London, 1931; reprinted, 1951).

colonies under discipline and control.[2] Government in the colonies was in fact more popular, more subject to the feelings of a wider electorate than in Britain, so that historians had much valid material with which to argue that the conditions of American life predisposed the colonists to resist such a program as well as to prejudice British officials against them.

Colonial assemblies, which deliberately claimed the rights and adopted the procedures of the British House of Commons, saw themselves as carrying on a struggle against the royal (or proprietary) governors analagous to that of Parliament in the seventeenth century against the king. So that when a tyrannical king, with the British Parliament ranged on his side, tried to impose taxation and other types of arbitrary rule on colonists who were unrepresented in the British Parliament, the whole process fell naturally into place as an extension, on the imperial scale, of the struggle for British liberties which had once been so honorably known as "the Good Old Cause."

The purposes of the present volume do not extend to an examination of the causes of the American Revolution, but they do include its consequences. For independence not merely gave Americans the opportunity, but also the necessity to declare their intentions as to their methods and principles of self-government. But this challenge did not find the colonists ready with radically new plans for remodeling their own institutions; their leading spokesmen had given much attention to the rights and wrongs of the quarrel with Britain but not much thought to the basic institutions of their own domestic politics. There existed a number of scattered areas of discontent, some of it directed against exploitation by landlords, and some against domination by highly unrepresentative assemblies, but there was no such thing as a coordinated movement for reform within the colonies. And where signs of such opposition appeared, as in New York, they were apt to encounter the resistance of those very leaders who were conducting the colonial case in the argument with Britain.

Since the French Revolution, historians have grown accustomed to looking for plans and theories underlying major upheavals. But the colonists were working on the basis of experience rather than of theory, and the theory that mattered to them was a rather attenuated and colonialized version of the English Constitution; the Whig interpretation has always been right in holding that the primary motive of the colonial resistance was defensive and their constitutional doctrine conservative. It

---

[2] George Bancroft, *History of the United States*, 6 vol. (Boston, 1879); Sir George Otto Trevelyan, *The American Revolutuion*, 3 vol. (London, 1889–1903).

was consistent with this standpoint that when they came to make their own state constitutions, they proved themselves content with resounding declarations of human rights and equality but linked them to political institutions that placed a far-reaching variety of restrictions on the equal exercise of those rights.

What, then, was the existing nature of colonial institutions? The question has been tackled with great courage and with single-minded research by Professor Robert E. Brown and his wife, B. Katherine Brown.[3] They have established that the suffrage franchise was widespread in the late colonial period, that moderate amounts of property were widely distributed, and that public life was decidedly more democratic than was formerly supposed. But these findings do not prove the existence of democracy before the Revolution, and in a sense they make the problem more complicated. For the political opinions of the acknowledged leaders throughout most of the colonies, translated into specific institutional form in the new state constitutions and backed up by numerous public pronouncements, certainly did not imply faith in the direct rule of the mass of the people. What Professor and Mrs. Brown have done is to draw very accurately one indispensable line in a figure; but the figure when complete is many-sided, and its completion involves an understanding of both political ideas and social attitudes.

The effort of Professor Brown to establish that America was democratic even before the Revolution represents a somewhat new form of old Whig history. It says, in effect, not only that the colonists were defending their constitutional rights against British encroachments but, further, that those "rights" meant "democracy" in a fully modern sense of the word and that colonial institutions were good enough to make them safe. From this position one may assume that very little further development could be expected, either in theory or in concrete political reform.

Every history of American democracy must take account of the ringing preamble to the Declaration of Independence.[4] Seeing this as a starting point, older works which carried "Whig" history over into America took the view that American government, at the time of Independence and the drafting of the first state constitutions, had achieved what may be called a condition of "imperfectly realized democracy."[5] Thus the Revolution

[3] Robert E. Brown, *Middle-Class Democracy and the Revolution in Massachusetts* (Ithaca, N.Y., 1955); Robert E. Brown and B. Katherine Brown, *Virginia 1705–1776: Aristocracy or Democracy?* (East Lansing, Mich., 1964).

[4] For a fascinating study, see Carl L. Becker, *The Declaration of Independence* (New York, 1922; reprinted, 1958).

[5] Professor Brown, when he recognizes imperfections in the Massachusetts constitution of 1780, comes significantly close to restating this view. *Middle-Class Democracy*, p. 402.

seemed to have made useful progress toward the attainment of true democracy but had left the work incomplete. A second great wave of reform arose about the figure of Thomas Jefferson and crashed down on the Federalist structure in the Presidential election of 1800, sweeping away much that remained of aristocratic power; but new forms of privilege arose while some old ones remained, and the work was not complete until after Jackson's election in 1828, which carried popular power further forward in a period when fully democratic government was extended through constitutional reform in most of the states where such progress had not already been made. This view might be summarized by saying that Jackson's administration was "the completion of the unfinished business of the Revolution."[6]

This view of American democracy as coming in three separate waves has certain merits which cannot be lightly overlooked. In the first place it is clear, and does offer an account of events which are of major importance from any view. This theory recognizes the differences between the eighteenth- and nineteenth-century American social orders and accepts that political development was related to changes in the social order; and it recognizes the advance of democratic government as a theme of central significance. It is typically Whig, in the older English sense, and typically American, in its sense of direction. The history that matters is not seen merely as the history of change, but as that of progress towards certain desirable ends.

One consequence of this attitude is that, as the story approaches modern institutions, the historian becomes less and less critical. Historians who are not particularly sympathetic to Jacksonian democracy point out that it deprived Negroes of rights and Indians of land they had enjoyed before; they add that opponents of reform during that period did more to defend the rights of minorities than the Jacksonian democrats.[7] Another consequence is that earlier institutions tend to be seen not so much for what they were in the context of their own time, but rather as temporary expedients and often as impediments to further progress. From this point of view the institutions of the eighteenth century appear at best as imperfect forms of what nineteenth-century democracy achieved.

What this view fails to encompass is that earlier institutions were ex-

---

[6] The division of American historical series by period and subject has sometimes implied the adoption of this view. See, for example, William MacDonald, *Jacksonian Democracy, 1829–1837* (New York, 1906) in the first of the American Nation series; and Carl Russell Fish, *The Rise of the Common Man, 1830–1850* (New York, 1927) in *A History of American Life*. Jacksonian spokesmen could see their cause in much the same light; see Joseph L. Blau, *Social Theories of Jacksonian Democracy* (Indianapolis, 1954), p. 155–56.

[7] Samuel Eliot Morison, *The Oxford History of the American People* (London and New York, 1965) chap. xxvi, xxvii.

pressions of a different social order and embodied different ideas about political relationships. It leads to a common mistake about the objects of earlier political movements, for it assumes that reformers in past eras, who were dissatisfied with some aspect of their lives, must have been aiming to achieve remedies that would lead to modern democracy. It assumes that they must somehow have sought modern democracy as their own ultimate objective.

To adopt this standpoint is to show a disregard for the fullness and complexity of eighteenth-century minds and to inculcate a disrespect for the meaning of their experience. For example, the preamble to the Declaration of Independence is by no means self-explanatory and must have meant different things to different subscribers, while to many contemporaries it probably meant very little; but people in later generations, bent on specific objects, have often said, "We know exactly what the Declaration meant, and any other reading is false." Clearly, the words of the Declaration give aid and comfort to equalitarian and democratic principles and state strong views about the equality of individual rights; yet just as clearly, persons who did not hold such views found they could subscribe to the Declaration as a statement of American colonial claims against Britain.

In trying to understand the advance of democracy in America the historian is obliged first to soak himself in the meanings that contemporaries could have attached to those ideas of rights, and then to discover why—and how far—the more "modern" implications did in fact eventually supersede the others. That they have not completely done so is only too obvious.

Most political leaders in the Revolutionary era would have been horrified by much that is taken for granted in modern democratic and industrial society. They particularly disapproved of organized political parties; they believed as firmly in the rights of property as of individuals, and consequently, their theories of political representation usually held that property should have specific safeguards in the laws of elections. They had for the most part little conception of racial equality, and many had serious reservations about religious toleration. Many of them would have been dismayed by the fierce economic competitiveness, the urge for quick wealth, that had already become a leading feature of America before the time of Jackson.

Another significant difference between the attitudes of the Jacksonian era and that of the Revolutionary period concerned the individual and his relationship to authority. The emphasis of Revolutionary politics on equality of rights, together with certain prevalent ideas about the virtue of republican simplicity, brought out a new questioning of the weight of tradition and family connections. Yet such ties still had enormous influence. Plain people might vote freely to choose their rulers, but they nearly always voted for their social and economic superiors.

Walter Bagehot, in writing on the British constitution in the middle of the Victorian era, described England as a "deferential" nation,[8] and the same description helps to explain the attitudes which shaped American politics before the rise of the more modern style of equalitarian democracy. There was a large amount of a somewhat genial corruption in colonial elections, which went on merrily despite the purer air of republican independence, but there is relatively little evidence of force or intimidation at elections either before or after the Revolution. Votes were given freely, but even so, they were given within distinct social limits. Americans inherited, and in some states they long retained, an enormous respect for family names and traditional leadership. Dr. Jack P. Greene[9] has recently demonstrated with a wealth of new evidence the hold on legislative leadership exercised by a small number of families in the southern colonies, while as long ago as 1787, John Adams made the same point on the basis of local experience in New England.[10]

This deference, challenged as it was by some articles of republican doctrine, was not entirely unearned. Inherited renown had to be maintained by merit and by an interest in public affairs consistent with social rank. Many eighteenth-century Americans were frugal, most were hardworking, and they would not have been content to be ruled by mere opulence, any more than they would have accepted the spoils system or have tolerated any organized political party. The coming of democratic politics represented much more than the reform of laws on eligibility to office, or the extension of the suffrage. It meant an upheaval—and in the fuller sense, a revolution—in the life and mind of American society. The essays presented in this volume are intended to explain this momentous transformation, and they have been grouped to follow various avenues of development.

One of the needs met by earlier historical writing was to establish the course of political history, both state and federal. The dimension of economic interpretation was added when Charles Beard published his views on the motives and interests of the makers of the Constitution and later of the Jeffersonian Republicans;[11] although his influence has nar-

[8] Walter Bagehot, *The English Constitution* (London, 1867; new ed., Intro. by R.H.S. Crossman, London, 1964), p. 247–251.

[9] Jack P. Greene. *The Quest for Powers: The Lower Houses of Assembly in The Southern Royal Colonies, 1639–1776* (Chapel Hill, 1963), esp. chap. 2.

[10] John Adams, *Defence of the Constitutions . . . of the United States,* 3 vol., (Philadelphia, 1797) I, p. 110–111.

[11] Charles A. Beard, *An Economic Interpretation of the Constitution of the United States* (New York, 1913); *The Economic Origins of Jeffersonian Democracy* (New York, 1915).

rowed and in some ways has prejudiced the discussion, the importance of these elements can never again be ignored. But more recent work, conducted perhaps with more patience, has done much to deepen the available knowledge of the social conditions underlying political change. Professor Chilton Williamson's careful analysis of the suffrage makes clear the influence of the Revolution itself in helping to bring suffrage extension, while Professor Jackson Turner Main's thorough study of social structure establishes the context of these changes.[12] A brilliant interpretation of the transforming effects of revolutionary republican thought has been contributed by Professor Bernard Bailyn in his Introduction to *Pamphlets of the American Revolution.*[13]

When American political parties arose in the 1790s, out of the tense domestic and foreign policy questions of the time, they did so in the face of a prevalent disapproval of political organization, which was widely held to interfere with electoral freedom. Great advances have been made in the study both of the origins of parties and their influence on the ensuing character of politics. An earlier tendency to dramatize the struggle as being a personal feud between Alexander Hamilton and Thomas Jefferson, and to explain Jefferson's movement as being a kind of resumption of the interrupted Revolutionary democracy, has given way to greater sophistication. One of the more interesting discoveries of this recent research is that the central organization, principally in the early Congresses themselves, had the most influence on party development. The Democratic-Republican societies, which sprang up spontaneously in the early 1790s, and which undoubtedly exerted some influence on a variety of localities, do not seem to have had any direct connection with the emergent Jeffersonian group in Congress.

From Congress the lines ran back to the election districts. As divisions over issues of policy hardened around the leading personalities, so party rivalry became intense. The preparations for the election of 1800 stirred numerous citizens into action and stimulated a keen sense of the power of the vote. All this activity resulted in a very big practical extension of the exercise of the suffrage and very naturally excited demands for its further extension by constitutional right. Professor Williamson has traced the course of this gradual and somewhat haphazard process in the various states, while Professor Noble E. Cunningham's studies of the Jeffersonian

[12] Chilton Williamson, *American Suffrage from Property to Democracy* (Princeton, 1960). Jackson Turner Main, *The Social Structure of Revolutionary America* (Princeton, 1966).

[13] Bernard Bailyn, ed., *Pamphlets of the American Revolution,* Vol. I (Cambridge, Mass., 1965). Reprinted separately as, *The Ideological Origins of the American Revolution* (Cambridge, Mass., 1967).

party[14] have revealed the part played by central direction and organization. The great problem has always been to relate different state and regional developments, often proceeding at different speeds and not always in precisely the same direction. These recent studies of institutions, of social structure, and of political parties have gone far to advance our understanding of the eighteenth century and to give us a basis for the development of democracy; they represent a high degree of scholarly competence, and the best of them avoid the simplicities sometimes found in the more powerful of the earlier works which attribute complex events to single causes.

The most influential of all these earlier works was Frederick Jackson Turner's famous essay, "The Frontier in American History" (1893), followed up by a series of limited studies of the frontier in various sections. Turner treated democracy as the fundamental American institution and attributed it to the presence of a constantly receding frontier of free land. It was all very exhilarating, particularly because Turner wrote like an epic poet, and because his thesis, which had an engaging simplicity, appealed to American nationalist pride by rejecting all debts to European influence. Turner put a generation of students to work on the details of frontier history, but he also succeeded, like Beard, in arousing potent animosities. He had failed to explain how the influence of the frontier of free land (itself a vague and partly misleading expression) had translated itself into the specific institutional forms of democracy; and while economic historians debated the question of whether the frontier operated as a "safety valve" against explosive labor unrest, others challenged Turner's methods, his perspective, and his rhetoric.

Yet Turner had drawn attention to a dimension of the experience of settlement that could never again be wholly ignored. In America the traditional land hunger of Europe could be easily satisfied, bringing into existence a society of freehold farmers whose properties alone qualified them as participants in the politics of their country. Yet the frontier was not a region of innovation, and most new state constitutions were in large measure imitative rather than inventive; while the Ohio Valley was settled in the early nineteenth century, state constitutions new and old reflected the pressure for democratic advances. The steam is dying out of the fierce controversies about the role of the frontier, and modern scholarship examines the relationships between natural resources and political institutions with a more dispassionate eye than in earlier days. The history of city development in new areas of settlement has also been

---

[14] Noble E. Cunningham, *The Jeffersonian Republicans* (Chapel Hill, 1957); *The Jeffersonian Republicans in Power* (Chapel Hill, 1963).

opened up by Professor Richard C. Wade,[15] whose work reminds us that the city rather than the farm tends to be the center of economic development and of the corresponding nexus of political influence.

Turner's influence, at some distance now, can still be discerned in the works of Professor Daniel J. Boorstin.[16] But these books are too learned and too subtle to be attributed to any one "influence," and they give an account not only of the rise of democracy but of what was peculiarly American in American institutions.

Boorstin, better than perhaps any of his contemporaries, conveys a vivid sense of what life was like for the ordinary person. If one follows his method through local history and through local economic enterprise, one is led inevitably into that vein of social history which is the substratum for the political historian but the stuff of life for most people, most of the time. At this level, the reader comes up against the irresistible force of the rising popular element in politics during and after the War of 1812.

It is here that the interests developed by historians in recent years give not only more detailed information than was advanced by Turner and his immediate followers, but help to explain the democratic phenomenon in its social context. Turner was plainly open to criticism on grounds of method; but criticism of his method, though it weakened his specific hypothesis, did not get the discussion much further; there was need for research into regional and state history.

One team of historians, led by Professor Merle Curti, has investigated the development of a single community in Wisconsin;[17] Professor Charles Sellers has dug deeply into the connections between business, banking, and political management in Jackson's Tennessee and has shown, in his biography of James K. Polk,[18] that the demands for alleviation of local economic distress gave the impetus, at the state level, to the new wave of "democratic" reform. Many of the tools for this movement had already been forged. A wide suffrage existed, and the remaining restrictions could not exclude any class of people who would clearly range themselves on one side or another and tip the balance of an election. The problem was rather to break down the habits of deference, the apathetic tendency to leave politics to the managers, and to instill into the ordinary citizen the feeling that his vote could affect his fortunes. This was the work of those local politicians whose activities revitalized state politics long before the movement for Jackson reached presidential proportions. But for some

[15] *The Urban Frontier* (Cambridge, Mass., 1959).

[16] Daniel J. Boorstin, *The Americans: The Colonial Experience* (New York, 1958) and *The National Experience* (1965).

[17] Merle Curti, *The Making of An American Community* (Stanford, 1959).

[18] Charles G. Sellers, Jr., *James K. Polk, Jacksonian* (Princeton, 1957).

reason, Jackson himself—as a figure, as a symbol—succeeded in catching the people's imagination as none of his predecessors had; and he gave to many different voters, with varied hopes and grievances, a distinctly personal feeling that he could speak for them, that he could personify their feelings, as no other President had ever done. American democracy would have come into being if Jackson had never existed, but it is more than mere tautology to say that the "Jacksonian" movement would not.

This movement grew out of a social and economic texture that was increasingly equalitarian, while at the same time it was keenly and often cruelly competitive. Some of the most important of the recent research has been that of Professor Lee Benson, whose study of New York State[19] has broken the components of political society down into groups that have little bearing on the larger and more "ideological" themes of Jacksonian politics. Professor Richard P. McCormick endorses Benson in holding that deep issues of principle have very little to do with the realities of political struggle, even of divisions between parties.[20] Genuine differences of opinion did exist, of course, and so did the most acute conflicts of interest, but parties sought to cater for and offered to represent as many interests as they could hold. Consistently with this reasoning, McCormick has shown that extensions of the suffrage did not lead to profound upheavals in legislative policies.

These vast changes were not in any direct sense the intended consequences of the American Revolution. The effect of the Revolution was permissive; but equally, it was of decisive importance.

After independence, there is no single keynote, there is no one line to follow. Americans were offered a new variety of choices, some resettling in new territories, some opening up overseas trade, many developing new technical skills, some advancing their fortunes, and others failing or standing still.

Not all the aspects of this ferment are adequately covered in the selections that follow, because the issues themselves have been very unevenly covered by historians. Although much of the enterprise of Americans must be classified as economic, comparatively little study has been made of the connections between local economic activity and politics. The issues come to light from time to time and have to be disentangled from the general welter of political history. The cities threw up an advanced form of participation in politics but, with one or two valuable exceptions,[21] we

[19] Lee Benson, *The Concept of Jacksonian Democracy* (Princeton, 1961).

[20] Richard P. McCormick, *The Second American Party System* (New Brunswick, 1966).

[21] For example, Carl and Jessica Bridenbaugh, *Rebels and Gentlemen: Philadelphia in the Age of Franklin* (Philadelphia, 1940).

have little guidance on the relationship of city life to democratic growth. Yet the city was the true seedbed of democratic politics in America; there political organization began, newspapers and pamphlets flourished, and voters swarmed to the polls. The countryside followed at a more quiet and gentle pace.

While this outflow of variously directed energies drove Americans forward, democratic institutions seemed not so much an end in themselves as the political instrument most suited to the kind of economic and social life Americans wanted to live. These activities went on at the pace dictated by the energy of the people themselves, by the capital available, and by the obstacles to overcome; but Americans were free of the deadening restraints of obsolete customs or entrenched privilege. They were under no single, unified control, no central program, and not even one unified code of law. Law could be changed; rules could be remolded. American democracy sprang from all these sources and thrived in an absence of restraint.

THE PREVIOUS CONDITIONS
OF DEMOCRACY IN AMERICA

By the middle of the eighteenth century the British colonies in North America and the West Indies lay on the fringes of a very complicated structure of old-world power politics. They were instruments of British policy; but having grown under the protection of British commercial and naval power, their institutions had developed a very marked independence. Just as the British Parliament put British interests first, so colonial assemblies put colonial interests first. In doing so, they were applying British principles and methods of government to their own problems—they were serving as representatives of their own people. These assemblies were outgrowths of ancient forms, which had themselves been the center of civil conflict in seventeenth-century England. Yet American experience was gained under American conditions—and the ages of history, the accumulated powers and customs, that kept English society in order but yielded so slowly to change—these things lay very lightly on American shoulders. Conditions were favorable for self-government, and within that self-government they also favored experiment, local initiative, and diffused responsibility.

Professor Louis Hartz is the leading proponent of a very direct and persuasive thesis which accounts for the advance of democracy under American conditions.[1] He has argued, in effect, that the basic "liberal" character of the English institutions exported to America accounted for their subsequent ad-

[1] Louis Hartz, *The Liberal Tradition in America* (New York, 1955).

vance to full democracy. No aristocratic order, no feudal heritage, no privileged landowning church lay across the path of popular government. Given the strength of the initial impulse, and the absence of obstacles, republican government was bound to take root. Professor Hartz has further developed a more general theory that in the founding of new societies, the decisive influence is that of the prevalent institutional practices of the founding group, the fragment torn off from the mother country, which subsequently develops, not as the mother country does, but according to interior laws. Thus, the English founders of the American colonies did not represent and did not reproduce the *whole* order of their native society; what they took to America was a cutting from its "liberal" branch—from the sector whose own natural tendency was republican and libertarian. Similarly, Australian society owes its fundamental character to the "radical" tradition of which it is an offshoot.[2]

In the present essay, Professor Hartz develops this argument, which explains democracy as the politics of what Alexis de Tocqueville called "the equality of conditions" in America—meaning conditions of men, not of nature. It is very cogent; but does it tell the whole story? Certain questions which a historian of democracy must ask still deserve attention. First, the thesis does not seem to account for different developments that took place under different climatic conditions, the most obvious being the very material differences between levels of democracy under the "republican" government in northern and southern American states. Further, the argument does not explain the *pace* of progress towards democracy.

If the pace differed according to areas and different circumstances, then we are led to a third difficulty: the thesis tends to overlook history itself— the variety of contingencies, of unexpected changes and new circumstances, that must occasionally modify the substance of institutional development. It is not necessarily a question here of slowing or speeding the pace: the outcome itself is involved. Different regions do not possess identical methods of government, and the differences are a result of history.

Yet, having raised these objections, we are left with a forceful element of unmistakable truth. Another European experience, however, was missing in the colonies, and it may be added to the negative elements which Professor Hartz emphasizes. Americans had no powerful enemies on their frontiers. Neither the French in the Ohio Valley and in Louisiana, nor the Spaniards in Florida, nor the numerous Indian tribes who periodically counter-attacked white aggression ever confronted the Americans with the sort of immediate and general military threat to which European states were accustomed.

This condition did not free the Americans from war, but it did free them from the need to depend on a large, permanent army. It freed them from the growth of a military class needing peacetime support and capable of battening on the people. Consequently, the American institutions that grew up in such luxurious freedom were not only predominantly republican, but profoundly civilian.

[2] Louis Hartz (ed.), *The Founding of New Societies* (New York, 1964).

The Rise of the Democratic Idea

LOUIS HARTZ

I

WHAT ACCOUNTS FOR THE EARLY TRIUMPH OF DEMOCRACY IN America? In many ways this is the classic question of American history, the question which each of our major interpretations of the American past has sought most ardently to answer. And yet each of the answers has encountered difficulty because it has not been able to withstand the test of comparative analysis. The Germanic tradition stressed by Herbert Baxter Adams is of course to be found in Germany, hardly notorious for its democracy; the frontier cherished by Turner is to be found in many lands where democracy did not arise; the farmers and debtors discovered by Beard are a commonplace of Western politics in the early nineteenth century. Let us see if we can answer the question in another way: by a running analysis of America and Europe, of the part which came to the New World and the whole which it left behind.

In the Europe of the nineteenth century we see, first of all, an analogue of the early Whiggery of Hamilton and Fisher Ames, the chief obstacle in America to democratic success. It is a stern movement, marked on the one hand by a powerful capitalist ambition and on the other by an unchangeable fear of the people. We find it everywhere in the Western nations—in the English Whigs of the Reform Act era, in the French Liberals of the July Monarchy, in the conservative German liberals and Constitutionalists of 1848. But we must not assume that Whiggery in Europe serves merely the satisfaction of its own ambition, the ambition of the wealthier bourgeoisie. This drive, of course, comes out well enough when it assails the old European reactionary establishments, as in the liberal revolutions of the nineteenth century, ending up when victorious with severe limitations on the popular suffrage. But in the course of these upheavals, which utilize the people only to prevent them actually from coming to power, it performs an important educative function, serving to prepare the ground for later democracy. In a world of mass passivity

Reprinted from *Paths of American Thought,* edited by Arthur M. Schlesinger, Jr., and Morton White, Boston, 1964, by permission of the Houghton Mifflin Company and Chatto and Windus Ltd.

and relative ignorance its exploitation of the people is the route by which they are in fact brought into the political arena. There is a striking contradiction between the splendid liberal slogans of the British bourgeoisie when it fights an unreformed Parliament and the almost hysterical fear of popular rule which immediately follows the issuing of these slogans. That is a contradiction which British democracy, as in the case of the Chartists, ultimately exposes. But the process of exposing it is one of the things which brings British democracy to consciousness.

In Europe, however, the opposition to Whiggery is not the simple, unified, and easily perceptible thing that it is in America. There, it is not a flat case of Jefferson versus Hamilton. And the reason is that the opposition to Whiggery is split up into various parts, some of them hating each other more bitterly than they hate Whiggery itself. There is first of all the peasant population which has strong affinities for the old feudal conservatism and which, if it is touched for a moment by the liberalism or the radicalism of the towns, can easily lapse back into reaction or into a Napoleonic authoritarianism, as in France. Next there is the lower middle class, which in Jacksonian America constitutes practically the whole of the democracy, but which is split off in Europe not only from the peasantry but from the workers as well. The painful relations between petit-bourgeoisie and labor are a part of the Marxian legend of the nineteenth century, documented in everything Marx and Engels wrote on the age. They may have drawn their categories sharply, and twisted them into a romantic proletarian pattern, but the facts they described were relevant.

Nevertheless, the American Whig and American democrat had analogues in the European setting from which they both ultimately derived. Why is it that the democrat wins out so easily here?

II

There are various ways of answering this question. One is to say what I have already implicitly said, that the democracy is vastly more unified in America and hence can rise up and with a single stroke bring Whiggery down. The notion that one of the central characteristics of American democracy is its unity of alignment is bound to come as a surprise to anyone studying the subject in the American context alone. For in that context what always seems impressive is the looseness of the popular combination. A political historian like Binkley will look at the elections of 1800 and 1828 and he will be struck with the hodgepodge of groups which brought the democracy to power: city wage-earners, small traders, landowners of a certain type.[1] From this angle, Jefferson and Jackson emerge as master politicians whose genius lay in their capacity to weld a unity out of a hopelessly disparate mass. But the truth of the matter is—and one does not need to deny the political genius of American democratic politicians to affirm this—that the unity was already there. The American farmer was hardly as alienated from the spirit of democracy as the German peasant of 1848, the American worker hardly in the same position as the British worker in 1832. Indeed the apparent looseness of the democratic combination is itself a clue to the point involved. For what the European scene presents us with is a series of sharp class breaks, involving deep mutual suspicions, and the bridging of these so effectively not even a master American politician could have accomplished. Could Jackson have done much better than Carl Schurz in the Germany of 1848?

But the unity of the American democratic alignment points to other things. Alone it is simply a matter of numbers, a wider combination of democrats overwhelming the Whig force, a matter of the Benthamite numerical majority. But this could not have come about if the mass of the American people were not capable of a very high degree of independent political activity. I have spoken of the function which Whiggery served in Europe of gradually leading the people into the political arena, educating them at the very moment it was making sure that they would not threaten its political or economic interest. Now we must not make the mistake of assuming that some such phenomenon did not take place in America too. The average American was not always the viable political unit that he appears to be at the hands of Jacksonian organizers. There is a background of political indifference, of submission to paternalism in the American people, which we are only now beginning to appreciate. The research of Robert E. Brown[2] and others has shown that electoral rights existed before they were fully used and that the rise of democracy in America is not simply a matter of obtaining the suffrage. It is a matter of political consciousness as well.

But this ought not to obscure the central fact that the shell of passivity and alienation cracked with comparative ease in the United States, bringing into existence the unified democratic alignment of American politics. There was from the outset no authentic feudal submissiveness; and if, during moments like 1776 and 1828, men of the type of Fisher Ames lamented that the average man no longer knew his place, those men did not have in mind the place of the European serf. In the agrarian sphere, for all of the delicate sense of status that may have prevailed in the South, the

---

[1] Wilfred E. Binkley, *American Political Parties: Their Natural History* (New York, 1955), chaps. IV-VI.

[2] Cf. Robert E. Brown, *Middle-Class Democracy and the Revolution in Massachusetts,* 1691–1780 (Ithaca, N. Y., 1955).

mood of the independent entrepreneur was a dominant one from the outset. Labor in the towns was never a mob in the European sense, despite the fears of Jefferson; and even before the arrival of the Loco-Foco movement in New York, the sense of political alienation and depression which characterized the urban proletariat almost anywhere in Europe was not to be found among the workers of that city. It is indeed a difficult matter to define the precise quality of American popular passivity prior to the outbreaks of democratic organization and passion in the nineteenth century. We are dealing with something midway between the European mood and the mood of a truly awakened democracy, something for which no precise category exists. But one thing is clear. Once the democratic organization began, a degree of mass political enlightenment was manifested which had no parallel in the world. Participation was continuous, and sentiment crystallized easily around the great democratic slogans of economic monopoly and the suffrage itself. Here again we find a place where our perspectives need to be altered when the European angle is considered. We do not ordinarily think of American democratic activity as continuous but are rather impressed with its cyclical character, rising and falling with the succession of democratic movements after the Revolution. But truly sporadic activity is what we find in the case of the French peasantry which leaps to a moment of glorious life in 1789 only to lapse back for a long period after that into shadows so deep that they can scarcely be dissipated by historical research. The American had a genius for political participation.

A wider and more unified majority, an enlightened electorate—these two factors were the woe of early American Whiggery. But they implied automatically a third which, in some measure, I have already touched upon: a simplification of political alignment. One cannot ever number with finality the forces in a political struggle, since any group can be broken down into other groups. But it is not wholly unfair to say that in the Europe of the early nineteenth century there were four major elements at work in the political arena: the feudal, aristocratic right, in various shades of strength and decline, ranging from a repatriated Bourbonism to the German princes; Whiggery, the analogue of the American right, fortified by industry in England, mainly by commerce and finance in France; the petit-bourgeoisie, sharply delineated on the Continent where big wealth is a class unto itself, much harder to find in England where the middle class has a more unified outlook; and finally labor, in different stages of political development and awakening. After one has taken all the shadings into account, these are the forces which stand out in the European world that the Americans left behind in the seventeenth century.

It is not hard to see what frustrates democracy in such a pattern. The fact that it is distributed in so many places, and lacks political confidence and awareness, means that it cannot assume command of the situation. It is an enemy of the right—but not quite, since on the land there is still a strong attachment to the aristocratic order. In the towns, where the press and industry are at work, democracy in its lower-middle-class and labor manifestations is clearly an enemy of the right. But even if it were powerful enough in these manifestations to lead the campaign against the right, it lacks the political education to do so, and in the end it follows Whiggery in that campaign. Limited reforms are made by Whiggery, and the natural instinct of democracy is to follow them up with wider demands for itself: a Jacksonian era in Europe. But this it cannot successfully do, first because Whiggery has turned around and joined the *ancien régime* against it, secondly because it thus loses its leadership, and thirdly because it begins to crack up itself as the leftward movement advances. On the Continent the lower middle class, not already incorporated into the Whig reform as in England in 1832, becomes terrified of labor as labor begins to increase its demands. Battles break out, and democracy is defeated. This is the old European story.

The situation is different in America. The very wideness of the democratic alliance is proof that the political situation has been simplified, and the very enlightenment of the American electorate is proof that in this simplified picture it cannot be defeated. The right is absent, never transported to America in the first place. Whiggery stands alone. But American democracy does not need it as an ally, or at least not for very long. Not only do the German princes not exist: even if they did, it is very likely that Jackson could take care of them without the help of Rufus Choate. But one thing is certain. It is not hard for Jackson to defeat Choate. The American farmer is Jackson's ally, not his sullen enemy; the small American trader is behind him; and the worker, however controversial his role may be in Jacksonian democracy, is not likely to strike out on terrifying revolutionary paths. The democracy has widened, and its capacity for political participation has insured the defeat of Whiggery. There are two contenders in America, as it were, not four, and one is vastly larger than the other, subsuming the two European contenders that are missing: an unenlightened peasantry and a threatening proletariat.

It is evident that the factors I have mentioned are analogues of each other. A wider and more cohesive democratic combination implies a larger degree of mass enlightenment, for it means that the predemocratic and antidemocratic dross in the European popular mind has been eliminated: the feudal spirit is gone from the land, the proletarian outlook from the towns. And this necessarily means a simpler political alignment, for the right is gone and the democracy has greatly grown. It was fortunate indeed for the democratic idea to find such a home, and Bancroft, for all of his nationalist piety, was right in terms of sheer political inter-actions when he said that a democratic Providence had fulfilled itself in the New World. But if one factor in the strategic rise of American democracy always turns out to be the analogue of another, there must surely be some deeper factor behind them all. What is it that works itself out through all the phases of the American political battle? What really is Bancroft's Providence?

III

The decisive moment in American history is the time of the great migration of the seventeenth century: this is our real "revolution," and what happened in 1776 is an aftermath, an experience determined by the earlier era. I do not mean this only in the sense that the American Revo-lution finally sundered the tie with England, completed, as it were, the original act of detachment. I mean it also in the sense that the domestic upheavals of the revolutionary age, which brought the democracy to power, prefiguring the victories of Jefferson and Jackson, were manifes-tations of the logic of the New World settlement. For it was precisely then that the complex world in which European Whigs and democrats moved was left behind, that the American political scene shrank at the moment that American democracy expanded. But more than complexity was left behind. There was the whole of the historic feudal culture, from which the liberal element, common to both antagonists in the American political struggle, was extricated. A liberal tradition arose in the New World, and this is the factor which, like some ultimate Hegelian force, keeps showing its face in the various aspects of American politics.

Now this was an idea, nothing more. In its Puritan form it was charged with immense passion; but on a more secular level, not unknown to the Puritans themselves, the level of land-hunger and economic ambition, it was still an idea. Elsewhere I have referred to Locke as a symbol of this idea,[3] but there is no need to overemphasize his significance, especially since in the actual historic sense there is much in his life and work which contradicts the American scheme of thought. We must not forget that he was the author of the Fundamental Constitutions for the Carolinas, one of the historic ill-fated efforts to establish feudal relations in the New World. What is involved is a set of concepts concerning the social order which come out well, to be sure, in Locke's *Second Treatise* but which can be found in any of the classical liberal thinkers of the seventeenth and the eighteenth centuries. These concepts, transformed into operating

[3] Louis Hartz, *The Liberal Tradition in America* (New York, 1955).

modes of behavior, yielded the swift victories of American democracy.

They were responsible for the breadth of the democratic alignment. For what eliminated the barriers that divided European democracy into so many parts if not the sharing in America of liberal values? How did the English tenant or the German peasant become a vital part of the democratic force in the United States? How did the proletariat of Birmingham or Lyons become in the New World respectable members of the bourgeoisie? One can point to an abundance of land, which certainly aided the process, or to industrial conditions which were not so severe as those in Europe. But the explanatory power of these factors must be denied when one remembers that there was an abundance of land as well as comparable working conditions in other countries where the same results did not take place. Fundamentally we are dealing with a psychic matter, the transforming impact of an idea which, long before the American political manipulators got to work, brought both the farmer and the worker into the framework of democratic liberalism. Then a Jefferson could arise, and historians could marvel at his political genius. Then a Jackson could emerge, the wonder of students of political pressure groups. But from a European point of view there was an incongruity in this expansion of the experience of democratic liberalism. For in Europe that experience was the product essentially neither of farmers nor of workers; it was the experience of the small urban entrepreneur, the Jacobin. What happened by contrast in America was that this figure mushroomed to enormous proportions as the American political scene contracted.

The impact of the liberal idea is reflected also in the political activism of the American public. We must be careful not to be too idyllic here. It would certainly be false to portray the American democracy as a set of splendid citizens reading their Calvin or their Locke, and then rationally exercising individual responsibility. This was somewhat the image that Jefferson had of politics, and it did of course pursue American political thinking all the way into the Progressive era. The fact is that the slogans of democratic liberalism, whether they had to do with the natural rights of Samuel Adams or the popular will of William Leggett, were quite as irrational in their appeal as the deferential slogans of European feudalism or the proletarian outcries of the emergent working class of Europe. The issue is not one of rationalism, or at least of rationalism in the classical sense, but rather of the behavioral consequences of an allegiance to different types of symbols. The symbols of democratic liberalism produced a type of political participation which kept the people continuously in the political arena. Leadership was no less essential here than in Europe, ballyhoo, as it were, no less essential, but the public could be relied upon as a political force.

How the liberal idea simplified political alignments is obvious enough from what I have already said. When that idea is universal, the politics of four dimensions becomes the politics of two dimensions, and the latter is contained within the bourgeois framework. We can lament, if we like, the missing components of the American experience, the European things that the seventeenth century in America left behind. We can long with the American Whigs of the eighteenth century for the aristocracy they could not lean on, or with the socialists of a later time for the proletarian outlook they could not find. America in the early nineteenth century might actually have been a more exciting place if Fisher Ames could have fulfilled his dream, or if Fanny Wright had had a better break. The simplification of American political alignments, which led to the burgeoning triumph of democracy, was a simplification also of cultural experience. It meant the elevation of the liberal idea to the rank of a national absolute. The virtue of this may be a debatable point. Some may prefer a quick democracy even if it means a contraction of perspective: others may not. Perhaps the question is whether one good experience is better than a multiplicity of experiences, some of them not so good. But there can be little doubt that the shrinking of the context of American politics, which yielded the giant figure of Jackson, was traceable to the dominion of the liberal spirit.

Wherever one looks, then, amid the excitement of early American political battles, one sees the power of the idea that was extracted from Europe and carried to the New World in the seventeenth century. The width of the democratic combination, the torchlight parades of the voters, the duality of the political struggle, all are traceable, in some final sense, to the *Mayflower*. Now one is tempted to be truly Hegelian, for the men in American politics do not really know this: they are victims of the universal mind. They call each other names—Tory, leveler[4]—which prove that they do not realize, or at least that they do not consciously care about, the process that is at work. But is not this the final proof of the process itself? When a unifying idea has sunk so far beneath the surface of a culture that it can support a raging hyperbole which contradicts it, then surely it has attained no mean victory.

IV

In such a world the search for "democratic theory," or even "political theory," is a beguiling quest. For it is the talent of such a world to take

---

[4] For these slogans as they appear in the popular literature see, for example, Joseph L. Blau, ed., *Social Theories of Jacksonian Democracy* (New York, 1955).

a single idea out of the conscious intellectual struggles of Europe and plunge it deep into unconscious behavior where it reigns, without philosophy, without criticism, as an operational absolute. This is the death of theory as theory is studied, the beginning of fetishism. A hundred books may be written on "American political thought," a score of "neglected American thinkers" may be discovered, but no amount of scholarly energy will ever, I think, alter this fact. Let us not then really search for "democratic theory" and confuse a social with a philosophic process. Let us try to find out rather how the thoughts of the Americans in the early nineteenth century disclose the actual process which brings democracy to power.

The amalgamation of the land and the workshop into the province of the small entrepreneur, which generated the greatness of the popular combination, and which was rooted in a universal liberal conception of life, is reflected in the multicolored character of the American democratic polemic. It has, to begin with, a strong agrarian strain, which in Europe is for the most part to be located in the theory of the reaction. Jefferson takes the rustic feudal philosophy of Bonald, with its picture of benign seigneurs and happy peasants, and dynamizes it with the image of countless independent bourgeois entrepreneurs. Of course the actual capitalist hunger among American landowners was far more intense than even Jefferson suggested, and we have to go into the story of land speculation to document it. But in contrast to Europe, Jefferson shows us enough, and so does John Taylor. There is a confusing issue here in the "anticapitalism" of democratic ruralism in America, the opposition to the Hamiltonian program which seems to link the American democrat with the hatred of commerce and industry that the European reactionary had. Indeed there is some connection, for the antagonism of city and farm cuts, in a sense, across all social alignments. But agrarian "anticapitalism" in America, for all of the grand historical concepts which Taylor mustered, and which give him a Marxian touch, is not really "anticapitalism." It is in fact a defense of the capitalist farmer against other capitalist interests.[5]

There is a comparable confusion which can hide the liberal nature of the American labor movement: the high-flown slogans of Stephen Simpson and Ely Moore about class struggle. During the thirties it used to be the fashion to find here a native American radicalism which had gone unnoticed before. Actually the thinking of the Jacksonian labor movement is shot through and through with individualistic aspirations. Its language is the language of natural right, and it is in the name of this concept that the whole range of labor demands, from lien legislation to shorter hours, is rationalized. The fate of true collectivists in the American labor

[5] Cf. Whitney Griswold, *Farming and Democracy* (New York, 1948).

movement was not a happy one, as the history of the movement in New York vividly shows. What touched labor, say, in the France of 1848—Fourierism for example—was shoved out to the frontier in America, and the Lockean combination was not impaired.[6] Capitalist proletarianism united with capitalist agrarianism to make the Jacobin spirit, rather uninviting in its petty trader form, blossom into a many-splendored thing. The huge figure of Jackson moved amid the romance of log-cabin clearings and striking carpenters.

The issue of mass participation, however, as it comes out in American argument, has a comic rather than a romantic quality. For the Whigs conjure up a necessity for their existence which is false, while the democrats belabor the obvious to prove their right to power. There is John Adams with his mixed state in which the Senate was to represent wealth alone, in which an impartial executive was to mediate between rich and poor, all designed to keep the threatening mob under control. There is Thomas Jefferson ardently protesting that the people, at least the agrarian people, are fit for political participation. But in and through this argument, which does not really die until 1840, when the Whigs themselves have become log-cabin democrats, the Whigs are being defeated badly and the people are participating without catastrophic results. Whiggery dies a complete but easy death: it is laid to rest, not with an axe, but with a pat on the back. And this is of the very essence of the American story. For if the barricades had been thrown up in 1800 or 1828, the point of Whiggery about the people would have been proved, and the European pattern would instantaneously have appeared. Instead of democratizing itself, and generating the tradition of Lincoln and Grant, Whiggery would have made a triumphant return, displaying precisely that capacity for perpetual resurrection which the Whiggery of Europe manifested in the nineteenth century.

The spiritual transformation of American Whiggery in 1840 produces a duality of images which fulfills the democratic idea but confuses it forever in American thought. Who is the real democrat: the new Edward Everett or the old Van Buren; Harding or Wilson? It is rare in intellectual history that a nation has spent its time trying to disentangle two claims to the same principle, and surely there can be no better proof that this principle has succeeded. But for Whiggery, of course, this confusion is a much more fruitful matter than the false clarity of its earlier thinking. It is a method of seizing precisely those forces in the democratic combination which destroyed it, well worth the sacrifice of Fisher Ames to the

[6] Cf. Donald Drew Egbert and Stow Persons, eds., *Socialism and American Life* (Princeton, N. J., 1952), Vol. 1, chaps. 4 and 5.

egalitarian gods. Nor is everything given up. Big wealth is still there, and if the average man is linked to it by the magic of capitalist ambition, by the dream of Horatio Alger, that wealth has not been destroyed. There is only a psychological leveling, not an actual redistribution of goods. On the contrary—and this is one of the secrets of the Whig achievement —the elitism of the millionaire can be more openly flaunted now than in the age of Hamilton because he has become in origin and spirit an average man. Of course some gentility is lost, some Eastern hankering after an association of money and manners. But in America this is a luxury that Whiggery simply cannot afford, and Hamilton must be accounted lucky that there existed in American life that law of compensation which permitted him to live at least in the garb of Andrew Carnegie.

And this was indeed a law. For it was a matter of inevitable logic that the universality of the bourgeois spirit which isolated Hamilton should make the nation peculiarly susceptible to him when he preached the message of democratic capitalism. Actually throughout the entire earlier era the reality of Horatio Alger existed even if his novels had not yet been written in political thought. While Hamilton was sagely speaking in class economic terms, and embroidering the virtues of the employment of women and children in factories, American economic life was distinctly democratic in cast. While Jefferson was spinning out the virtues of the puritanical farmer, the speculative frame of mind, which reached vivid heights during the Jacksonian era, had already thrust itself forward. Alger was bursting beneath the surface of American life before he actually appeared. And if his appearance produced Whig victories, could the democratic politician complain? The Whig law of compensation works in reverse. What had given the democratic politician his success if not the unification of popular power that the individualist ethic had yielded? What had made him great if not the capitalist culture itself? Brownson might lament, but you cannot have the virtues of precapitalist and postcapitalist Europe and the virtues of capitalist America at the same time. If Jackson was to arise, he was bound in the end to be defeated too. But at least he was defeated by being enchanted with a millionaire's dream, not by being crushed beneath the complexities of the class politics of Europe. One may oppose that dream, and find it unsuitable as a way of life, but it was an inherent manifestation of the democratic idea in America.

Here then are the consequences of the liberal principle in American thought: the image of a many-faceted democrat proving his capacity to make and unmake politicians. But where in the American argument do we find the liberal principle itself? Where do we find a celebration of the historic act of the seventeenth century? Actually we do not find it. Folklore and ceremony will always of course remember the Pilgrims, but the significance of the middle-class extrication from Europe for the character of the American political struggle does not figure centrally in American thought. We are back again to the unconscious nature of the power of the liberal principle. One ought not to assume, of course, that overt political argument should always reflect actual political reality. Indeed this is almost never the case. English thought is Hobbesian but the English people are encrusted with a thick general will, French thought is Rousseauian but the French are individualists, German thought is nationalistic but Germany has had its problems with national unity. Political thought is as much the record of a yearning as it is the record of a reality. But the American case is not of this sort. American thought does not seek to reverse the liberal nature of American reality, although in a few cases of the Adams type this may be so. The hidden nature of the liberal premise is testimony, in fact, to its general acceptance, and what we are dealing with is not a misery the Americans seek to escape but a satisfaction so universal that they do not bother to mention it. The rise of American democracy, with its radical expansion of the small liberal, its popular activism, and its simplification of political culture, is traceable in the end to a bourgeois trip that was taken in the seventeenth century which everyone has forgotten.

V

This interpretation of American democratic success, based on the wider European context from which the American experience was extracted, is not wholly incompatible with other interpretations that have reigned in the past. The liberal idea could not have flourished so successfully unless there had been an open place to put it, and in this sense Turner was right. The American democratic combination did consist in large measure of farmers and workers, and in this sense Beard was right. But what this interpretation does is to place these factors in a perspective which comparative analysis cannot destroy. If there is a frontier in feudal French Canada, that need not now trouble us, for the liberal principle was not exported there. If there were farmers and workers in England, that is no problem, since they did not have the bourgeois mentality to unite them.

Indeed from the European angle, from the angle of the context and the part, the rise of American democracy is a fated thing, even though it is not duplicated there. For the analysis I have presented is based on the course of European history itself, and can be checked by it, so that if one were in a reckless mood, one might almost be tempted to say that if American history had not existed it could have been conjured up by an acute student of the European experience: observe England, abstract the bourgeois element, put it on open ground, watch its democratic logic unfold. What is wrong with this view, however, is that abstraction is itself a process, yielding many of the crucial aspects of the American story, and it is not uniquely related to the liberal principle or for that matter to America itself. In any case the concept of a liberal tradition, if it modifies Turner and Beard, puts them on stronger ground. In American historical study, especially in connection with the rise of democracy, we have grown accustomed to a kind of cyclical excitement in which theories reign for a moment and then are dramatically "disproved." Actually all the major analyses of American democracy, from Bancroft's nationalism to Beard's proletarianism, seized on lasting insights. I believe that the idea of a liberal society puts these insights into a meaningful relationship to one another.

THE CHARACTER AND PROCESS
OF REVOLUTION POLITICS

The American Revolution was both a beginning and an end. It was the beginning of independence for the Republic, which meant the assumption of all the responsibilities of self-government through representative institutions. For this responsibility the colonists had been prepared by a century and a half of experience in running their own home affairs while developing and refining their own institutions; the "previous conditions" for republican government had given them ample experience.

But in the second sense, the break with the mother country was an end— a culmination of all that earlier experience. Americans had inherited from English whigs of the seventeenth-century school the doctrine that the supreme power in the state was the "legislative" power. Both English and Americans used this concept to distinguish between the power derived from the estates of the realm and embodied in assemblies or houses of Parliament, and the royal prerogative or "executive" power. The colonial assemblies had long been very conscious of both the doctrines and practices associated with the "legislative power," which they gradually appropriated during the eighteenth century. But during the latter part of this period—roughly, since about the 1720s—the balance of power had shifted within the colonial structures; the elective assemblies gained power at the expense of the governors' councils.

These movements went on at different rates and with differences of emphasis, but there was a notable degree of comparable development among the colonies. The crisis in relations with Britain hastened the process and forced it towards completion. When that final phase occurred, it took the shape of a convergence of the two major trends of the last fifty years: the assemblies firmly seized the "legislative power" in their own hands, and this seizure of power by the Americans converged with the rise of the *representative* branch of the colonial assembly. In this sense the Revolution was a culmination of at least half a century of political development.

Such a revolution, arising in large part from the British challenge to colonial claims to self-taxation and representative government in general, could never have taken place without a large measure of genuine representation. The colonial assemblies were based on a property franchise and controlled by prevailing standards of conformity, deference, and leadership, but they were remarkably effective in really "representing" their own society. Their representatives stood closer to their own communities than did members of the British House of Commons, and their members often took more seriously the duty of speaking for specific local interests. The experience of controlling domestic affairs had produced in the assemblies a trained and seasoned leadership; they were capable men, and they combined authority and representation in a manner which produced, not colonial democracy, but certainly a high measure of political capability. Professor Hartz gave in the first section an account of the original "liberal" content of American institutions which produced this situation; the business of our selections in this section is to explain the ways in which the Revolution itself transformed those institutions in more democratic directions.

Mr. Richard Buel's contribution sets up a "frame of reference" for the study of the themes of democracy and representation. But why should this have been necessary? The answer lies mainly in the article itself; but certain points may be mentioned by way of introduction. In the first place, controversy over the idea of "democracy" has arisen from confusion about the meaning of words. As men of the eighteenth century used "democracy" in a stricter sense than we do, it is clearly necessary to decide whether we are talking about our meaning or theirs; and when, for example, Lieutenant-Governor Thomas Hutchinson writes in 1767, "The town of Boston is an absolute democracy," it is clear that he disapproves, but not that he means what we would mean by the same expression.

The painful process of developing a case for colonial rights against the claims of Parliament threw the colonists back onto the seventeenth-century Whig idea of an original "social compact" between sovereign and people— an idea which implied the right of revolution when the sovereign was guilty of breaking the agreement. But no clear rules existed for this procedure of revolution; and it was here that the colonists had to make use of their existing institutions of representation. The relationship of this process to the advance of democratic ideas is part of Mr. Buel's theme.

So far as colonial resistance went, independence might be the extreme remedy, but colonial leaders certainly did not intend to go on and lead a social revolution. Yet the consequences of their resistance far exceeded their original aims. This simple statement is borne out and amplified in two further essays in this section. Professor Jensen gives a broad interpretation of the full process. Professor Main's structural analysis of the history and composition of the state legislative bodies shows us in detail exactly what happened. These two articles do much to support each other and explain in what ways independence turned into political revolution.

The War of Independence caused deep internal disturbances, a violent depreciation of the various colonial currencies, the ruin of old fortunes and the rise of new ones. Men of property new or old were confirmed in their conviction that the rights of property must be secured by firm constitutional safeguards, and these safeguards in state constitutions introduce a form of "interest" representation that is difficult to reconcile with the more democratic principle of the simple representation of persons.

At the same time, the emphasis placed on equality of rights, and the inner logic of much of the colonial argument, did form the basis of a case for a very extensive participation by citizens in the government which was to rule them. Exigencies of a practical as well as a doctrinaire kind helped to bring about a greater emphasis on the individual than had been usual in the colonial—or in English—electoral system; and this new emphasis, as the editor's own article shows, laid the foundations for the principle of majority rule. It was to be majority rule within limits, but it was indispensable as a foundation of later democratic development.

These essays also bring out that the Revolution was in its complex reality a variety of movements. One consequence was certain: it threw the American people back on themselves, it forced them more than ever before to rely on their own institutions. As George Washington remarked, they would be wholly responsible for their own success or failure.

Democracy and the American Revolution

MERRILL JENSEN

THE HISTORIAN WHO VENTURES TO TALK ABOUT DEMOCRACY IN EARLY
America is in danger because there are almost as many opinions as there
are writers on the subject. The Puritans have been pictured as the founders
of American democracy, and it is vigorously denied that they had anything to do with it. Some have seen in Roger Williams the father of
American democracy, and others have denied that he was a democrat,
whatever his putative progeny may be. The conflict is equally obvious
when it comes to the American Revolution, and the problems of solution
are far more complex than they are for the seventeenth century. The difficulty is compounded, for all too often men's emotions seem to become
involved.

It is sometimes suggested that we avoid the use of the word "democracy" when discussing the seventeenth and eighteenth centuries. It seems
to me that this is a flat evasion of the problem, for the Americans of
those centuries used the word and they meant something by it. Our task,
then, is not to avoid the issue but to try to understand what they meant,
and understand what they meant in the context of the times in which they
lived. What we must not do is to measure the seventeenth and eighteenth
centuries in terms of our own assumptions about what democracy is or
should be. This is all the more important since many of us do not seem
to be too clear about our assumptions, even for the century in which we
live.

A number of years ago I took the position that "in spite of the para-
doxes involved one may still maintain that the Revolution was essentially,
though relatively, a democratic movement within the thirteen American
colonies, and that its significance for the political and constitutional history
of the United States lay in its tendency to elevate the political and economic status of the majority of the people." And then, with a somewhat
rhetorical flourish which I have sometimes regretted but have not as yet
withdrawn, I went on to say that "the Articles of Confederation were the

This article, which was originally delivered as a paper at the Conference on
Early American History at the Henry E. Huntington Library on February 9, 1957,
is reprinted from the *Huntington Library Quarterly* XX, 4, 1956–7, by permission of the Editors.

constitutional expression of this movement and the embodiment in governmental form of the philosophy of the Declaration of Independence."[1] One thing can be said for this statement at least: reviewers read it and quoted it, some with raised eyebrows, and some with approval, whether or not they said anything at all about the rest of the book.

During most of the present century historians have assumed that democracy was involved somehow or other in the American Revolution. They have assumed also that there were conditions within the American colonies that were not satisfactory to at least some of the American people. The causes of internal discontent were various, ranging all the way from religious to economic differences. The discontent was of such intensity that in certain colonies it led to explosive outbreaks in the 1760's such as the Regulator movements in the Carolinas, the Paxton Boys' uprising in Pennsylvania, and the tenant farmer revolt in New York, outbreaks that were suppressed by the armed forces of the colonial governments and with the help of British power.

Most historians have agreed also that the individual colonies were controlled politically by relatively small groups of men in each of them, allied by family, or economic or political interests, or by some combination of these. The colonial aristocracies owed their position to many things: to their wealth and ability, to their family connections and political allies, and to the British government which appointed them to office. As opposed to Britain, they had won virtual self-government for the colonies by 1763. Yet in every colony they were a minority who managed to maintain internal control through property qualifications for the suffrage, especially effective in the growing towns, and through refusal or failure to grant representation in any way proportional to the population of the rapidly growing frontier areas. Probably more important than either of these was the fact that in most colonies the aristocracies manned the upper houses of the legislatures, the supreme courts, and other important posts—all by royal appointment. Beyond this, their control extended down through the county court system, even in Massachusetts. In short, colonial political society was not democratic in operation despite the elective lower houses and the self-government which had been won from Great Britain.[2]

[1] Merrill Jensen, *The Articles of Confederation: An Interpretation of the Social-Constitutional History of the American Revolution, 1774–1781*, reprint with new foreword (Madison, Wis., 1948), pp. 15, 239.

[2] Ibid., ch. iii, "The Internal Revolution"; Leonard W. Labaree, *Conservatism in Early American History* (New York, 1948); and Robert J. Taylor, *Western Massachusetts in the Revolution* (Providence, 1954), as examples. For methods of local control see Charles S. Sydnor, *Gentlemen Freeholders: Political Practices in Washington's Virginia* (Chapel Hill, 1952).

This is a brief but, I think, fair summary of a widely held point of view concerning the political actualities at the beginning of the revolutionary era.

This view has been challenged recently. A writer on Massachusetts declared that "as far as Massachusetts is concerned, colonial society and the American Revolution must be interpreted in terms something very close to a complete democracy with the exception of Britsh restraints." It was not controlled by a wealthy aristocracy. There was little inequality of representation, and property was so widely held that virtually every adult male could vote.[3] The assumption that Massachusetts was an idyllic democracy, united in the fight against British tyranny, will be somewhat surprising to those who have read the letters of Francis Bernard and the diary of John Adams, not to mention the history of Thomas Hutchinson, and, I suspect, would be even more surprising to those gentlemen as well. Elsewhere, this writer has implied that what was true for Massachusetts was probably true for other colonies and for the United States after the Revolution.[4]

On the other hand it is asserted that democracy had nothing to do with the Revolution. Such an assertion made in connection with Pennsylvania is a little startling, for ever since C. H. Lincoln's work of more than a half century ago, down to the present, it has been held that there was a democratic movement in Pennsylvania during the revolutionary era. Not so, says a reviewer of the most recent study. He declares that "the attribution of democratic motivations and ideas to eighteenth-century colonists is a common fault among many historians of the colonial period. . . ." He argues that the struggle in Pennsylvania before 1776 was one between "radical and conservative variants of whiggism," which he defines as one between "those who held privilege most dear and those who valued property above all." The Pennsylvania Constitution of 1776 itself was not democratic, but a triumph of "colonial radical whiggism."[5]

It is clear that a considerable diversity of opinion prevails. It is also clear that the time has come to set forth certain propositions or generalizations which seem to me to have a measure of validity.

First of all, a definition of democracy is called for. And just to face the issue squarely, I will offer one stated at Newport, Rhode Island, in 1641

[3] Robert E. Brown, "Democracy in Colonial Massachusetts," *New England Quarterly*, XXV (1952), 291–313, and at length in *Middle Class Democracy and the Revolution in Massachusetts, 1691–1780* (Ithaca, N. Y. 1955).

[4] Robert E. Brown, "Economic Democracy Before the Constitution," *American Quarterly*, VII (1955), 257–274.

[5] Roy N. Lokken, review of Theodore Thayer, *Pennsylvania Politics and the Growth of Democracy, 1740–1776* (Harrisburg, 1953), in *William and Mary Quarterly*, XII (1955), 671.

when a meeting declared that "the government which this body politic doth attend unto ... is a democracy or popular government; ... that is to say: It is in the power of the body of freemen, orderly assembled, or the major part of them, to make or constitute just laws, by which they will be regulated, and to depute from among themselves such ministers as shall see them faithfully executed between man and man." That such an idea was not confined to Newport was shown six years later when the little towns in Rhode Island formed a confederation, the preamble of which states: "It is agreed, by this present assembly thus incorporate, and by this present act declared, that the form of government established in Providence Plantations is democratical; that is to say, a government held by the free and voluntary consent of all, or the greater part of the free inhabitants."

These are simple but, I think, adequate definitions. I will go even further and offer as a theoretical and philosophical foundation for democracy the statement by Roger Williams in the *Bloudy Tenent* of 1644. After describing civil government as an ordinance of God to conserve the civil peace of the people so far as concerns their bodies and goods, he goes on to say: "The sovereign, original, and foundation of civil power lies in the people (whom they must needs mean by the civil power distinct from the government set up). And if so, that a people may erect and establish what form of government seems to them most meet for their civil condition. It is evident that such governments as are by them erected and established have no more power, nor for no longer time, than the civil power or people consenting and agreeing shall betrust them with. This is clear not only in reason, but in the experience of all commonweals where the people are not deprived of their natural freedom by the power of tyrants."[6]

The central issue in seventeenth-century New England was not social equality, manhood suffrage, women's rights, or sympathy for the Levellers, or other tests which have been applied. The central issue was the source of authority for the establishment of a government. The English view was that no government could exist in a colony without a grant of power from the crown. The opposite view, held by certain English dissenters in New England, was that a group of people could create a valid government for themselves by means of a covenant, compact, or constitution. The authors of the Mayflower Compact and the Fundamental Orders of Connecticut operated on this assumption, although they did not carry it to the logical conclusion and call it democracy as did the people in Rhode Island. It is

[6] *English Historical Documents*, IX, *American Colonial Documents to 1775*, ed. Merrill Jensen (London and New York, 1955), pp. 168, 226, 174.

the basic assumption of the Declaration of Independence, a portion of which reads much like the words of Roger Williams written 132 years earlier.

The second proposition is that colonial governments on the eve of the Revolution did not function democratically, nor did the men who controlled them believe in democracy. Even if we agree that there was virtually manhood suffrage in Massachusetts, it is difficult, for me at least, to see it as a democracy. In 1760 the government was controlled by a superb political machine headed by Thomas Hutchinson, who with his relatives and political allies occupied nearly every important political office in the colony except the governorship. The Hutchinson oligarchy controlled the superior court, the council, the county courts, and the justices of the peace; with this structure of appointive office spread throughout the colony, it was able to control the house of representatives elected by the towns. For six years after 1760 the popular party in Boston, lead by Oxenbridge Thacher and James Otis, suffered one defeat after another at the hands of the Hutchinson machine. The popular leaders in the town of Boston tried everything from slander to mob violence to get control of the government of the colony but it was not until after the Stamp Act crisis that they were able to win a majority of the house of representatives to their side. Even then, men like James Otis did not at first realize that the Stamp Act could be turned to advantage in the fight against the Hutchinson oligarchy.[7] In terms of political support between 1760 and 1765, if Massachusetts had a democratic leader, that man was Thomas Hutchinson, a charge to which he would have been the first to issue a horrified denial.

The third proposition is that before 1774 or 1775 the revolutionary movement was not a democratic movement, except by inadvertence. The pamphleteers who wrote on political and constitutional questions, and the town and county meetings and legislatures that resolved endlessly between 1763 and 1774, were concerned with the formulation of constitutional arguments to defend the colonies and their legislatures from interference by parliament.

The colonial theorists wrote much about the British constitution, the rights of Englishmen, and even of the laws of nature, but they accepted the British assumption that colonial governments derived from British charters and commissions. Their essential concern was with the relationship that existed, or ought to exist, between the British government and the colonial governments, and not with the relationship between man as man, and government itself. Such writers showed no interest in domestic

---

[7] See Ellen E. Brennan, *Plural Office Holding in Massachusetts 1760–1780* (Chapel Hill, 1945), and "James Otis: Recreant and Patriot," *New England Quarterly*, XII (1939), 691–725.

problems, and when it was suggested that the arguments against taxation by parliament were equally applicable to the taxation of under-represented areas in the colonies, or to dissenting religious groups, such suggestions were looked upon as being quite out of order.

The same indifference was displayed in the realm of political realities. The ardent leaders of the fight against British policies showed no interest in, or sympathy for, the discontent of back-country farmers or religious groups such as the Baptists. Instead, they temporarily joined with their political enemies to suppress or ignore it. Such sympathy as the discontented got, they got from the British government, or from colonial leaders charged with being tools of the British power.

The fact is that the popular leaders of the revolutionary movement had no program of domestic reform.[8] Instead, their program was a combination of a continuous assault on the local officeholding aristocracies and an ardent attack on British policies; and in the course of time they identified one with the other. It is sometimes difficult to tell with which side of the program the popular leaders were more concerned. In Massachusetts, for instance, before 1765 they were so violent in their attack on Hutchinson that they prevented Massachusetts from joining the other colonies in making formal protests against British legislation.

The fourth proposition is related to the third. It is that although the popular leaders in the colonies showed no interest in internal political and social change, they were still able to build up a political following, particularly in the seacoast towns. They were superb organizers, propagandists with a touch of genius, and possessed of an almost demonic energy in their dual fight against the local political aristocracies and British policies. After a few false starts such as that of James Otis, who at first called the Virginia Stamp Act Resolves treason,[9] the popular leaders took an extreme stand on the subject of colonial rights. The political aristocracies might object to British policies, as most of them did, but considering what they owed to British backing, they displayed an understandable caution, a caution that made it impossible for them to pose as patriotic leaders.

The popular leaders were also willing to take extreme measures in practical opposition to British policies, ranging all the way from mob violence to non-importation agreements forced upon unwilling merchants. And with ever more force and violence they accused Americans who did

[8] For example, see Irving Mark, *Agrarian Conflicts in Colonial New York, 1711–1775* (New York, 1940); *The Carolina Background on the Eve of the Revolution*, ed. Richard J. Hooker (Chapel Hill, 1953); and Elisha Douglass, *Rebels and Democrats* (Chapel Hill, 1955).

[9] Brennan, "James Otis: Recreant and Patriot," p. 715.

not agree with them or their methods of knuckling under to British tyranny and of readiness to sell the liberties of their country for a little pelf. In the course of this campaign they appealed to the people at large. Men who normally could not or did not take part in political life, particularly in the cities, were invited to mass meetings where the rules of suffrage were ignored and where they could shout approval of resolutions carefully prepared in advance by their leaders. In addition, the mob was a constant factor in political life, particularly in Boston where it was efficiently organized. Mobs were used to nullify the Stamp Act, to harass British soldiers, to hamper the operations of the customs service, and to intimidate office holders.

All these activities on the part of the disfranchised, or the hitherto politically inactive, accustomed men to taking part in public affairs as never before; and it gave them an appetite for more. From the beginning of the crisis in 1774 onward, more and more "new men," which was the politest name their opponents called them, played an ever more active role, both on the level of practical politics and on the level of political theory. They began writing about and talking about what they called "democracy." And this was a frightening experience, not only to the conservative-minded leaders of the colonies, but to many of the popular leaders as well.

For instance, when a New York mass meeting gathered in May 1774 to answer the letter of the Boston Town Meeting asking for a complete stoppage of trade with Britain as an answer to the Boston Port Act, the people talked about far more than letter writing. One alarmed observer wrote: "I beheld my fellow-citizens very accurately counting all their chickens, not only before any of them were hatched, but before above one half of the eggs were laid. In short, they fairly contended about the future forms of our government, whether it should be founded upon aristocratic or democratic principles." The leaders had "gulled" the mob for years, and now, said Gouverneur Morris, the mob was waking up and could no longer be fooled. The only salvation for the aristocracy of New York was peace with Britain at almost any price.[10]

Another witness to the stirrings among the people was John Adams. Unlike Gouverneur Morris, he never wavered in his belief in independence, but at the same time he was constantly concerned with the danger of an internal upheaval. Years later in his "Autobiography," he recalled as vividly as if it had happened the day before an event that took place while he was home in Massachusetts in the fall of 1775. While there he

[10] Gouverneur Morris to [John] Penn, May 20, 1774, in *English Historical Documents*, IX, 861–863.

met a man who had sometimes been his client. "He, though a common horse jockey, was sometimes in the right, and I had commonly been successful in his favor in our courts of law. He was always in the law, and had been sued in many actions at almost every court. As soon as he saw me, he came up to me, and his first salutation to me was, 'Oh! Mr. Adams, what great things have you and your colleagues done for us! We can never be grateful enough to you. There are no courts of justice now in this province, and I hope there never will be another.' " Then Adams goes on: "Is this the object for which I have been contending? said I to myself, for I rode along without any answer to this wretch. Are these the sentiments of such people, and how many of them are there in the country? Half the nation for what I know; for half the nation are debtors, if not more, and these have been, in all countries, the sentiments of debtors. If the power of the country should get into such hands, and there is great danger that it will, to what purpose have we sacrificed our time, health, and everything else? Surely we must guard against this spirit and these principles, or we shall repent of all our conduct."[11]

In May of 1776, with the talk of independence filling the air and the Virginia convention planning to draft a constitution, old Landon Carter of Virginia wrote to Washington bewailing the "ambition" that had "seized on so much ignorance all over the colony as it seems to have done; for this present convention abounds with too many of the inexperienced creatures to navigate our bark on this dangerous coast. . . ." As for independence, he said, "I need only tell you of one definition that I heard of Independency: It was expected to be a form of government that, by being independent of the rich men, every man would then be able to do as he pleased. And it was with this expectation they sent the men they did, in hopes they would plan such a form. One of the delegates I heard exclaim against the Patrolling Law, because a poor man was made to pay for keeping a rich man's slaves in order. I shamed the fool so much for it that he slunk away; but he got elected by it."[12]

One could go on endlessly giving examples like these from the hectic days between 1774 and 1776, examples of the fear among leaders of all shades of opinion that the people would get or were getting out of hand. Meanwhile there was an increasing amount of political writing in the newspapers, writing which was pointing in the direction of independence and the creation of new governments in America. More than a year before

[11] John Adams, "Autobiography," *The Works of John Adams,* ed. Charles F. Adams (Boston, 1856), II, 420–421.

[12] *American Archives,* ed. Peter Force, 4th ser. (Washington, 1837–1846), VI, 390–391. May 9, 1776.

Common Sense, a piece which appeared first in the *Pennsylvania Packet* declared that "the history of kings is nothing but the history of the folly and depravity of human nature." "We read now and then, it is true, of a good king; so we read likewise of a prophet escaping unhurt from a lion's den, and of three men walking in a fiery furnace without having even their garments singed. The order of nature is as much inverted in the first as it was in the last two cases. A good king is a miracle."[13]

By early 1776 the debate over future governments to be adopted was in full swing. Disliking intensely the ideas of government set forth in *Common Sense,* John Adams drafted his *Thoughts on Government.* His plan was modeled on the old government of Massachusetts, with an elective rather than a royal governor, of course, but it certainly contemplated no radical change in the political structure.[14] John Adams was no innovator. He deplored what he called "the rage for innovation" which had appeared in Massachusetts by June of 1776. The projects, said he, are not for repairing the building but for tearing it down. "The projects of county assemblies, town registers, and town probates of wills are founded in narrow notions, sordid stinginess, and profound ignorance, and tend directly to barbarism."[15]

There was equal alarm in the South at demands for change and new governments. Among those who sought to defend the old order was Carter Braxton. In a long address to the Virginia convention he praised the British constitution and declared that it would be "perverting all order to oblige us, by a novel government, to give up our laws, our customs, and our manners." The spirit or principles of limited monarchy should be preserved. Yet, he said, we daily see it condemned by the advocates of "popular governments. . . . The systems recommended to the colonies seem to accord with the temper of the times, and are fraught with all the tumult and riot incident to simple democracy. . . ." Braxton declared that democracies would not tolerate wealth, and that they could exist only in countries where all the people are poor from necessity. Nowhere in history could he find an example of a successful democracy. What he proposed for Virginia was a three-part government with a house of representatives elected by the voters for three years. The house, in turn, would choose a governor to serve during good behavior and a council of twenty-

---

[13] *English Historical Documents,* IX, 816–817.

[14] *Works of John Adams,* IV, 189–200.

[15] To John Winthrop, Philadelphia, June 23, 1776, in Mass. Hist. Soc. *Collections,* 5th ser. (Boston, 1878), IV, 310. This was in reply to a letter of John Winthrop, written on June 1, in which he reported to Adams on the various schemes afoot in Massachusetts. Ibid., 305–308.

four to hold their places for life and to act as an upper house of the legislature.[16] Braxton in Virginia, like John Adams in Massachusetts, hoped to make the transition from dependence to independence without any fundamental political change.

But change was in the air, and writer after writer sought to formulate new ideas about government and to offer concrete suggestions for the theoretical foundations and political structures of the new states to be. In 1775, on hearing that congress had given advice to New Hampshire on the establishment of a government, General John Sullivan offered his thoughts to the revolutionary congress of his colony. All government, he wrote, ought to be instituted for the good of the people. There should be no conflicting branches in imitation of the British constitution "so much celebrated by those who understand nothing of it...." The two houses of the legislature and a governor should all be elected by the people. No danger can arise to a state "from giving the people a free and full voice in their own government." The so-called checks upon the licentiousness of the people "are only the children of designing or ambitious men, no such thing being necessary...."[17]

In the middle colonies appeared an address "To the People of North America on the Different Kinds of Government." After defining monarchy, aristocracy, oligarchy, and democracy, the anonymous writer said: "Popular government—sometimes termed democracy, republic, or commonwealth—is the plan of civil society wherein the community at large takes the care of its own welfare, and manages its concerns by representatives elected by the people out of their own body."

"Seeing the happiness of the people is the true end of government; and it appearing by the definition, that the popular form is the only one which has this for its object; it may be worth inquiring into the causes which have prevented its success in the world."

This writer then undertakes to explain the failure of former democracies. First of all, he says that past republics tried democracy too late and contained within them remnants of aristocracies and military cliques which disliked it. A second cause was that men did not have adequate knowledge of representation and that their large and tumultuous assemblies made it possible for unscrupulous men to charge all troubles to the constitution.

[16] *The Virginia Gazette* (Dixon and Hunter), June 8, 1776. This had been printed earlier in pamphlet form. For similar ideas see the letter of William Hooper, North Carolina delegate to the Continental Congress, to the North Carolina Provincial Congress, October 26, 1776, in *The Colonial Records of North Carolina*, ed. W. L. Saunders, X (1890), 866–869.

[17] John Sullivan to Meshech Weare, Winter Hill [Mass.], December 11, 1775, in *American Archives*, IV, 241–242.

A third cause of failure has been the political writers who from ignorance or ulterior motives have tried to discredit democracy. "This has been carried to such a length with many, that the mentioning a democracy constantly excites in them the idea of anarchy; and few, except such as have emancipated themselves from the shackles of political bigotry and prejudice, can talk of it with patience, and hearken to anything offered in its defence." Such are the causes of the destruction of former republics, but the Americans have the best opportunity ever open to mankind to form a free government, "the last and best plan that can possibly exist."[18]

In "The Interest of America," another writer says that new governments must soon be created in America and that "the good of the people is the ultimate end of civil government." Therefore, "we should assume that mode of government which is most equitable and adapted to the good of mankind . . . and I think there can be no doubt that a well-regulated democracy is most equitable." The annual or frequent choice of magistrates is "most likely to prevent usurpation and tyranny; and most likely to secure the privileges of the people." Legislatures should be unicameral, for a plurality of branches leads to endless contention and a waste of time.[19]

In New England, where the revolutionary congresses of Massachusetts and New Hampshire were controlled by leaders along the seacoast, there was a growing discontent among the people of the back-country counties. Out of it came one of the clearest democratic statements of the times: "The People are the Best Governors." The author starts with the premise that "there are many very noisy about liberty, but are aiming at nothing more than personal power and grandeur." "God," he said, "gave mankind freedom by nature, made every man equal to his neighbor, and has virtually enjoined them to govern themselves by their own laws." Representatives in legislatures should have only the power to make laws. They should not have power to elect officials or to elect councils or senates to veto legislation. Only the people have this power. If there must be senates, they should be elected by the people of the state at large and should have only advisory powers. Representation should not be according to taxable property, for "Nature itself abhors such a system of civil government, for it will make an inequality among the people and set up a number of lords over the rest." Representation according to population also has its difficulties. The solution is for each town to have one representative, with more for larger towns if the legislature thinks fit. So far as property qualifications for representatives are concerned, there should be none. "Social

[18] *American Archives*, V, 180–183. [March 1776.]
[19] Ibid., VI, 840–843. [June 1776].

virtue and knowledge . . . is the best and only necessary qualification of
the person before us." If we have property qualifications "we root out
virtue; and what will then become of the genuine principle of freedom?"
"Let it not be said in future generations that money was made by the
founders of the American states an essential qualification in the rulers of a
free people." The writer proposed annual elections of a one-house legislature, of a governor, and of the judges of the superior court. The people
in the counties should elect annually all their own officials—judges,
sheriffs, and others—as should the inhabitants of the towns. And in all
elections "any orderly free male of ordinary capacity" should have the
right to vote if he has lived in a town for a year.[20]

From such discussions one may sum up certain of the essential ideas.
(1) They agree that the "good" or the "happiness" of the people is the
only end of government. (2) They agree that "democracy" is the best
form of government to achieve that end. (3) They show a distrust of
men when in power—a distrust shared with far more conservative-minded
writers of the times.

As to details of government there are variations, but they do agree on
fundamentals. (1) The legislatures, whether one or two houses, are to be
elected by the people. (2) Public officials, state and local, are to be elected
by the people or by their representatives in the legislatures. (3) There
should be annual elections. (4) Some argue for manhood suffrage, and
one writer even advocated that tax-paying widows should vote. (5) There
should be freedom of religion, at least for Protestants; in any case, freedom from taxation to support established churches.

One may well ask: did such theoretical discussions have any meaning
in terms of practical politics, or were they idle speculations by anonymous
writers without influence? The answer is that they did have meaning. I
have already cited the discussion of the principles of government in New
York in the spring of 1774, and the litigious jockey in Massachusetts in
1775 who hoped that the courts would remain closed forever. These are
not isolated examples. By the end of 1775 all sorts of organized activity
was under way, ranging in place from North Carolina to New Hampshire, and from militia groups to churches.

In North Carolina the defeat of the Regulators in 1771 had not ended
discontent but merely suppressed it. By September 1775, Mecklenburg
County was instructing its delegates in the provincial congress to work
for a plan of government providing for equal representation and the
right to vote for every freeman who supported the government, either
in person or property. Legislation should not be a "divided right"; no

[20] Reprinted in Frederick Chase, *A History of Dartmouth College and the Town
of Hanover, New Hampshire* (Cambridge, 1891), I, Appendix D, 654–663.

man or body of men should be "invested with a negative on the voice of the people duly collected. . . ."[21] By November 1776, when North Carolina elected a congress to write its first state constitution, Mecklenburg County was even more specific in its instructions. It told its delegates that they were to endeavor to establish a free government under the authority of the people of North Carolina, and that the government was to be a "simple democracy, or as near it as possible." In fixing fundamental principles, the delegates were to "oppose everything that leans to aristocracy or power in the hands of the rich and chief men exercised to the oppression of the poor."[22]

In the middle colonies militia organizations made demands and suggestions. Pennsylvania was in turmoil, with the assembly controlled by the opponents of independence and the revolutionary party working in large measure through a voluntary militia organization called the Associators. In February 1776, a committee of privates from the Philadelphia Associators told the assembly "that it has been the practice of all countries, and is highly reasonable, that all persons . . . who expose their lives in the defense of a country, should be admitted to the enjoyment of all the rights and privileges of a citizen of that country. . . ." All Associators should be given the right to vote.[23]

In June the committee of privates again protested to the legislature. This time they denied the right of the assembly to appoint two brigadier generals for the Associators as recommended by the Continental Congress. The privates declared that since many of them could not vote, they were not represented in the assembly. Furthermore, many counties where the Associators were most numerous did not have proportional representation. And for that matter, since many members of the assembly were members of a religious profession "totally averse to military defense," they could not possibly be called representatives of the Associators.[24]

While such ideas were being expounded in Pennsylvania, some militia in Maryland were proposing a new constitution. There was a growing discontent in Maryland with the revolutionary convention which was opposed to independence, and whose members were appointing one another to military posts. Government by convention should stop, said one writer, and regular government be instituted.[25]

Late in June 1776 deputies from the militia battalions in Anne Arundel

[21] *Colonial Records of North Carolina*, X, 239–242. [Sept. 1775.]
[22] Ibid., 870, a–f. [Nov. 1776.]
[23] Votes and Proceedings of the Assembly, Feb. 23, 1776, in *Pennsylvania Archives*, 8th ser. [Harrisburg, 1935], VIII, 7406.
[24] Ibid., 7546–47. June 14, 1776.
[25] "An American" in "To the People of Maryland," *American Archives*, VI, 1094–96.

County met and proposed a constitution to be submitted to the people of the county. They started out with the declaration that the right to legislate is in "every member of the community," but that for convenience the right must be delegated to representatives chosen by the people. The legislature must never form a separate interest from the community at large, and its branches must "be independent of and balance each other, and all dependent on the people." There should be a two-house legislature chosen annually "as annual elections are most friendly to liberty, and the oftener power reverts to the people, the greater will be the security for a faithful discharge of it." All provincial officials, including judges, should be elected annually by joint ballot of the two houses. All county officials should be chosen annually by the people of each county. Nothing is said of property qualifications for either voting or office-holding. So far as taxes are concerned, "the unjust mode of taxation by poll" should be abolished, and all monies raised should be according to a fair and equal assessment of people's estates.[26]

In New Jersey the revolutionary congress, like that in other colonies, was trying to prevent change and was maintaining the land qualification for voting for its members. But the complaints grew so loud that it was forced to yield. One petition in 1776, for instance, declared that "we cannot conceive the wise author of our existence ever designed that a certain quantity of earth on which we tread should be annexed to a man to complete his dignity and fit him for society. Was the sole design of government either the security of land or money, the possession of either or both of these would be the only necessary qualifications for its members. But we apprehend the benign intentions of a well regulated government to extend to the security of much more valuable possessions—the rights and privileges of freemen, for the defense of which every kind of property and even life itself have been liberally expended."[27]

In Massachusetts the Baptists were quick to draw a parallel between the fight for civil liberty. Baptists were being jailed for refusal to pay taxes to support churches. Their leader, the Reverend Isaac Backus, put Sam Adams squarely on the spot in January 1774. "I fully concur with your grand maxim," wrote Backus, "that it is essential to liberty that representation and taxation go together." Hence, since the representatives in the Massachusetts legislature have only civil qualifications, how can they levy ecclesiastical taxes? "And I am bold in it," Backus goes on, "that taxes laid by the British Parliament upon America are not more

[26] Ibid., 1092–94. June 26-27, 1776.
[27] Richard P. McCormick, *The History of Voting in New Jersey . . . 1664–1911* (New Brunswick, 1953), pp. 66–68.

contrary to civil freedom, than these taxes are to the very nature of liberty of conscience. . . ." He hopes, he says, that Adams will do something about it so that a large number of peaceable people "may not be forced to carry their complaints before those who would be glad to hear that the legislature of Massachusetts deny to their fellow servants that liberty which they so earnestly insist upon for themselves. A word to the wise is sufficient."[28]

Samuel Adams was not interested in liberty of conscience, particularly for Baptists, and he did not reply. But Backus pursued him to the first Continental Congress in Philadelphia where a four-hour meeting was held in Carpenter's Hall one night. The Massachusetts delegation met with the Baptists, but with a large audience present, among whom were the Quaker leaders James and Israel Pemberton, and members of congress like Joseph Galloway. The Backus diary gives a picture of Sam and John Adams quite literally squirming as the Baptists cited the facts of religious life in Massachusetts.[29] One can well imagine with what delight Galloway and the Pembertons looked on as the Massachusetts delegation vainly tried to wriggle out of a dilemma produced by the contradiction between their theory and their practice.

The Declaration of Independence was taken seriously by many Americans, or at least they found its basic philosophy useful in battling for change in the new states. Nowhere was this done more neatly than in Grafton County, New Hampshire. The Provincial Congress was in the control of eastern leaders and they refused to grant representation that the western towns thought adequate. In calling elections in the fall of 1776, the Congress grouped various towns together for electing representatives and told them that the men they elected must own real estate worth £200 lawful money. Led by professors at an obscure little college at Hanover, the people of Grafton County went on strike. They refused to hold elections, and town after town met and passed resolutions. The whole procedure of the Congress was unconstitutional. No plan of representation had been adopted since the Declaration of Independence. By the Declaration, said Hanover and two other towns in a joint statement, "we conceive that the powers of government reverted to the people at large, and of course annihilated the political existence of the Assembly which then was. . . ." Six other towns joined together and declared it to be "our humble opinion, that when the declaration of independency took place, the Colonies were absolutely in a state of nature, and the powers

---

[28] To Samuel Adams, Jan. 19, 1774, in Alvah Hovey, *A Memoir of the Life and Times of the Rev. Isaac Backus* (Boston, 1859), pp. 195–197.

[29] Ibid., ch. xv.

of government reverted to the people at large. . . ." Such being the case, the Provincial Congress has no authority to combine towns, each of which is entitled to representation as a corporate entity. And it has no right to limit the choice of representatives to the owners of £200, said the people of Lyme, because "every elector in free states is capable of being elected."[30]

It seems clear, to me at least, that by 1776 there were people in America demanding the establishment of democratic state governments, by which they meant legislatures controlled by a majority of the voters, and with none of the checks upon their actions such as had existed in the colonies. At the same time there were many Americans who were determined that there should be no changes except those made inevitable by separation from Great Britain.

The history of the writing of the first state constitutions is to a large extent the history of the conflict between these two ideals of government. The conflict can be exaggerated, of course, for there was considerable agreement on structural details. Most of the state constitutions worked out in written form the structure of government that had existed in the colonies, all the way from governors, two-house legislatures, and judicial systems, to the forms of local government. In terms of structure, little that is revolutionary is to be found. Even the much maligned unicameral legislature of Pennsylvania was only a continuation of what Pennsylvania had had since the beginning of the century.

The significant thing is not the continuity of governmental structure, but the alteration of the balance of power within the structure, and in the political situation resulting from the break away from the supervising power of a central government—that of Great Britain.

The first and most revolutionary change was in the field of basic theory. In May 1776, to help bring about the overthrow of the Pennsylvania assembly, the chief stumbling block in the way of independence, Congress resolved that all governments exercising authority under the crown of Great Britain should be suppressed, and that "all the powers of government [be] exerted under the authority of the people of the colonies. . . ." John Adams described it as "the most important resolution that ever was taken in America."[31] The Declaration of Independence spelled it out in terms of the equality of men, the sovereignty of the people, and the right of a people to change their governments as they pleased.

Second: the Revolution ended the power of a sovereign central govern-

---

[30] *American Archives*, 5th ser. (Washington, 1848–1853), III, 1223–24, and Chase, *History of Dartmouth*, I, 426–433.

[31] *Warren–Adams Letters*, I. (Boston, 1917), 245; in Mass. Hist. Soc. *Collections*, Vols. 72, 73.

ment over the colonies. Britain had had the power to appoint and remove governors, members of upper houses of legislatures, judges, and other officials. It had the power to veto colonial legislation, to review cases appealed from colonial supreme courts, and to use armed force. All of this superintending power was wiped out by independence.

Third: the new central government created in America by the Articles of Confederation was, in a negative sense at least, a democratic government. The Congress of the United States had no power over either the states or their citizens. Hence, each state could govern itself as it pleased, and as a result of some of the new state constitutions, this often meant by a majority of the voters within a state.

Fourth: in writing the state constitutions, change was inevitable. The hierarchy of appointed legislative, executive, and judicial officials which had served as a check upon the elective legislatures was gone. The elective legislature became the supreme power in every state, and the lower houses, representing people however inadequately, became the dominant branch. The appointive houses of colonial times were replaced by elective senates, which in theory were supposed to represent property. They were expected to, and sometimes did, act as a check upon the lower houses, but their power was far less than that of pre-war councils.

Fifth: the office of governor underwent a real revolution. The governors of the royal colonies had, in theory at least, vast powers, including an absolute veto. In the new constitutions, most Americans united in shearing the office of governor of virtually all power.

Sixth: state supreme courts underwent a similar revolution. Under the state constitutions they were elected by the legislatures or appointed by governors who were elected officials. And woe betide a supreme court that tried to interfere with the actions of a legislature.

What such changes meant in terms of political realities was that a majority of voters within a state, if agreed upon a program and persistent enough, could do what it wanted, unchecked by governors or courts or appeals to a higher power outside the state.

There were other areas in which changes took place, although they were only beginnings. A start was made in the direction of ending the property qualification for voting and office-holding. A few states established what amounted to manhood suffrage, and a few years later even women voted in New Jersey although that was stopped when it appeared that woman suffrage meant only a means of stuffing ballot boxes. A few states took steps in the direction of representation according to population, a process as yet unsolved in the United States. A large step was taken in the direction of disestablishing state churches, but on the whole one still had to be a Protestant, and a Trinitarian at that, to hold office.

In connection with office-holding, there is one eighteenth-century American idea that is worthy of a whole study by itself, and that is the concept of rotation in office. Many Americans were convinced that office-holding bred a lust for power in the holder. Therefore there must be frequent, if not annual, elections; and there must be a limitation on the time one might spend in certain offices. There is probably no more remarkable self-denying ordinance in the history of politics than the provision in the Articles of Confederation that no man could be a member of Congress more than three years out of any six. I have often been accused of wanting to go back to the Articles of Confederation, which is nonsense, but there are times when I do wish that this one provision might be revived in the twentieth century.

What I have done in this paper is to set before you some of the reasons for believing that the American Revolution was a democratic movement, not in origin, but in result. Certainly the political leaders of the eighteenth century thought the results were democratic. Whether they thought the results were good or bad is another story.

Democracy and the American Revolution: A Frame of Reference

RICHARD BUEL, JR.

AMERICAN HISTORIANS HAVE NEVER BEEN FAMOUS FOR AGREEMENT, but in one respect they seem curiously united. All have tried to measure the significance of the Revolution in relation to the development of American democracy. However, beyond the limits of this initial premise their unity dissolves into a rich multiplicity of interpretations. Such a state of affairs is not necessarily to be lamented, for the diversity of opinions has helped to illuminate the complexity of our Revolutionary experience.

There is a point, though, where multiplicity ceases to enlighten and

Reprinted from the *William and Mary Quarterly*, XXI, 2, April 1964. Copyright 1964 by Richard Buel, Jr.

NOTE: By the author's permission the original footnote citations have been curtailed for reasons of space. They can of course be found in the original article.

instead merely creates confusion. We are approaching, though we may not yet have reached, that point on the question of whether or not the Revolution was a democratic movement. While it is impossible, and even undesirable, to have complete agreement on the substance of interpretations, to be still debating such a fundamental question indicates a critical weakness in our knowledge. The crux of our confusion lies more in the realm of intellectual history than in institutional history. After almost a century and a half of historical speculation, we are still not agreed on the democratic nature of Revolutionary ideas, let alone on precisely what "democratic" changes took place in American thinking between 1760 and 1789.

The problem transcends simple divergencies in individual points of view and relates more fundamentally to the methods employed. Our confusion in the realm of ideas stems largely from the reluctance of historians to define a point of departure in historical context. Because we have failed to clarify the manner in which mid-eighteenth-century Americans viewed the people's role in the polity, it has been difficult to interpret the significance of institutional and intellectual changes throughout the Revolutionary period.

The institution of representation serves as a useful illustration both because it was subject to rigorous scrutiny during the Revolution and because it has been traditionally associated with democracy. The colonists themselves referred to their representative assemblies as the democratic branch of their constitutions. But were they using the word "democratic" in the same context we use it today? Though modern representative institutions are popularly regarded as the principal mechanism through which the people express their will in politics, this does not mean they were viewed in the same light by the Revolutionary generation almost two centuries ago. If, in fact, representation was conceived to perform quite a different function, then the meaning of such institutional developments as the extension or contraction of the franchise may have to be reassessed.

What we need, then, is an imaginative reconstruction of the values and assumptions as well as the explicit ideas of colonial political thought immediately prior to the Revolution. Generally American historians have dismissed such an enterprise as impractical. They have assumed that American political ideas were unformed or ambiguous at the beginning of the imperial crisis and that colonial thought remained inchoate until the eve of independence. Confirmation for this view has been sought in the instability of the colonists' ideas about the jurisdiction of Parliament throughout the first decade of crisis. The assumption that American thought started from no fixed point and achieved no uniform expression until independence has made it difficult to define with precision the meaning of its development throughout the Revolutionary era.

It is possible, however, that American historians have unduly despaired of defining a point of departure from which to assess the meaning of the Revolutionary experience. Though colonial leaders differed in their initial definitions of Parliament's power, in a more fundamental sense they were in basic agreement. Their agreement sprang from their common experience within the British imperial system which, despite the diffuse heterogeneity of the thirteen colonies, had by 1760 given birth to a surprisingly homogeneous leadership on the provincial scene. During the bitter factional disputes that had infected all the colonial polities throughout the eighteenth century, local political magnates devoid of transatlantic connections had acquired an elaborate conceptual arsenal from the dissenting tradition in English thought[1] with which they sought to protect themselves from the superior power of their adversaries.

Provincial leaders had been attracted to dissenting thought by a combination of circumstances. For one thing a vast majority of them shared a religious affinity with the British dissenters. But of greater importance was the ability of this tradition to interpret unique aspects of the American experience. If the seething factionalism of provincial politics left many colonists disenchanted with the exercise of political power in general, dissenting thought was characterized by a profound distrust of all power, no matter by whom possessed. Most important of all, however, was the fact that these colonists occupied an analogous position to the dissenters in relation to the sovereign power. Because dissenting thought had been developed throughout the seventeenth and eighteenth centuries by men who were excluded from the centers of influence within the state, it had sought to enlist the resources of a virtuous people against the potential aggressions of a hostile sovereign. This, of course, was precisely the same situation local colonial politicians found themselves in during the mid-eighteenth century. In many cases they too possessed no other available resource with which to defend their local autonomy than the united support of the provincial populace.

[1] By the "dissenting tradition in English thought," I do not mean to refer only to the ideas of English thinkers who were nonconformists, but also to the work of such men as John Trenchard, Thomas Gordon, and Benjamin Hoadly, all of whom were members of the Church of England and whose ideas, for reasons explained below, proved to be especially congenial to the English dissenters. I call it the "dissenting tradition" only because the nonconformists gradually became the exclusive custodians of this strand of thinking in Britain after 1745. For a complete description of the participants in the dissenting tradition, see Caroline Robbins, *The Eighteenth-Century Commonwealthman* . . . (Cambridge, Mass., 1959), passim.

It was also the situation which confronted all Americans simultaneously when the ministry undertook to reorganize the empire in 1763. Ironically the colonists' initial reaction to parliamentary taxation was not to think radically new thoughts but to apply the familiar political ideas of the English dissenting tradition to an unprecedented situation. If there was any change in the structure of basic concepts, it was one of crystalization and clarification rather than innovation as these ideas were diffused to a wider circle. Many who had been familiar with dissenting notions but had not been accustomed to rely on them were now forced to appropriate them by the common jeopardy in which American rights had been placed. At least in the substratum of fundamental premises, if not in their precise application, the impact of crisis produced uniformity rather than confusion, a uniformity which was only to dissolve under the grueling strain of long years of controversy. Even after independence the ideas and assumptions that were characteristic of dissenting thought continued to dominate the minds of many individuals and were an important influence in the creation of our nation's unique political institutions.

As we have indicated, the dissenting tradition was forced to rely heavily upon the power of the populace. But how was its power to be applied? This paper will explore the colonists' ideas about the contract theory of government, the right of revolution, and representation. These ideas were part of a systematic theory about the role of the people in the polity which lay at the heart of the colonists' initial confrontation with parliamentary taxation.[2] By explicating this theory we can define an initial frame of reference from which the "democratic" significance of subsequent events can be more readily assessed.[3]

I

Like all eighteenth-century English thinkers the provincial leadership sought to control power by limiting and dividing it. What was novel in their solutions was not the principle behind their techniques, but the

[2] One facet of the people's power will be omitted from consideration, however, because it was not subject to major revision during or after the Revolution and because it is not germane to the interpretive question of whether or not the American Revolution was a democratic movement. This is the power of the people to participate in the execution of the law through juries.

[3] As the New England clergy were instrumental in disseminating dissenting thought to wide sectors of the population in the northern colonies, much reliance has been placed on their political sermons. Political pamphlets bearing directly on the imperial crisis have been the other major source used. Whenever possible an attempt has been made to refer the reader to relevant English sources from which the colonists derived their ideas.

scope with which they were applied. Rather than confine the balance of the constitution to the autonomous composition of the supreme power, to the parliamentary components of Kings, Lords, and Commons, Americans turned to a conception of balance between two broad, countervailing forces in political society, the rulers and the ruled. In their elaboration of the relationship between rulers and ruled they defined arrangements whereby society might benefit from the exercise of power without suffering from its corresponding abuses.

By enlarging the constitutional balance to embrace not only the rulers but also the ruled, Americans indicated that the real lines of conflict to be anticipated within the polity were not between the constituent parts of the supreme power but between magistrates and people.[4] In doing so they challenged the idea that in a conflict of interests between rulers and ruled the subject should passively acquiesce in the determinations of the magistrate. Though they lamented the existence of such a conflict, they were nonetheless willing to accord the subject's interests a legitimacy which the interests of power did not necessarily possess. Their willingness to reverse the dominant presumptions of eighteenth-century English thought did not proceed from a belief that the people were incapable of mischief. Rather, it proceeded from a theoretical recognition that the ruler's peculiar position made his power even more liable to abuse than was that of the subject.

By virtue of his office a ruler possessed presumptive control over society's combined resources while the subject's power was confined entirely to his own person, or at most, to the resources of those whose immediate co-operation he could secure. In a predominantly agrarian community where groups of individuals tended to live in isolation from one another, uninformed of each other's needs and opinions, it was difficult enough to get all the people to unite in one common course of action after extensive persuasion and virtually impossible to have them all unite spontaneously. The magistrates, on the other hand, were a compact and potentially disciplined group which constituted a formidable force against a flock of helpless and disunited subjects.

Furthermore, the possession of power exposed the ruler to temptations to which the subject, by virtue of his impotence, was immune. Because of the difficulties obstructing the people's concerted action, history had demonstrated that the populace were usually quiescent under good government and loath to stir even when oppressed with substantial injustices. While the magistrates in full possession of the powers of the state might

---

[4] By "magistrate" I refer to any civil officer, either legislative or executive, to whom presumptive obedience was due.

not only find it within the range of their capabilities but also to their *immediate* interest to erect a tyranny, that is to enhance their own welfare at the expense of the subjects', the people in their naturally unconnected state could rationally desire nothing else but the public welfare in which their own personal welfares would be maximized. Thus the people were not under such temptations to thwart their own interests as powerful rulers were to abuse those of the people. It was precisely because those in power were more likely to pursue interests distinct from the common interest than were those without power that the subject was entitled to some means of influencing the magistrate's actions as security against oppression.

However, in constructing a broad balance between rulers and ruled, all eighteenth-century thinkers had to face the problem of how this balance could be rendered stable. The difficulty of the task was compounded by the apparent absence of a mediating third force, such as the House of Lords in the parliamentary balance, and by the potentially unstable nature of the people's power. If you were willing to give the subject sufficient power to maintain the legitimacy of his interests against the encroachments of the magistrates, how could you in turn render the subject's power incapable of abuse?

Superficially it looked as though this problem could be bypassed. A balance between the rights of the subject and the prerogatives of the magistrate might be stabilized by an agreed on jurisdictional definition of the magistrate's power. Once it was acknowledged that rulers were more likely to violate the common interest than were subjects, was it not reasonable to endow the people with a right to frame a constitution "as the standing measure of the proceedings of government" for their own protection and to solicit their ruler's consent to it? Even if there was no express compact, "yet it has been necessarily implied, and understood, both by governors, and the governed, on their entering into society."[5] In these covenants both rulers and ruled could mark out the fundamental law by which the rights of each would be guaranteed against infringement by the other. If the magistrates transcended the formal boundaries of power delegated to them, then and only then did the people have a right to withdraw their obedience and ultimately to form new governments.

However, Americans took pains to emphasize that slight infringements of the compact would not justify a rebellion. Only when the ruler trampled wholesale upon the rights of the subject and violated the welfare of society was resistance justified, and then only insofar as it was necessary

[5] Gad Hitchcock, *A Sermon preached before his excellency Thomas Gage . . . May 25th, 1774 . . .* (Boston, 1774), 7; Whitney, *Transgression,* 10.

to preserve the rights of the people and their welfare from destruction. Until such an emergency occurred, the people were morally bound to obey the magistrate's commands as well as it being their interest to do so. Hopefully the existence of such a fundamental law and the ultimate threat of revolution would preclude all emergencies and enable the people to confine their role to obeying their superior's lawful commands.

But the compact theory of government enforced by the sanctions of possible revolution did not provide the subject with practical guarantees against aggression by the magistrates. In the first place, as was often pointed out, the magistrate's office could not be adequately defined by explicit reference to fundamental laws. The extent of the magistrate's power was determined by the ends which his office was designed to realize. He had plenary power for the good of society, but when he used power to society's detriment he was exceeding his lawful commission. What constituted the "good of the society" could not be completely anticipated in a fixed law, but depended upon the changing circumstances in which a society was placed. The plea which was made during the imperial crisis by some of the New England clergy for a clarification of the fundamental law so that neither party could misconstrue it merely indicated the difficulties with which this means of resolving political conflict was beset.

Even had the magistrate's powers been capable of full and complete definition, the basic problem would still have remained of rendering such jurisdictional definitions of equilibrium real, in other words of making these arrangements self-enforcing. Both magistrates and subjects had an interest in guarding their rights against each other's encroachments. But under the compact theory of government, once encroachments were made, the only remedy was violence which, by obstructing the force of government, placed the very existence of the "social fabric" in jeopardy and threatened to dissolve all into one wild tumult of confusion and anarchy.

The difficulties associated with the compact theory of government were compounded by the fact that according to the premises of dissenting thought, amply reinforced by colonial experience, violations were to be anticipated from one's rulers. But if the magistrate violated the compact, the people were left only with the unpalatable alternatives of submission or resistance by force. Though a people might be perfectly justified in their resistance, this right when exercised could as effectually destroy a free society as would the arbitrary sway of a tyrant. If to enforce the covenant you had to be continually breaking it, you would never derive the benefits of it in the first place. The real problem was to prevent these encroachments from occurring. What was needed was some special power lodged in the people, short of revolution, with which they could peacefully restrain the misuse of political power by their superiors.

One such peaceful restraint might be found in selective as opposed to wholesale or violent disobedience. Eighteenth-century thinkers persisted in emphasizing the co-operative nature of human society. If laws were to be duly executed, the magistrate needed the co-operation of the subject. The exercise of political power was not the autonomous function of the ruler's command, but depended equally on the subject's willingness to obey. Against the possibility of the magistrate issuing oppressive commands the subject always had the choice of yielding or withholding obedience. New England election sermons continually raised the question of when obedience was due and when it was proper to disobey. In telling the people that obedience was a matter of choice and that the subject should not obey the ruler's commands blindly but only in response to his conscience, the New England clergy was advocating a doctrine of selective disobedience which would not necessarily overturn society. If their rulers persisted in oppressing the people, might not the people withdraw their obedience to such oppressive measures so as to deprive their authors of all benefit from them? And might not this serve as an admonishment to wicked rulers to return to their duty?

Opponents of this school of thought could legitimately object that if obedience to the commands of a political superior was a matter which each member of society could decide for himself, then what security was there that society would not disintegrate in the unrelated disobediences of private men? Such an objection could be leveled equally at admitting the right of revolution, for many felt selective disobedience was the practical consequence of such an admission. Why would not this lead to anarchy?

One could reply that conscience was not an entirely arbitrary standard to which to appeal. Men could agree on questions of conscience, particularly when there was an objective standard by which the lawfulness of authority was to be tested which was independent of the subject's will. It was the subject's duty to resist only when the ruler acted contrary to God's law and the constitution. But when the magistrate remained within the bounds of his commission to rule, his authority was fortified by conscience as well as interest, for the subject's temporal and eternal happiness depended upon obedience to all the ruler's lawful commands.

However, the colonists were willing to admit that in our imperfect condition men with sincere intentions could disagree on matters of conscience. Then there was the added consideration that depraved men unmindful of the dictates of conscience lived in society. But Americans pointed out that the power of the magistrate was so great in proportion to that of the populace that only the united opposition of the people could defeat the magistrate's power. In any conflict an isolated subject would make a very poor match for a magistrate armed with the power of the state. To counter the weight of the magistrates' power, subjects had to act in concert, which in itself constituted a substantial check on the people's ability to express their will in politics. When contemporary literature referred to the people as a "rope of sand," the image reflected the obstacles obstructing their effective group action and the tendency of their potential power to dissolve in disunity. The unrelated disobediences of depraved men or the sincere mistakes of a few misguided souls could not disturb the stability of society or the magistrate's power because their opposition, lacking a unifying principle, would not enable them to act in a concerted fashion. Only ordered resistance could successfully challenge the magistrates' power and this could spring only from a general agreement among the individual consciences of the people that the ruler had transcended the legitimate bounds of his authority.

The trouble with the idea of selective disobedience was that it assumed the ruler could not wield the instruments of coercion without the co-operation of the subject. While it was true that the ruler's power to contribute to the public good did depend on the subject's cooperation, and while the notion of selective disobedience might have some remedial effect so far as the operation of oppressive laws was concerned, it could not affect the manner in which the ruler wielded other instruments of power at his disposal such as command of the army or control over the administration of justice. True, the subject might push disobedience to the point where the sinews of government had virtually dissolved in order to destroy some of the advantages the ruler hoped to reap from his oppression, yet when he did so selective disobedience became in effect the right of revolution, and the people were infinitely more vulnerable in a state of anarchy than were their rulers. The fact that by partial resistance the subject could diminish the benefits the ruler sought in oppression provided no guarantee that the ruler would return to a respect for the common interest. The only real sanction which the people possessed in the compact theory of government was the right of revolution for this alone could halt the march of a determined tyrant.

While colonial thinkers of the mid-eighteenth century were perfectly aware of the limitations and abuses to which the right of revolution might be put, they continued to affirm it, both as a last resort and because power exercised without the threat of this right was liable to even greater abuse. Acknowledgment of the right of resistance protected rulers as well as subjects because it helped to prevent the evil of the magistrate's encroachments in the first place, and thus ultimately protected rulers from the wrath of the populace. But it provided no guarantee, and as a remedy was likely to prove worse than the disease. For the practical maintenance of a stable constitutional balance between rulers and ruled the people needed subtler and more discriminating means of persuading their superiors to respect their rights. What more acceptable techniques could be devised for protecting the subject from the overwhelming power of the magistrates which were not equally liable to abuse?

II

The contract theory of government was plagued by two essential weaknesses. The first related to the inflexible and unprecise nature of the fundamental law; the second to the procedures of enforcement. Both could be obviated through the institution of representation.

Despite its recognized limitations, eighteenth-century Americans continued to regard the law as an essential device in demarcating the boundary between the rights of the subject and the prerogatives of the magistrate. If power were confined within the channels the law had marked out for its circulation, the subject—provided his behavior conformed to certain pre-established standards—would have security that the power of the magistrate would not affect him. The security that the law might afford in turn depended on the character of the laws which were made. The more supple the law was in confronting new situations, the more agile it was in nipping tyranny in the bud, the more effective a barrier it would provide against the potential encroachments of power.

But the possibility still existed that no matter how good the laws were the magistrates would nonetheless overstep them. Against this contingency the colonists invoked a sanction short of revolution which was at the same time calm, gentle, and forceful. This was the power of the purse. Errant rulers could be starved into compliance with the law by the withholding of supplies.

If the people were to be secure from oppression, it seemed necessary that they have a role in the making of laws and levying of taxes. Their role could be either active or passive. They could actively enter into the formation of statutes by framing and enacting them, or they could passively give their consent to what the magistrates proposed. However, both alternatives were open to objection. If the people had the power merely to accept or reject what questions were proposed to them, history demonstrated that in their naturally disconnected state they would prove an easy prey for ambitious rulers, who could divide, deceive, and trick them with impunity into assenting to whatever the magistrate desired. But on the other hand allowing subjects an active voice in policy was liable to all the objections which had been raised about their potential instability and incompetence.

Many observers in the eighteenth century felt that the British constitution had resolved this dilemma through the institution of representation. Similarly, contemporary colonial thinkers hoped, by providing that the power of the people should be exercised by their representatives, to obviate various objections which were raised against the people's active participation in politics while at the same time providing the people with adequate protection against oppression from their rulers.

The concept of representation specifies the existence of a certain relationship between the representative and the represented. This relationship is one of consensus or agreement.[6] In the modern democratic context we are apt to think of this consensus in a way which was not necessarily congenial to the dominant values of eighteenth-century political science. Democracy means rule by the will of the people, and within a framework of democratic assumptions the representative must place himself in agreement with at least a majority of his constituents if he is to remain a representative. Theoretically, in a democracy agreement is the result of the representative adjusting himself to his constituent's views rather than the constituent adjusting himself to his representative's views.[7]

Such democratic notions had shortcomings from the eighteenth-century point of view. Aside from the practical difficulties the people would confront in making decisions upon all the contingencies of government without access to information and without the leisure to devote their best energies to the problems at hand, theoretically to make the representative nothing more than the obedient lackey of his constituents was the height of folly because it threatened to deprive society of the benefit of its most talented personnel. In a world of radically unequal political competencies, where the least competent would obviously compose the majority of the population, to surrender the power of political decision to a majority of the people would be to surrender this important trust to those in society least capable of executing it, if not to unprincipled demagogues who might control the mob in their own interests. For eighteenth-century thought, representation not only solved the obvious difficulties that prevented a whole people from assembling in one place and rationally conducting a debate, it also was an institution which utilized the political *expertise* of the realm in the people's behalf. The representative was not supposed to be an average man who reflected the defects as well as the virtues of his constituents, but in theory he was supposed to be the best man, the wisest and most virtuous.

Far from being the humble servant of his constituents, eighteenth-century thinkers tended to regard the representative as a quasi-magistrate to whose commands constituents owed presumptive obedience. Though

---

[6] Alfred de Grazia, *Public and Republic: Political Representation in America* (New York, 1951), 4.

[7] Elisha P. Douglass, *Rebels and Democrats: The Struggle for Equal Political Rights and Majority Rule during the American Revolution* (Chapel Hill, 1955), 51, 185; such a definition reflects popular expectations about the democratic process more than it represents the actual operations of a democracy.

rhetorically representation involved a delegation by the people of their powers to the representatives, once the representatives had made laws for the people, the people were expected to obey the decisions of their "delegates." Right down until the crisis of independence the New England clergy proceeded to preach obedience to one's political superiors, and representatives were as much within the category of "political superiors" as were governors and councilors.

Of course, as we have noted, conditions were attached to obedience, and the clergy continued, as the imperial crisis deepened, to confirm to the people their right to judge when the magistrate's power was exercised in violation of the constitution and the public felicity. But the extent of the people's commission was confined to granting or withholding obedience. When the clergy finally urged the people to withdraw their obedience from the royal government, they were not then told to express their will in politics or to riot in a state of nature, but to obey the commands of the provincial and continental congresses. John Adams proudly boasted in 1774 that throughout the dispute with the Mother Country the people of Massachusetts had "arranged themselves under their house of representatives and council, with as much order as ever." For the colonial leadership, independence was not a democratic movement which dissolved all the ligaments of subordination in colonial society and "liberated" the people. It was much more the orderly transference of allegiance from one set of magistrates to a slightly different set who happened to be called representatives of the people.

If the representative was not the tool of his constituents but the equivalent of a magistrate or political superior, was the consensus which all thinkers anticipated between rulers and ruled, between representative and constituent, to be derived solely from the latter's obedience to the former's commands? Though most colonial thinkers rejected such an extreme position, British proponents of parliamentary power in the colonies were forced to rely on a peculiar notion of virtual representation which implied as much.

Not all British spokesmen rejected the colonists' contention that according to the constitution no subject might be taxed without his own consent or the consent of his representative. Rather some claimed that the colonists were in fact "represented," or what was more frequently the case, did in fact "consent" to Parliament's acts in exactly the same sense that the nonvoting Briton was virtually represented and consented in Parliament. To this end British pamphleteers attempted to demonstrate that the nonvoting Briton and American occupied identical positions relative to parliamentary power. However, any attempt to convince the colonists that their interests would be considered equally with British interests in Parliament's concern for the common good was foredoomed to failure after the passage of the Stamp Act if not by the century of commercial regulation which had preceded it.[8] Therefore, British writers were forced to draw other parallels between the disfranchised in the Mother Country and the colonies in their attempts to prove Americans were in fact virtually represented in Parliament.

Crucial to British logic in this matter was the reception of the Navigation Acts in the colonies. If the colonists could not be taxed by Parliament because they were not represented, neither could they be bound by any parliamentary laws, for the constitution, it was argued, made no distinction between taxation and legislation. On the other hand, since everyone knew the colonists had never disputed the binding force of the Navigation Acts, their reception by the colonists could be taken as presumptive evidence that Americans were represented in Parliament, because "every Argument in support of an Exemption from the Superintendance of the *British* Parliament in the one Case is equally applicable to the others."[9] For the colonists to submit to the Navigation Acts when they nonetheless considered themselves unrepresented in Parliament was inconsistent with their current objections to the constitutionality of taxation without representation, particularly when they claimed that the trade regulations were "a tax" upon them.

Even if one refused to admit that the colonial position was inconsistent, British writers could still claim that by receiving the Navigation Acts in the colonies, Americans had virtually consented to be bound by parliamentary power. For "the reception of any law draws after it by a chain which cannot be broken, the unwelcome necessity of submitting to taxation. . . . We virtually and implicitly allow the institution of any Government of which we enjoy the benefit and solicit the protection."[10]

The crux of the British argument supporting parliamentary power in the colonies remained the same throughout the imperial crisis. Americans were bound to obey Parliament's authority for precisely the same reasons that nonvoting Englishmen were bound. However, the colonists felt the only real similarity British writers were able to point to between the virtually represented or consenting American and Briton which they did not share in common with all mankind, was that neither had voted for representatives in Parliament and yet both had obeyed Parliament's

---

[8] Such attempts were made; see Whately, *Regulations lately made,* passim. For the colonists' reactions to such pleas, see "Novanglus," in C. F. Adams, ed., *Works,* IV, 49; Thomas Jefferson, *A Summary view of the rights of British America* . . . (Williamsburg, 1774), 9–10, 16.

[9] Whately, *Regulations lately made,* 104.

[10] Johnson, *Taxation no tyranny,* 33; see also William Knox, *The controversy between Great Britain and her colonies reviewed* (London, 1769), 67–69, 90.

statutes.[11] For British thinkers, then, the mark of whether or not one was represented in Parliament lay in whether or not he had obeyed Parliament's commands. Such a logic, which had assumed what it had set out to prove, could only seem plausible to minds which likewise assumed that the consensus existing between the representative and the constituent would invariably depend on the latter's obedience to the former's commands.

The concept of representation which British pamphleteers had advanced seemed to provide no security for the subjects against the oppressions of their representatives, let alone of their other rulers. If obedience were the central ingredient of representation, the subject would have no recourse against the magistrate issuing unlawful commands except the ultimate and unpalatable one of revolution. If representation was to offer the subject practical protection against encroaching power some method of reaching a consensus between the rulers and the ruled had to be devised which did not demand the total compliance of one party to the wishes of the other party, but at least struck a balance between the two.

However, obedience to the commands of a political superior, in this case one's representative, might provide some protection to the subject against oppression if the interests of the subject and the representative were so intimately connected if not identical as to preclude the possibility of the one injuring the other without at the same time injuring himself. Moreover, if the consensus which was finally created between the rulers and the ruled proceeded not from the total compliance of one to the arbitrary commands of the other, but was rather the product of an organic unity of interests which would naturally predispose the representative and constituent to agreement, obedience would be more attractive to the subject because it would be his interest as well as his duty to obey. In this sense Americans might be said to consent to laws and taxes framed by their representatives in the legislature.

The basic ingredient of the colonial notion of representation lay in maintaining just such an organic relationship of interest between the representative and the constituent. If such a relationship could be established, it would afford the subject security against the arbitrary decrees

---

[11] One could say that Americans and nonvoting Britons also shared in the benefits and protection offered by British power. But so had the Portuguese, and this had not made them liable to parliamentary taxation; see *The Late Regulations Respecting the British Colonies on the Continent of America* . . . (Philadelphia, 1765), in *Political Writings of John Dickinson*, I, 82–83; Jefferson, *Summary View*, 6–7. The benefits and protection argument ultimately resolved itself into a disagreement over whether Parliament was in fact benefiting and protecting the colonies. British spokesmen proposed to resolve this disagreement by exacting obedience from America.

of his political superiors without at the same time absolving him from his obligation to obey their commands. Ideally, it would lead to a situation where no law or tax could be passed affecting the liberties or property of the subject which did not directly affect the legislator. Thus every burden which the representative attempted to lay on his constituents would be equally borne by himself. It was to precisely such a circumstance that John Adams and others referred when they said a republic was a government of laws and not of men.

Nor was an intimate association of interests between rulers and ruled valued solely as security against the abuse of power. It was equally important as a standing incentive to the ruler to promote actively whatever interests he might share in common with his constituents. In binding together the interests of rulers and ruled lay a guarantee of positive advantages to be reaped by all as well as of protection against unreasonable oppression.

It was the realization that the magistrate's power enabled him to pursue interests distinct from those of the community at large and therefore constituted a temptation to do so, from which the ordinary subject was immune, that had ultimately shifted the presumption of distrust from the subject to the magistrate. What a free society really needed, then, was some force to oppose the insidious tendency of power to separate the interests of the rulers from the ruled and thereby preserve the nation from the tyranny to which it was perpetually liable, both from the inherently passionate nature of man and from the rational calculations of a few malignant intelligences. It was precisely this power of keeping the ruler's interest dependent on the interest of the ruled which the provincial leadership was willing to bestow on a populace which they nonetheless considered incompetent to participate directly in the esoteric decisions of government and which they still regarded with suspicion as a potential source of disorder within the polity. But in confiding a power of such importance to the people, colonial thinkers had also to demonstrate that the populace would not misuse their trust.

The device which permitted the people to accomplish their important function was the franchise, the power to choose whom their magistrates or representatives were to be. Their experience as colonials of being subject to an external political authority and of having officials imposed on them from without had taught Americans to value the privilege of electing rulers from among themselves. By virtue of the franchise the people were empowered to choose representatives whose virtues and abilities were known to them and whose interest was organically related to their own. Moreover, the effect of naturally shared interests was reinforced by the very act of choice which bound the representative by ties of honor and gratitude to observe and protect the interests of those who nominated him. While such an identity of interests was maintained the populace could safely be urged to bestow their favor on the leading men in the community with some security that their superior abilities would not be turned against the interests of the people.

However, the power the people possessed to nominate rulers whose interests, at least initially, were intimately related to those over whom they presided did not by itself provide the populace with sufficient security against the potential abuse of the representative's power. Though each representative by himself was endowed with insufficient power to have any incentive but to promote those interests he might share in common with his constituents, even the smallest power possessed for an indefinite length of time gave the possessor opportunities to study the ends to which it might be put, ends which the momentary possession of great power even could not necessarily procure. Prolonged power gave the representative an opportunity to pool his limited resources with other representatives in a general conspiracy against the public. Such a union could not be easily effected in a short time because of the difficulty in reconciling the conflicting interests and passions of any large group of men. However, if once chosen a representative remained in office either permanently or for a long period of time, not only would he be subject to greater temptations to join with his fellow representatives in pursuing interests distinct from those of their constituents, but prolonged tenure would give permanent magistrates, who invariably existed in mixed monarchies, greater incentives as well as opportunities to corrupt the representatives of the nation away from the people's interests.

It was against the operation of forces such as these that colonial thinkers invoked an additional power in the people, the power they had periodically to re-elect their representatives. If the representative betrayed his trust and sacrificed the public interest to the gratification of his private appetites, if he disregarded or dissolved the natural ties of interest, which had initially been an incentive for him to pursue his constituent's welfare, by idemnifying himself from their oppression, the subjects still possessed the power to return their representatives to the body of the people.

The power of the people to deny re-election to erring representatives not only involved a mortifying disgrace, it also proved to be a convenient means of subjecting those who were responsible for oppressive measures to the full force of their handiwork. If the representatives participated in the making of oppressive laws from the operation of which they exempted themselves, all immediate restraints upon their power would be dissolved. Through the power of re-election the people could bring oppressive laws to bear upon all by reducing the authors of these laws to the condition of subjects at the next election. Faced with the sustained threat of being made to feel the consequences of their own actions, no representative could contemplate the enslavement of his constituents while the franchise was still effective. An elected ruler had no immediate, rational alternative but to pursue the interests he shared in common with his constituents.

Thus the power of the people to punish their representatives by returning them to the body of the people was an essential technique in binding the interests of rulers and ruled together. However, many colonial thinkers refrained from asserting that a man could not be represented unless he voted for a representative. They were careful to distinguish between the franchise as a technique in achieving the status of being "represented" and the essential attribute of being represented, namely an identity or intimate connection of interests. Thus there was no necessary contradiction between the colonists' insistence that they could be represented only by men chosen within the colonies by themselves and their assertions that the nonvoting Englishman was nonetheless represented in Parliament. However, few Americans would have gone to the other extreme and held that when a whole society was denied the franchise, as indeed the colonists had been so far as Parliament was concerned, it could still be represented. What was a technique with respect to individuals was a necessity for any distinct interest in the community.

Instructions tended to be viewed in the same light as the franchise, as a means to an end but not to be confused with the end itself. They were not considered as the commands of the people with which the representative was bound to comply, but as an aid in preserving a harmony or unity of interest between representative and constituent. If the problem of diverging interests had never arisen, instructions would have been unnecessary. Through instructions the people were able to inform their representatives what their sense of the common interest was in extraordinary circumstances. But the representative relationship did not confine the channels of communication to one direction only. The representative was equally at liberty to persuade his constituents that their sense of the common interest was wrong, in fact it was his duty to do so if he really thought the people were misled in their judgment. If the people finally refused to re-elect a representative, it was not because he neglected to obey their specific orders, but because he had betrayed their interest. In a society of unequal political abilities the representative was still thought of as a political superior. The mass of the people elected representatives not to order them around like lackeys to do the people's bidding, but to reap benefit from the distinguished abilities of the few upon which the safety of society might in large measure depend.

What power the people actually possessed over their representatives was not easily misused. In the first place the scope of their power was limited and precisely defined. It was not part of their commission to dictate terms to their representatives, but only to apply the brakes when their rulers went off the track. The object of their power was merely to maintain an identity of interests between rulers and ruled, and the means at their disposal to accomplish this end allowed the people a minimum of discretion. They could either accept or reject a delegate, and if they rejected him choose another in his place. As the New England clergy pointed out, the people had no incentive to betray their limited trust for the abuse of their powers would bring civil calamities on them in this world and damnation on them in the next.

Thus representation performed a dual function in refining the people's power through their representatives. On the one hand it enabled a diffuse and unorganized people to make common cause against their oppressors. Through representation their disorderly, uncohesive power could be focused and brought to bear in effectual opposition to the potential tyranny of magistrates not elected by the people. On the other it helped restrain the populace from the extremes which men dreaded from a united people, even when they acted for legitimate reasons. Here representative devices served a useful function by compartmentalizing the subjects into divisions beneath their representatives. The representative relationship facilitated communication vertically between subject and representative but not horizontally between subjects of different constituencies. Since the constituents' legitimate powers were confined to the election of their particular representatives, the only normal communication they had with their fellow subjects in the political arena was through the medium of their delegates. Representative institutions helped to limit and divide the power of the people as much as they served to restrain the passions of rulers.

III

The complex model of assumptions about the people's power with which Americans entered the imperial crisis bore little relation to American democracy as it is popularly conceived today. What power the people did possess was not designed to facilitate the expression of their will in politics but to defend them from oppression. Nor were such ideas easily abandoned. They lingered on throughout the period of constitutional formation and even into the nineteenth century, helping to account for the many "undemocratic" features of the state constitutions.

However, the jarring effect of the Revolutionary experience administered a series of decisive challenges to this web of undemocratic assumptions which made it impossible to retain the full integrity of the model after independence. As the logic of events thrust rebellion upon the colonists, many were forced to revise their estimate of the people's competence. Moreover, once British authority had been removed from the provincial arena, Americans were explicitly confronted with a problem which before had been only implicit, of protecting themselves from each other. The new danger demanded new solutions which were forever to destroy the notion of virtual representation. Finally the Revolution brought new men into politics who had not been thoroughly schooled in the dissenting tradition. Often these men represented minority groups struggling for recognition within the state. Because the elitist orientation of dissenting theory gave scant support to their aspirations, they turned elsewhere for their ideas.

However, the subversion of dissenting thought was an insidious rather than a dramatic development. It has been difficult to trace precisely because it crept upon many Americans unawares. We today can hardly hope to understand a process which often eluded our forebears without defining the point of departure from which it proceeded.

Government by the People:
The American Revolution and the
Democratization of the Legislatures

JACKSON TURNER MAIN

AN ARTICLE WITH "DEMOCRACY" IN ITS TITLE, THESE DAYS, MUST account for itself. This essay holds that few colonials in British North America believed in a government by the people, and that they were content to be ruled by local elites; but that during the Revolution two interacting developments occurred simultaneously: ordinary citizens in-

Reprinted from the *William and Mary Quarterly*, XXIII, 3, July 1966, by permission of the Editor.

NOTE: By the author's permission the original footnote citations have been curtailed for reasons of space.

creasingly took part in politics, and American political theorists began to defend popular government. The ideological shift can be traced most easily in the newspapers, while evidence for the change in the structure of power will be found in the make-up of the lower houses during the revolutionary years.

Truly democratic ideas, defending a concentration of power in the hands of the people, are difficult to find prior to about 1774. Most articulate colonials accepted the Whig theory in which a modicum of democracy was balanced by equal parts of aristocracy and monarchy. An unchecked democracy was uniformly condemned. For example, a contributor to the *Newport Mercury* in 1764 felt that when a state was in its infancy, "when its members are few and virtuous, and united together by some peculiar ideas of freedom or religion; the whole power may be lodged with the people, and the government be purely democratical"; but when the state had matured, power must be removed from popular control because history demonstrated that the people "have been incapable, collectively, of acting with any degree of moderation or wisdom." Therefore while colonial theorists recognized the need for some democratic element in the government, they did not intend that the ordinary people —the *demos*—should participate. The poorer men were not allowed to vote at all, and that part of the populace which did vote was expected to elect the better sort of people to represent them. "Fabricus" defended the "democratic principle," warned that "liberty, when once lost, is scarce ever recovered," and declared that laws were "made for the people, and not people for the laws." But he did not propose that ordinary citizens should govern. Rather, "it is right that men of *birth and fortune,* in every government that is free, should be invested with power, and enjoy higher honours than the people." According to William Smith of New York, offices should be held by "the better Class of People" in order that they might introduce that "Spirit of Subordination essential to good Government." A Marylander urged that members of the Assembly should be "ABLE in ESTATE, ABLE in KNOWLEDGE AND LEARNING," and mourned that so many "little upstart insignificant Pretenders" tried to obtain an office. "The *Creature* that is able to keep a little Shop, rate the Price of an Ell of Osnabrigs, or, at most, to judge of the Quality of a Leaf of Tobacco" was not a fit statesman, regardless of his own opinion. So also in South Carolina, where William Henry Drayton warned the artisans that mechanical ability did not entitle them to hold office. This conviction that most men were incompetent to rule, and that the elite should govern for them, proved a vital element in Whig thought and was its most antidemocratic quality. The assumption was almost never openly challenged during the colonial period.

Whether the majority whose capacity was thus maligned accepted the insulting assumption is another question. They were not asked, and as they were unable to speak or write on the subject, their opinions are uncertain. But the voters themselves seem to have adhered, in practice at least, to the traditional view, for when the people were asked to choose their representatives they seldom elected common farmers and artisans. Instead they put their trust in men of the upper class. In the colonies as a whole, about 30 per cent of the adult white men owned property worth £500 or more. About two thirds of these colonials of means had property worth £500 to £2,000; their economic status is here called *moderate*. The other third were worth over £2,000. Those worth £2,000 to £5,000 are called *well-to-do,* and those whose property was valued at more than £5,000 are called *wealthy.*[1] The overwhelming majority of the representatives belonged to that ten per cent who were well-to-do or wealthy. Government may have been for the people, but it was not administered by them. For evidence we turn to the legislatures of New Hampshire, New York, New Jersey, Maryland, Virginia, and South Carolina.

In 1765 New Hampshire elected thirty-four men to its House of Representatives. Practically all of them lived within a few miles of the coast; the frontier settlements could not yet send deputies, and the Merrimack Valley towns in the south-central part of the colony, though populous, were allotted only seven. New Hampshire was not a rich colony. Most of its inhabitants were small farmers with property enough for an adequate living but no more. There were a few large agricultural estates, and the Portsmouth area had developed a prosperous commerce which supported some wealthy merchants and professional men; but judging from probate records not more than one man in forty was well-to-do, and true wealth was very rare. Merchants, professional men, and the like comprised about one tenth of the total population, though in Portsmouth, obviously, the proportion was much larger. Probably at least two thirds of the inhabitants were farmers or farm laborers and one in ten was an artisan. But New Hampshire voters did not call on farmers or men of average property to represent them. Only about one third of the representatives in the 1765 House were yeomen. Merchants and lawyers were just as numerous, and the rest followed a variety of occupations: there were four doctors and several millers and manufacturers. One third of the delegates were wealthy men and more than two thirds were at least well-to-do. The relatively small upper class of the colony, concentrated in the southeast, furnished ten of the members. They did not, of

---

[1] A discussion of the distribution of property and income is contained in Jackson Turner Main, *The Social Structure of Revolutionary America* (Princeton, 1965).

course, constitute a majority, and the family background of most of the representatives, like that of most colonials, was undistinguished. Probably nearly one half had acquired more property and prestige than their parents. In another age New Hampshire's lower house would have been considered democratic—compared with England's House of Commons it certainly was—but this was a new society, and the voters preferred the prosperous urban upper class and the more substantial farmers.

New York was a much richer colony than New Hampshire. Although most of its population were small farmers and tenants, there were many large landed estates and New York City was incomparably wealthier than Portsmouth. In general the west bank of the Hudson and the northern frontier were usually controlled by the yeomanry, as was Suffolk County on Long Island, but the east bank from Albany to the City was dominated by great "manor lords" and merchants. The great landowners and the merchants held almost all of the twenty-eight seats in the Assembly. In 1769 the voters elected only seven farmers. Five others including Frederick Philipse and Pierre Van Cortland, the wealthy manor lords from Westchester, were owners of large tenanted estates. But a majority of New York's legislators were townspeople. Merchants were almost as numerous as farmers, and together with lawyers they furnished one half of the membership. The legislators were no more representative in their property than in their occupation. At most, five men, and probably fewer, belonged to the middle class of moderate means. At least 43 per cent were wealthy and an equal number were well-to-do. The members' social background was also exceptional. Ten came from the colony's foremost families who had, for the times, a distinguished ancestry, and two thirds or more were born of well-to-do parents. Taken as a whole the legislators, far from reflecting New York's social structure, had either always belonged to or had successfully entered the colony's economic and social upper class.

New Jersey's Assembly was even smaller than that of New York. The body chosen in 1761, and which sat until 1769, contained but twenty men. Half of these represented the East Jersey counties (near New York City) which were in general occupied by small farmers, but only three of the ten members came from that class. The others were merchants, lawyers, and large proprietors. Although several of these had started as yeomen they had all acquired large properties. West Jersey, which had a greater number of sizable landed estates, especially in the Delaware Valley region, sent the same sort of men as did East Jersey: three farmers, an equal number of large landowners, and an even larger number of prosperous townsmen, some of whom also owned valuable real estate. Merchants and lawyers made up one half of the membership. As usual, a considerable proportion—perhaps forty percent—were self-made men, but the colony's prominent old families furnished at least 30 per cent of the representatives. Four out of five members were either well-to-do or wealthy.

In contrast to the legislatures of New Hampshire, New York, and New Jersey, Maryland's House of Delegates was a large body and one dominated by the agricultural interest. Like its northern equivalents, however, its members belonged to the upper class of the colony—in Maryland, the planter aristocracy. The 1765 House supposedly contained over sixty members, but only fifty-four appear in the records. About one half of these came from the Eastern Shore, an almost entirely rural area. Except for Col. Thomas Cresap who lived on Maryland's small frontier, the remainder came from the Potomac River and western Chesapeake Bay counties, where agriculture was the principal occupation but where a number of towns also existed. About one sixth of the Delegates belonged to the yeoman farmer class. Most of these lived on the Eastern Shore. Incidentally they did not vote with the antiproprietary, or "popular," party, but rather followed some of the great planters in the conservative "court" party. As in the northern colonies, a number of the Delegates were *nouveaux riches,* but in Maryland's stable and primarily "Tidewater" society, fewer than one-fifth had surpassed their parents in wealth. The overwhelming majority came from the lesser or the great planter class, and probably one-third belonged to the colony's elite families. Four-fifths were well-to-do or wealthy. Lawyers and merchants (among whom were several of the self-made men) furnished about one-sixth of the principally rural membership.

Virginia's Burgesses resembled Maryland's Delegates, but they were even richer and of even more distinguished ancestry. The Old Dominion's much larger west helped to make the House of Burgesses twice as large a body, with 122 members in 1773. Small property holders, though they formed a great majority of the voters, held only one out of six seats. Half of the Burgesses were wealthy and four fifths were at least well-to-do. Merchants and lawyers contributed one fifth of the members, much more than their proper share, but most of them were also large landholders and the legislature was firmly in control of the great planters. Indeed the median property owned was 1,800 acres and 40 slaves. Virginia's social structure was quite fluid, especially in the newly-settled areas, but between five-sixths and seven-eighths of the delegates had inherited their property. A roll call of the Burgesses would recite the names of most of the colony's elite families, who held nearly one half of the seats.

The planters of South Carolina, unlike the Virginians, were unwilling to grant representation to the upcountry, and its House of Commons was an exclusively eastern body. The colony was newer and its society may have been more fluid, for in 1765 between 20 and 40 per cent of the representatives were self-made men. The legislature also differed from its southern equivalents in Maryland and Virginia in that nearly half of its members were merchants, lawyers, or doctors. But these figures are deceptive, for in reality most of these men were also great landowners, as were almost all of the representatives; and prominent old families contributed one half of the members of the House. All were at least well-to-do and over two thirds were wealthy. The rich planters of South Carolina's coastal parishes held a monopoly of power in the Assembly.

These six legislatures, from New Hampshire to South Carolina, shared the same qualities. Although farmers and artisans comprised probably between two thirds and three fourths of the voters in the six colonies, they seldom selected men from their own ranks to represent them. Not more than one out of five representatives were of that class. Fully one third were merchants and lawyers or other professionals, and most of the rest were large landowners. Although only about 10 per cent of the colonials were well-to-do or wealthy, this economic elite furnished at least 85 per cent of the assemblymen. The mobile character of colonial society meant that perhaps 30 per cent had achieved their high status by their own efforts; but an even larger percentage were from prominent, long-established families.

Collectively these "representatives of the people" comprised not a cross section of the electorate but a segment of the upper class. Although the colonials cherished the democratic branch of their governments, and although a majority may have hoped to make the lower house all powerful, they did not yet conceive that the *demos* should actually govern. The idea of a government by as well as for the people was a product of the Revolution. It should be noted here that Rhode Island and Connecticut are exceptions to this general pattern, though the upper house of Connecticut was composed entirely of well-to-do men. As for Massachusetts, the number of representatives with moderate properties exceeded that in the royal and proprietary colonies; but the Massachusetts legislature was still controlled by the well-to-do. Of the 117 men in the House in 1765, at least fifty-six were not farmers and thirteen were large landowners; of the remaining forty-eight, thirty-seven were ordinary farmers and the occupations of eleven are unknown. Among those representatives whose economic status can be discovered (about nine tenths), well over one half were well-to-do or wealthy and two fifths of these had inherited their property.

Widespread popular participation in politics began during 1774 with the various provincial congresses and other extralegal organizations. Although the majority of these bodies seem to have been made up of men of standing, both artisans and farmers appeared in greater numbers than they had in the colonial legislatures. There were several reasons for this. Whereas heretofore the more recently settled areas of most colonies had been underrepresented—at times seriously so—the legal prohibitions on their sending representatives to the colonial assemblies did not apply to the extralegal congresses, and they chose delegates when they wished. Moreover the congresses were much larger than the colonial assemblies, and consequently the over-all number of men who could be elected was greatly increased. For instance, South Carolina's House of Commons contained forty-eight men in 1772, but almost twice that number attended the first Provincial Congress in December 1774 and four times as many were present in January 1775. By 1775 the western districts were sending about one third of the members. Similarly, nothing now prevented New Hampshire's country villages from choosing representatives, and they seized the opportunity. By the time the fourth Provincial Congress met in New Hampshire, four times as many men attended as had been admitted to the 1773 legislature, and nearly one half of them came from the inland counties.

Perhaps an even more important reason for the greater participation in politics by men of moderate means than simply the enlarged and broadened membership of the Provincial Congresses was that the interior areas often contained no real upper class. They had no choice but to send men of moderate property. Furthermore, many men of the upper classes who had previously held political power were not sympathetic with the resistance movement and either withdrew from politics or did not participate in the extralegal Congresses. At the same time events thrust new men forward, as for example in Charleston where the artisans became increasingly active. As the Revolution ran its course, many new men came to fill the much larger number of civil offices, and new men won fame in battle. These developments were quickly reflected in the composition of the legislatures, and by the time the war ended the legislatures were far different bodies from what they had been in colonial days. At the same time democratic ideas spread rapidly, justifying and encouraging the new order.

With the overthrow of royal government, the previously unrepresented New Hampshire villages hastened to choose representatives to the state legislature. The number of men present in the lower house varied considerably, for some smaller communities were too poor to send a man every year, while others combined to finance the sending of a single delegate; but during the 1780's between two and three times as many attended as before the war. The House chosen in 1786 had eighty-eight members. The balance of power had shifted into the Merrimack Valley, for fewer than half of the delegates came from the two counties near the coast, and even these included frontier settlements.[2]

The socio-economic composition of the New Hampshire legislature also changed. All but four of the 1765 legislators can be identified, but more than one fifth of the post-war representatives are obscure, and the parentage of very few can be established despite the existence of many town histories, genealogies, and published records. Before the war fewer than one third were farmers, exclusive of large landowners but including the men whose occupation is doubtful; by 1786 at least 50 per cent were yeomen and if those whose occupations are unknown are added, as most of them should be, the proportion rises to over 70 per cent. Merchants and lawyers, who had furnished about one third of the members of the 1765 legislature, now comprised only one tenth of the membership. Similarly men of wealth totalled one third of the former legislature but less than one-tenth of the latter. The well-to-do element who had dominated the prewar Assembly with 70 per cent of the seats were now reduced to a minority of about 30 per cent. Thus a very large majority of the new legislature consisted of ordinary farmers who had only moderate properties. Ten members of the prominent old families had seats in the 1765 house; by 1786 there were only four in a body two and one half times as large. Even if the newly-represented towns are eliminated, the trend toward the election of less wealthy and less distinguished representatives remains the same, though the degree of change was less. If only the towns which sent men to both legislatures are considered, one finds that whereas farmers formed between 20 and 30 per cent in 1765, they accounted for 55 to 67 per cent twenty years later. Similarly, in these towns the proportion of representatives having moderate properties rose from 30 per cent to more than twice that. Thus the economic and social character of the members in the lower house had been radically changed.

The pattern of change was much the same in other states. New York's society was fundamentally less egalitarian than that of New Hampshire, having more men with large estates and proportionately fewer areas dominated by small farmers. The agricultural upcountry had not yet extended much beyond Albany to the north and Schenectady to the west, so that most New Yorkers still lived in the older counties. As might be expected the changes which occurred in New York were not as striking as in New Hampshire but they were still obvious. By 1785 the counties west of the Hudson, together with those north of Westchester, increased their representation from about one third to nearly two thirds of the total. That

[2] Strafford County, which contained the commercial center of Dover, extended north through what are now Belknap and Carroll Counties, then just under settlement.

fact alone might not have guaranteed a social or economic change in the composition of the Assembly, for every county had its upper class, but the new legislature differed from the old in many respects. The voters selected far fewer townspeople. In the 1769 Assembly some 57 per cent of the members had been engaged primarily in a nonagricultural occupation; by 1785 the proportion had been halved. Farmers, exclusive of large landowners, had made up 25 per cent of the total in 1769; now they furnished about 42 per cent. In contrast, one half of the 1769 legislators had been merchants and lawyers, but now such men held less than one third of the seats. Similarly the proportion of wealthy members dropped from 43 per cent to 15 per cent, whereas the ratio of men of moderate means increased from probably one seventh to nearly one half. New York's elite families, which had contributed ten out of twenty-eight Assemblymen in 1769, contributed the same number in 1785, but in a House twice as large. Meanwhile the number of men who had started without any local family background, newcomers to New York, increased from two to twenty-three. In general, the yeoman-artisan "middle class," which in colonial days had furnished a half-dozen members, now actually had a majority in the legislature. Under the leadership of George Clinton and others of higher economic and social rank, they controlled the state during the entire decade of the eighties.[3] In New York, as in New Hampshire, the trend was the same even within those counties which had been represented before the Revolution. If Washington and Montgomery counties are eliminated, the proportion of delegates who were well-to-do declines from 86 per cent to 60 per cent.

New Jersey's lower house, the size of which had increased in stages from twenty members to thirty-nine after the Revolution, retained equal distribution of seats between East and West Jersey. As in New Hampshire and New York, the economic upper class of well-to-do men, which in New Jersey had held three fourths of the seats before the war, saw its control vanish; indeed two thirds of the states' representatives in 1785 had only moderate properties. The typical legislator before the war held at least 1,000 acres; in 1785 the median was about 300 acres. Merchants and lawyers were all but eliminated from the legislature, retaining only a half-dozen seats. The colonial elite, once controlling one-third of the votes of the house, now had one-eighth; the overwhelming majority of the new legislators were men who had been unknown before the war and whose ancestry, where ascertainable, was uniformly undistinguished. Fully

---

[3] As far as the fathers of these legislators could be identified, 12 of the prewar 28 were merchants, lawyers, and large landowners, as were 12 or possibly 13 of the postwar 66.

two-thirds of the representatives were ordinary farmers, presumably men of more than average ability and sometimes with military experience, but clearly part of the common people. Again these changes occurred not just because new areas were represented but because the counties which had sent delegates in the prewar years now chose different sort of men. In New Jersey, the counties of Cumberland, Salem, Hunterdon, Morris, and Sussex had previously been underrepresented. If these are eliminated, we find that the proportion of men of moderate property rose from 20 per cent to 73 per cent and of farmers (exclusive of large landowners) from 23.5 per cent to 60 per cent.[4]

Southern legislatures were also democratized. Maryland's House of Delegates expanded to seventy-four by 1785, with the addition of a few members from the western counties. As had been true before the war, most of the representatives were engaged in agriculture, the proportion of those with a nonfarm occupation remaining constant at about 20 per cent. The most obvious change in economic composition was the replacement of planters by farmers, of large property owners by men with moderate estates. If the planter is defined as one who held at least twenty slaves or 500 acres, then they formed 57 per cent of the House in 1765 and only 36.5 per cent in 1785, while the farmers increased from 18.5 to 28 per cent. Wealthy men occupied about two fifths of the seats in the pre-Revolutionary period, one-sixth after the war, while delegates with moderate property, who had previously formed only one-fifth of the total, now comprised one-third. The yeoman farmer class, though still lacking a majority, had doubled in numbers while members of the old ruling families, in turn, saw their strength halved. By comparison with the northern states the shift of power was decidedly less radical, but the change was considerable. It was made more obvious, incidentally, by the great contrast between the postwar House of Delegates and the postwar Senate, for the large majority of the Senators were wealthy merchants, lawyers, and planters, who fought bitterly with the popular branch.

The planter class of Virginia, like that of Maryland, did not intend that the Revolution should encourage democracy, but it was unable to prevent some erosion of its power. The great landowners still controlled the lower house, though their strength was reduced from 60 per cent to 50 per cent, while that of ordinary farmers rose from perhaps 13 per cent in 1773 to 26 per cent in 1785. An important change was the decline in the number of wealthy members, who now held one quarter instead of one-half of the seats. Power thus shifted into the hands of the lesser planters, the well-to-do rather than the wealthy. Meanwhile men with

---

[4] Those of unknown property or occupation are excluded.

moderate properties doubled their share, almost equaling in number the wealthy Burgesses. Similarly the sons of the First Families lost their commanding position, while an even larger fraction of delegates were of humble origins. The general magnitude of the change is suggested by the decline in the median property held from 1,800 acres to about 1,100, and from forty slaves to twenty.

Thus, although the planter class retained control of the Burgesses, the people were now sending well-to-do rather than wealthy men, and at least one out of four representatives was an ordinary citizen. A roll call of the House would still recite the familiar names of many elite families, but it would also pronounce some never heard before. The alteration in the composition of the Virginia legislature undoubtedly sprang in part from the growing influence of westerners, for counties beyond the Blue Ridge sent many more representatives in 1785 than before the war, while the representation from the Piedmont also increased in size. However, the same shift downward also occurred within the older counties, those which had been represented in 1773. If we eliminate from consideration all of the newly-formed counties, we find that delegates with moderate property increased from 13.5 per cent to 23 per cent, and that wealthy ones declined from 48 to 30 per cent, while the proportion of farmers rose from 13 to about 25 per cent.

The South Carolina constitution of 1778 is noted as an expression of conservatism. Its conservatism, however, was much more evident with respect to the Senate than to the House of Representatives, which was now nearly four times as large. Although the eastern upper class refused to grant westerners as many seats in the House as were warranted by their population, the upcountry did increase its share from not more than 6 or 8 per cent (depending on one's definition of where the upcountry started) to nearly 40 per cent. The urban upper class of merchants, lawyers, and doctors dropped to 20 per cent of the total membership in 1785, as compared to 36 per cent in 1765. The agricultural interest greatly increased its influence, the principal gain being made by farmers rather than by planters. A significant change was a reduction in the strength of wealthy representatives, who made up four fifths of those whose property is known in 1765 and but one third twenty years later. The pre-Revolutionary House of Commons seems to have contained not a single man of moderate property, but the postwar representatives included more than fifty such—probably over 30 per cent of the membership. The median acreage held by the 1765 members was certainly over 2,000 and probably a majority owned over 100 slaves each. The lack of tax records makes it impossible to determine what land the 1785 representatives held, but they obviously owned much less; while the median number of slaves was about twenty-five. The scarcity of such records as well as of genealogies and other historical materials also makes it exceedingly difficult to identify any but fairly prominent men. This situation in itself lends significance to the fact that whereas before the Revolution the desired information is available for seven out of eight representatives and even for over two thirds of their parents, data are incomplete concerning 30 per cent of the postwar delegates and most of their parents. Equally significant is the different social make-up of the two bodies. The long-established upper class of the province controlled half of the 1765 house, but less than one fourth of the 1785 legislature. Although most of the representatives were well-to-do, the house was no longer an exclusively aristocratic body, but contained a sizable element of democracy. It should be pointed out that South Carolina was peculiar in that the change in the House was due almost entirely to the admission of new delegates from the west. In those parishes which elected representatives both before and after the war, the proportion of wealthy delegates decreased very slightly, while that of men with moderate property rose from zero to between 7 and 14 per cent.

All of the six legislatures had been greatly changed as a result of the Revolution. The extent of that change varied from moderate in Virginia and Maryland to radical in New Hampshire and New Jersey, but everywhere the same process occurred. Voters were choosing many more representatives than before the war, and the newly settled areas gained considerably in representatives. The locus of power had shifted from the coast into the interior. Voters were ceasing to elect only men of wealth and family. The proportion of the wealthy in these legislatures dropped from 46 per cent to 22 per cent; members of the prominent old families declined from 40 per cent to 16 per cent. Most of these came from the long-established towns or commercial farm areas. Of course many men who were well-to-do or better continued to gain office, but their share decreased from four fifths to just one half. Even in Massachusetts the percentage of legislators who were wealthy or well-to-do dropped from 50 per cent in 1765 to 21.5 per cent in 1784.[5]

[5] *Economic status of Mass. Representatives (percentages)*

	1765	1784 *duplicate towns*	1784 *total*
wealthy	17	8	6.5
well-to-do	33	17	15
moderate	40	55	51.5
unknown	10	20	27

Probably most of those whose property is unknown had only moderate incomes. Similarly the proportion of men from prominent old families dropped from 22 per cent to 6 per cent, college educated delegates from 27 per cent to 9 per cent, and representatives whose fathers were well-to-do from 30 per cent to 10 per cent, the change being greatest in the new towns but occurring everywhere.

Significantly, the people more and more often chose ordinary yeomen or artisans. Before the Revolution fewer than one out of five legislators had been men of that sort; after independence they more than doubled their strength, achieving in fact a majority in the northern houses and

TABLE 1. ECONOMIC STATUS OF THE REPRESENTATIVES[a]

| | N.H., N.Y., and N.J. | | Md., Va., and S.C. | |
	Prewar (percentages)	Postwar (percentages)	Prewar (percentages)	Postwar (percentages)
Wealthy	36	12	52	28
Well-to-do	47	26	36	42
Moderate	17	62	12	30
Merchants & lawyers	43	18	22.5	17
Farmers	23	55	12	26

[a] This table analyzes the property of about 900 representatives. The economic status of 85 per cent was discovered with reasonable certainty. Most of the rest were dealt with by informed guesswork. No one was admitted to the wealthy category unless their property was certainly known. Lawyers were assumed to be well-to-do, for almost all of them were. Merchants were also considered well-to-do if they lived in an important urban center, but inland shopkeepers were not. Doctors and judges were distributed on similar principles. Artisans were almost always of moderate property. Farmers and those whose occupation was unknown composed the two largest groups. Those who came from the inland, semi-subsistence communities were almost never well-to-do, the exceptions being conspicuous men, so that if nothing was discovered about them they were almost certainly of moderate means. On the other hand those who lived in the well-developed commercial farm areas were often well-to-do, so they were not assigned to any category unless other information was available. The basis for this procedure was derived from extensive study of property holdings as discussed in my *Social Structure of Revolutionary America*. By such an analysis the proportion of unknowns was reduced to 3 ⅓ per cent, most of whom were probably of moderate property. They are eliminated in the table. Percentages for occupation are less accurate, especially those for the post-war South.

constituting over 40 per cent generally. The magnitude of the change is suggested by the fact that the legislators of the postwar South owned only about one half as much property as their predecessors. Also suggestive is the great increase in the proportion of men of humble origin, which seems to have more than doubled. Therefore men who were or had once been a part of the *demos* totalled about two thirds of the whole number of representatives. Clearly the voters had ceased to confine themselves to an elite, but were selecting instead men like themselves. The tendency to do so had started during the colonial period, especially in the North, and had now increased so dramatically as almost to revolutionize the legislatures. The process occurred also in those areas which were represented both before and after the Revolution, as compared with those which were allowed to choose delegates for the first time after the war. Although

TABLE 2. ECONOMIC STATUS OF THE REPRESENTATIVES FROM PRE-REVOLUTIONARY DISTRICTS

	N.H., N.Y., and N.J.		Md., Va., and S.C.	
	Prewar	Postwar	Prewar	Postwar
Wealthy	35	18	50	38
Well-to-do	45	37	38	42
Moderate	20	45	12	20
Merchants & lawyers	41	24	22	18.5
Farmers	25	50	12	22

a similar change may not have taken place in Connecticut or Rhode Island, it surely did so in the states of Pennsylvania, Delaware, North Carolina, and Georgia, which have not been analyzed here.

The significance of the change may be more obvious to historians than it was to men of the Revolutionary era. Adherents of the Whig philosophy deplored the trend. They continued to demand a government run by the elite in which the democratic element, while admitted, was carefully checked. Such men were basically conservatives who conceived themselves as struggling for liberty against British tyranny, and who did not propose to substitute a democratical tyranny for a monarchical one. The states, observed a philosophical New Englander in 1786, were "worse governed" than they had been because "men of sense and property have lost much of their influence by the popular spirit of the war." The people had once respected and obeyed their governors, senators, judges, and clergy. But "since the war, blustering ignorant men, who started into notice during the troubles and confusion of that critical period, have been attempting to push themselves into office."

On the other hand democratic spokesmen now rose to defend this new government by the people. A writer in a Georgia newspaper rejoiced in 1789 that the state's representatives were "taken from a class of citizens who hitherto have thought it more for their interest to be contented with a humbler walk in life," and hoped that men of large property would not enter the state, for Georgia had "perhaps the most *compleat* democracy in the known world," which could be preserved only by economic equality. In Massachusetts as early as 1775 "Democritus" urged the voters to "choose men that have learnt to get their living by honest industry, and that will be content with as small an income as the generality of those who pay them for their service. If you would be well represented," he continued, "choose a man in middling circumstances as to worldly estate, if he has got it by his industry so much the better, he knows the wants of the poor, and can judge pretty well what the community can bear of public burdens, if he be a man of good common understanding." "A Farmer" in Connecticut boldly declared it a maxim that the people usually judged rightly, insisted that politics was not so difficult but that common sense could comprehend it, and argued that every freeman could be a legislator.

The change in men might be deprecated or applauded, but it could not be denied, and some found it good. To Jedidiah Morse the government of Virginia still seemed to be "oligarchical or aristocratical," but to a Virginian a revolution had taken place. The newly-chosen House of Burgesses, wrote Roger Atkinson in 1776, was admirable. It was "composed of men not quite so well dressed, nor so politely educated, nor so highly born as some Assemblies I have formerly seen," yet on the whole he liked it better. "They are the People's men (and the People in general are right). They are plain and of consequence less disguised, but I believe to the full as honest, less intriguing, more sincere. I wish the People may always have Virtue enough and Wisdom enough to chuse such plain men." Democracy, for a moment at least, seemed to have come to Virginia.

The Emergence of the Majority Principle in the American Revolution

J. R. POLE

RECENT JUDGMENTS OF THE SUPREME COURT OF THE UNITED STATES, coming nearly 200 years after the American Revolution, have declared as a constitutional doctrine that the majority principle must be regarded as fundamental to republican government.

Reprinted from *Études sur l'Histoire des Assemblées d'États,* Travaux et Recherches, Faculté du Droit and des Sciences Economiques de Paris, edited by François Dumont (Paris, 1966) by permission of M. Dumont.
NOTE: The original footnotes have been omitted.

The majority whose rights have thus been confirmed by the Supreme Court is clearly understood to be a purely numerical majority—a majority of persons in each constituency under a system in which the constituencies are all made up of equal numbers. On this basis, each representative in the legislature is held to represent a majority of his constituents, so that when a division takes place in the chamber, the majority of members will represent a majority of the electorate outside.

The main importance of this view both in history and in constitutional law lies in its necessary effect of displacing the claims of any other kind of majority. A majority of corporations, of unequal size but held to be equal to each other in their corporate capacity; a majority of 'interests,' economic or religious; or a majority of persons where each vote is compounded of property in addition to the person who owns it—all of these have historically contributed to the theory and practice of different forms and degrees of representative government.

The opinion of the Supreme Court—like so many other judgments affecting American constitutional law—requires a reconsideration of the formative period between 1774, when the Continental Congress began to meet in Philadelphia, and 1787, when the Constitution was drawn up in the same hall. The issues which were to enter into subsequent American history are to be sought among the internal struggles for the representation of different domestic interests, not in the American struggle with Britain or in the older story of the conflicts between the estates of the realm and the Crown.

Representation in the American colonies was never based on any single, uniform principle. In Massachusetts, the constituencies of the legislature, or General Court, were the corporate towns of which the province was made up. These towns, which were unequal to each other in population and wealth, were held to be equal within very narrow limits for purposes of representation. Each town was entitled to send one member to the General Court, with the exception of Boston, which was allowed four.

At times when the apportionment of representatives was being considered it seemed to be generally agreed that a correct representation would take account of both property and persons. The weight of property was to be assessed in accordance with taxation. This attitude was in no way confined to Massachusetts. In 1752 Philadelphia petitioned the Assembly of Pennsylvania for the right to increase its membership on the ground of its tax payments; and all Pennsylvania counties asking for increased representation mentioned their tax payments in support of their claims. In Massachusetts, Essex County also based a demand for a greater share of representatives on a statement of its proportion of the tax burden of the province.

American colonial institutions were not based on any assumption that political society was composed of autonomous individuals. An element of such political individualism was indeed present, partly because the suffrage was generally extensive, partly because the elector stood rather closer, socially and in fact numerically, to his representative, than could usually be the case in England. This element gained decisive strength during the period of the Revolution. By the time the Philadelphia Convention of 1787 had completed its labours, political individualism had emerged as the major principle among the interests competing for recognition. The character of this transformation can be followed most clearly in Massachusetts, where the responsibilities of electoral legislation and finally of constitution making produced, between the years 1775 and 1780, a distinct transition from a representative system based on corporations to one which, still using the corporate structure, used numbers of population to determine representation in the Assembly.

The leadership in Massachusetts politics had long lain with the eastern seaboard towns, dominated by Boston. These towns, for example, almost invariably gave the Assembly its speaker. But the leadership was exercised at the cost of considerable suspicion and hostility among the towns of the interior, and as the imperial crisis deepened, the domination of the seaboard depended to a large extent on the primacy of the question of relations with Britain over domestic issues. Even while western towns protested their determination to defend their liberties against Britain, they remained acutely suspicious of the intentions of the dominant group in the Assembly.

Representation in the Assembly was not the only issue. Much feeling was aroused by the distribution of patronage. But representation was the basic problem; and the Assembly juggled furiously with it in the crucial year before Independence was declared. The subject was regulated twice, in divergent senses, by acts of August 1775 and May 1776.

Unfortunately the military emergency reduced the output of newspapers and there is little information to be had about these measures from other sources.

The first Act, that of August 1775, was intended to correct the injustice that had developed gradually as a result of the eighteenth century practice of incorporating new towns without granting them the right of representation. This was the Massachusetts equivalent to the deliberate under-representation of the newer settlements as practised by the older counties in Pennsylvania; it was less effective, because Boston itself was restricted to four members by the Massachusetts charter of 1691—but the intention should not be mistaken. The new Act granted the right of sending one representative to every town or district of thirty or more qualified voters—

which meant approximately 150 inhabitants. Towns of 120 voters were to send two; Boston alone was entitled to four. Every district which had been invested with the rights and privileges of a town was declared to be a town for the purpose of representation; but only towns and recognised 'districts' could be represented, so that unincorporated plantations and settlements still lacked this privilege.

This step restored the basic position of 1691. The result was a great increase in the number of representatives from the towns of the interior. The obvious inference is that the measure was intended to rally support throughout the province—to give the townspeople a sense of attachment to their Assembly. If it achieved that, however, it also succeeded in producing great consternation on the seaboard.

The rejoinder came from Essex County, where a convention, held in April 1776, presented the legislature with a memorial holding out the new basis of representation as a major grievance. The memorialists declared that they would be satisfied with 'equality of representation, whether it has respect to numbers, or property, or both.' It was argued that a single town in Essex paid more taxes than thirty other towns and districts; though under the new distribution, a majority of the General Court could be obtained from towns which did not pay one fourth of the total taxes. Essex paid one sixth of the taxes but sent only one tenth of the representatives.

'Property, or numbers, or both.' The claim deserves attention. It was the first public challenge to the venerable tradition of town representation. The basic interest at stake, as the tax statement makes clear, was the great concentration of mercantile and city property on the seaboard; and this wealth was allied to the higher concentration of population. Thus a numerical scale could be introduced to undermine the principle of corporate representation. And, after all, was not the connection between taxation and representation the crux of the American case against Britain? To the memorialists of Essex, the principle seemed very clear cut; a plain matter of equality.

The tactical problem was how to get the basis of representation changed by an Assembly elected under the very Act that was to be attacked. The accomplishment of this delicate task showed much understanding of the management of representative bodies. The memorial appeared at the end of the session. It is clear from subsequent criticisms that the majority of members from the interior towns had already gone home when, in response to the petition, a new bill for reapportionment was introduced; the measure was propelled through its three readings in a single day.

The preamble of this new Act stated that representation in the colony was 'not as equal as it ought to be,' and the reform was drastic. Each town of 220 freeholders was thenceforth to be entitled to no fewer than three representatives while each additional hundred freeholders gave one additional member. Moreover the measure was to come into force at once, in time for the oncoming elections.

This last provision aroused as much protest as the substance of the Act. In the short interval before the election, the law was not properly circulated; one writer alleged that there were towns within twenty miles of the Court that had never heard of it—while others scorned to act on it, holding the measure to be illegal. A county convention held a year later in Worcester declared that the Act, passed 'in a very thin house, at the close of the Session, when members in general were returned home, expecting no further business of importance would be attended to, and even after writs were issued for a new choice,' was contrary to the general sentiments of the people; and ended by recommending the towns to instruct their representatives to vote for repeal. Two towns later used the unsatisfactory basis introduced by this Act as a reason for holding the General Court unqualified to draw up a new constitution for the State.

However, the composition of the new House, in consequence of the new basis, was highly satisfactory to the defenders of property. The number of members at the session of May, 1776 rose from 201 to 266, the increase from the seaboard being enough to account for the whole of the difference. The representation of Boston immediately went up from the traditional four to twelve.

One effect of this Act was to produce a House of unwieldy size. A Boston member gave it as his opinion that the object was to produce a period of confusion after which the leading men of property would be left in charge. The principal long-term result was to give the advantage in the making of policies to the commercial interests of the eastern section.

The General Court failed to satisfy the towns with a new draft constitution drawn up in 1777, and it was not until late in 1779 that a new convention, based on universal adult male suffrage, met to form a State constitution. The Constitution was adopted on ratification by the towns in 1780. By that time, the numerical principles of representation had gone far to undermine the older concept of corporate units. Towns were still to be represented: but on the basis of their populations.

The issue was not determined by size of population alone. There were no political demonstrations based on the rights of the majority. The determining factor was that the men of property who habitually exercised authority in the Assembly were allied by their interests with that of the numerical majority. The old corporation system was outflanked by this crucial combination of the interests of numbers and property. The fact was that much the greatest concentration of numbers occurred in the seaport cities where the great shipping and commercial interests were also centred. Effective political power was controlled by these interests. This combination of forces is the key to the advance of the principle of the numerical majority.

The Constitution of 1780 still recognised the need for an institutional safeguard for property. The Senate established by that Constitution was based on districts—actually the existing counties—and in each district, representation was based, not on numbers, but on taxes paid into the State treasury. The numerical basis of town representation in the House was thus made safe when the protection of property was confided to the Senate on a county basis. The numerical principle had not been established as the exclusive principle of representation in Massachusetts; but it had emerged as the dominant force—and subsequent political history would continue to confirm that domination.

Turning to the very different field of the organisation of the continental government, the same essential combination can be found at work.

At the Continental Congress, which began to meet at Philadelphia in September, 1774, each of the thirteen provinces was represented separately by its own delegation, appointed by a congress held in the province. Each province therefore amounted to a constituency, giving a Congress of thirteen very unequal units, each casting a single vote.

The delegates at Philadelphia accepted the prevailing view that weight of property was always a factor of major importance in determining the political power to be exercised by any particular 'interest.' It proved to be the case that the large states held the essential combination: weight of property together with greatest numbers. It was these elements, moreover, which put forward the strongest arguments for basing the representation of the entire country on the numerical principle.

The problem of representation presented itself on the first day of the first meeting in 1774. Was each delegation to vote as a unit? Or should each province be apportioned a number of votes in accordance with its wealth and population—its 'weight' or 'importance?' The argument was settled, not on principles, but on the practical consideration that the material for a differentiated system was simply not available. But in order to avoid prejudicing future discussion the Congress recorded this difficulty, stating that the decision to give each colony one vote was taken because it was unable at the moment to 'procure proper materials for ascertaining the importance of each colony.'

When the debate was resumed, in 1776, the committee of the Congress which had been delegated to draw up Articles of Confederation reported its opinion that financial requisitions should be drawn on the states in proportion to the numbers of their inhabitants (except Indians); that a census should be taken every three years; but that 'In determining questions each colony shall have one vote.'

The view that the assessments of the states for requisitions to the Congress should be based on population was supported by the feeling that, on the whole, under the conditions prevailing in America, population was a fairly reliable guide to property. But it was not reliable enough to satisfy the delegates. The Articles of Confederation settled instead on the rule that each state was to be assessed according to the value of its land. The practice of limiting each state to one vote was maintained on the insistence of the smaller states, who were in the position of being able to exercise a kind of veto. The Articles incorporated the principle of state sovereignty, which necessarily meant state equality in the Congress.

This principle, for a variety of reasons, proved unworkable. A strong nationalist group of men whose experience had taught them to look on American government on a continental scale determined on a revision of the frame of government. In this movement the principal theoretical mind and the most effective parliamentarian were combined in the person of James Madison of Virginia, who has been called 'The Father of the Constitution.'

Shortly before the opening of the Convention at Philadelphia in 1787 he put his views to his colleague, Governor Edmund Randolph of Virginia. After noting the need to reform the system of representation and the danger of a splitting up of the states, he went on:

I hold it a fundamental point that an individual independence of the States is utterly irreconcileable to the idea of an aggregate sovereignty. I think at the same time that a consolidation of the States into one simple republic is not less unattainable than it would be inexpedient. [This view he was to modify after three weeks of struggle in the forthcoming Convention.] Let it be tried then whether any middle ground can be taken which will at once support a due supremacy of the national authority, and leave in force the local authorities so far as they can be subordinately useful.

The first step to be taken, is I think a change in the principle of representation.

Here Madison went on to argue in some detail for a system under which individuals, throughout the nation, would be represented on a numerical basis in a single, national legislature, whose composition would not be affected by state boundaries.

The change in the principle of representation [he concluded] will be relished by a majority of the States, and those too of the most influence. The Northern States will be reconciled to it by the *actual* superiority of their populousness: the Southern by their *expected* superiority in this point. This principle established, the repugnance of the large states to part with power will in great degree subside, and the small states must ultimately yield to the predominant will....

Madison, before the Convention assembled, had thought his way through the major problems that were to confront it.

A new form of government was offered by the delegation from Virginia to the Constitutional Convention. This draft became known as the Virginia Plan. In presenting this Plan the Virginian delegation assumed that, in accordance with the conventional view, the main objects requiring representation were the separate interests of *persons* and *property*. This well established doctrine of American whiggery embodied a pale reflection of the British distinction between Lords and Commons, and issued forth in the two houses of legislature, between which the Senate would represent the interests of property, the House of Representatives those of persons.

This Plan assumed that the whole of the national legislature would be put on a national basis—and therefore on a numerical basis. The nationalists, most of whom actually represented large states, had no fear of constituting the new Congress from numerical majorities on a popular basis. But when the small states, which feared for their independent existence, challenged this scheme and insisted on a compromise resulting in the specific, institutional representation of the states, then the Senate lost its original character as the house of property.

The great compromise adopted the principle of proportional representation in the House of Representatives. The electoral districts, equal in population, were to be drawn up by the state governments within the several states.

It was more on grounds of expediency than of democratic doctrine that this flat numerical ratio found favour with the Convention. The difficulties and disputes that would arise during the investigation and adjustment of apportionment on any mixed basis of numbers and wealth added to uncertainty as to whether any significant political value would be maintained, swung most of the delegates to the numerical side. In practice, the method adopted was bound to strengthen the interest of 'persons' and weaken that of 'property'. For property had lost almost its last institutional safeguard in the electoral system. Not quite its last, however: slave property was specially protected by the Federal ratio, which enumerated three fifths of the slaves as persons for computation of representatives. Nevertheless the voters who were to be consulted under the Federal Constitution were to be consulted as persons, not as the owners of specified amounts of property. Their state governments might and usually did impose property qualifications, but these were not the result of anything in the Federal Constitution. Once the Federal government was in operation, its electoral system gave a possibly unintentional but nevertheless an unmistakable impetus to the idea of political democracy.

After settling the dispute between large and small states, and the question of representation in Congress, the Convention nearly foundered on the problem of how to constitute the executive. And the question of the presidency was closely connected in principle with that of representation in Congress: the Nationalists, who had been ardent for proportional representation in both houses, were also strongest for popular election of the executive.

The Virginia Plan had envisaged an executive elected by the lower house of the legislature. But the objection to this proposal was that it would make the executive unduly dependent on the legislature, offending the doctrine of the separation of powers. The problem became extremely difficult. The Nationalists tended to favour a general election by the people at large; but this was firmly opposed by the defenders of the interests of small states and of local self-government, who argued that the people scattered over the country could not possibly know the characters of the candidates in states remote from their own, and that the elections would fall into the hands of small groups of intriguers. Eventually, at a very late stage, the Convention agreed to establish the College of Electors. Voters in presidential elections would not vote directly for presidential candidates; instead they would simply elect members of the electoral colleges in the several states; and these colleges, meeting separately, would proceed to give their own ballots for the president and vice-president, the winners being the candidates gaining the most electoral votes all over the country.

The system reflected a certain distrust of direct popular action. But the constitution of the electoral colleges in fact reflected the trend towards giving power to electoral majorities among the people. Each state was to be entitled to as many members in its own electoral college as it had members of the House of Representatives and senators; so that voting strength in the full College of Electors would turn on population. Each state was free to decide how to elect its own electoral college—some did it by legislative appointment, others by popular election. It later became the custom for the winning side in each state to take *all* the electoral votes in that state; so that a narrow popular majority would result in a unanimous slate of voters in the state electoral college. The system therefore produced, in presidential elections, some marked distortions of the majority principle.

The Nationalists—or National Whigs, as they might better be called—showed no fear or hesitation about the wholesomeness of the popular will. They had undertaken to model a government based on the consent of the governed. Though such consent had long stood, in some form, as an English constitutional principle, it was a distinctive American contribution to insist that consent could no longer rest on legal fiction. American whiggery required more explicit procedure for the implementation of consent.

In the search for a procedure of consent, those who wanted special safeguards for property did not persist in the demand for the representation of property by itself but rather tried to find some way of mixing property with persons. It was this sort of mixture that gave to a state, or district, what was called 'weight' or 'importance'. And a decisive step had been measured in the forming of democratic institutions when it was decided that this great element of political authority was adequately determined by proportional representation—in short, by the majority.

In Massachusetts, the majority principle had made its decisive advance through the conjunction of the interests of mercantile wealth and the city populations of the seaboard. Something very similar happened in Maryland, under the dominating influence of Baltimore, and in New York. It was not population that carried the day, but population allied to the leading interests of the most politically influential form of property.

On the continental scene the operative principle, though not identical, was similar in character. The National Whigs, for a variety of reasons, saw the United States as a nation. The allegiance of every citizen, then, had to be drawn towards the national authority, and that authority had to draw its strength from the people of the Union, not from a congregation of unequal units exercising equal powers. The interests that brought the Convention into being were diverse, sometimes inharmonious; but the most powerful of those making for a stronger and more national form of government were in general (though not without exceptions) connected either with the larger states, or with the business interests more intimately allied to the leadership in those states than in their own.

The majority principle thus emerged as the one which would give a proper representation to 'weight' in the Union, as it had done in the states where, sooner or later, it was to gain a leading place in each constitution. But in spite of this victory, the principle of majority rule emerged from the Philadelphia Convention with an ambiguous authority in American government.

The truth was that a residual element of interest representation was frozen into the American Constitution. The form it took was that of the direct representation of the states on an equal basis in the Senate. As new interests, embodied in the great geo-economic sections of the growing Union, took shape during the next half-century, they took shelter beneath the interest principle in the Constitution. But even this procedure was made possible because, within the states themselves, the trend was towards more and more popular elections: wider suffrage (already extensive at the Revolution); wider eligibility to political office; numerical apportionment of legislative seats.

Thus, although the corporate or interest principle remained embedded in the Constitution, the course of American history gradually made it more anachronistic.

THE POLITICS OF INDEPENDENCE: DEMOCRACY AS AN INSTRUMENT OF COMPETITION AND CONTROL

The previous sections have sought to explain two major themes: the introduction of the basic principles of republican government into America, and the ways in which the quarrel with Britain and the long War of Independence helped to advance the popular elements in the republican system. The making of the United States Constitution is not a theme of this book, but it cannot be ignored when we try to understand how republican principles were applied in America or why, once applied, they tended further in the direction of modern democracy.

The federal Constitution could have only an indirect effect on politics within the several states, yet the nature of its influence was anticipated by James Madison, whose remarks in the fourteenth letter of *The Federalist Papers* are very close to the central point. In this letter Madison was concerned with refuting the almost universal belief that liberty could never be preserved by one government over a large territory. When he alludes to "some celebrated authors," he is replying principally to Montesquieu, whose book, *The Spirit of Laws,* had been widely read in both Britain and America since its appearance in 1748.

Madison's remarks were part of a propaganda campaign for the adoption of the Constitution; they were more favorable to state sovereignty and less favorable to the powers of the central government than some of the things he had said in the debates at Philadelphia. But he makes certain points here that deserve comment because of their bearing on democracy. It will be seen that he uses "democracy" in a purely classical sense, that of a small community in which all the citizens can meet to make laws; yet he goes on to say that a *republic* is a democracy by its system of representation (which he rather curiously attributes to "modern Europe," although English Parliaments had met on some sort of representative basis for nearly 500 years). He also describes America as an "unmixed" republic—one without orders or "estates" of the realm. These were sweeping generalizations, but it is significant that they were likely to appeal to Madison's readers; they were not a strict account of the facts everywhere in America, but they shrewdly anticipated the tendencies already in progress.

It is worth adding that during the debates in the Convention at Philadelphia, proposals were made to restrict the advance of democracy by placing property qualifications on the suffrage for federal representatives. These proposals were rejected in favor of the system by which the federal suffrage in each state was to be the same as for the popular house in that state. This was a wise decision. Much of the opposition to the new Constitution was based on a suspicion that the new federal government would take too much power into its own hands and would attack local liberties; if the document had begun by proposing to restrict the franchise, the opposition might well have been strong enough to defeat ratification in the state conventions.

The Constitution applied equally to all citizens in their capacities as Americans, not merely as citizens of separate states. It established a government which had power to tax and make laws equally for all citizens without regard to state sovereignty. The gradual effect of this system was to advance the idea of the political equality of individuals under the Constitution; this tendency was in part counteracted by the growth of sectionalism, but it nevertheless assisted the advance of a more democratic ideology.

That advance was given a much more immediate stimulus by the rapid rise of party rivalry on a national scale. Two separate events, one at home and the other in Europe, aroused in America the antagonism and conflict of principles that led directly to the bitter contest of the Presidential election of 1800. The first in point of time was the French Revolution, though it was not really until 1792, when the Revolution had gone into its more extreme phase, and Europe had been plunged into war, that the issues began to impinge on Americans in such a manner as to drive them into opposing political camps. The domestic issues, on the other hand, sprang from the economic policies of Alexander Hamilton, Washington's Secretary of the Treasury. Once Hamilton had gotten the Administration and Congress to go along with his policies of founding a central bank and funding the debts of the several states, he marked out ambitions and lines of policy that provoked the opposition of a wide range of agrarian, localist, and popular forces, some democratic in their orientation, some privileged, and most of them in their own way conservative.

The history of the American response to these events has been reconstructed in recent years largely through careful research into the origins of political parties. Professor Noble E. Cunningham, whose essay in the present collection forms the conclusion of his distinguished study of the origins of the Jeffersonian–Republican party, has shown that the party began to form as a result of the initiative taken by James Madison and a small circle of colleagues in Congress. The party did not spring up spontaneously throughout the country but had to be carefully nursed by a central leadership. The task of that leadership was to inform the country and to rally the local election districts, offering guidance on republican principles; party organization arose out of the need to win elections, and when issues of principle or interest began to take over from personal ambition, then the outlines of the modern political party had begun to appear.

Given the excitement of genuine rivalries, the leaders found a broad electorate willing to take part. Election statistics for this period show high proportions of the adult male populace actually casting their votes.[1] The main incentive was the desire to win. Local politics, often centered on elections of sheriffs or such questions as the location of the county courthouse, had already begun to attract widespread participation; much of the voting was illegal, votes were often challenged. The laws did not give the vote to everybody, yet practice often seemed to run ahead of law in extending the franchise. Already before the election of Jefferson, reformers in some states had begun to demand the removal of the property qualifications; and when the new states of Vermont and Kentucky came into the Union in 1792, they had already abandoned these restrictions.[2]

In this period, from the forming of the Constitution to the installation of the first Jeffersonian administration, the existing machinery of republican government was put into action, refined, and adapted; politics excited widespread interest and bitter animosity, and it was these feelings that spurred people deeper into political action. That action was itself a stimulus to the advance of democracy.

However, the process had not been completed and did not come to an end with the triumph of Jefferson. In a very able study of the Federalist party,[3] Mr. David Hackett Fischer has recently shown that an internal struggle, mainly between the older and younger generations of Federalists, resulted in a gradual but substantial reconstruction of their party. During the latter part of Jefferson's Presidency, and under the management of younger men, it became more aggressive, more systematic, and, by force of the sheer necessity for seeking votes, it became more popular. The newer Federalists accepted most of the presuppositions of a democratic political system. During Madison's terms as President, party rivalry reached extreme intensity and bitterness, and was once again reflected in the actual figures of participation in elections. Here again, in a more advanced stage, political parties fighting for power through elections stimulated political excitement, with practical consequences for the advance of democracy.

[1] J. R. Pole, *Political Representation in England and the Origins of the American Republic* (London and New York, 1966), Appendix II.

[2] The reasons, in counties containing comparatively sparse populations, were probably more practical than ideological. See Williamson, *American Suffrage,* pp. 97–99 and 209–211.

[3] David Hackett Fischer, *The Revolution of American Conservatism: The Federalist Party in the Era of Jeffersonian Democracy* (New York, 1965).

The Federalist No. 14

JAMES MADISON

November 30, 1787

To the People of the State of New York.

We have seen the necessity of the union as our bulwark against foreign danger, as the conservator of peace among ourselves, as the guardian of our commerce and other common interests, as the only substitute for those military establishments which have subverted the liberties of the old world; and as the proper antidote for the diseases of faction, which have proved fatal to other popular governments, and of which alarming symptoms have been betrayed by our own. All that remains, within this branch of our enquiries, is to take notice of an objection, that may be drawn from the great extent of country which the union embraces. A few observations on this subject will be the more proper, as it is perceived that the adversaries of the new constitution are availing themselves of a prevailing prejudice, with regard to the practicable sphere of republican administration, in order to supply by imaginary difficulties, the want of those solid objections, which they endeavor in vain to find.

The error which limits Republican Government to a narrow district, has been unfolded and refuted in preceding papers. I remark here only, that it seems to owe its rise and prevalence, chiefly to the confounding of a republic with a democracy: And applying to the former reasonings drawn from the nature of the latter. The true distinction between these forms was also adverted to on a former occasion. It is, that in a democracy, the people meet and exercise the government in person; in a republic they assemble and administer it by their representatives and agents. A democracy consequently will be confined to a small spot. A republic may be extended over a large region.

To this accidental source of the error may be added the artifice of some celebrated authors, whose writings have had a great share in forming the modern standard of political opinions. Being subjects either of an absolute, or limited monarchy, they have endeavored to heighten the advan-

From *The New-York Packet,* November 30, 1787. This essay appeared on December 1 in both *The Daily Advertiser* and *The Independent Journal.*

94

tages or palliate the evils of those forms; by placing in comparison with them, the vices and defects of the republican, and by citing as specimens of the latter, the turbulent democracies of ancient Greece, and modern Italy. Under the confusion of names, it has been an easy task to transfer to a republic, observations applicable to a democracy only, and among others, the observation that it can never be established but among a small number of people, living within a small compass of territory.

Such a fallacy may have been the less perceived as most of the governments of antiquity were of the democratic species; and even in modern Europe, to which we owe the great principle of representation, no example is seen of a government wholly popular, and founded at the same time wholly on that principle. If Europe has the merit of discovering this great mechanical power in government, by the simple agency of which, the will of the largest political body may be concentred, and its force directed to any object, which the public good requires; America can claim the merit of making the discovery the basis of unmixed and extensive republics. It is only to be lamented, that any of her citizens should wish to deprive her of the additional merit of displaying its full efficacy on the establishment of the comprehensive system now under her consideration.

As the natural limit of a democracy is that distance from the central point, which will just permit the most remote citizens to assemble as often as their public functions demand; and will include no greater number than can join in those functions; so the natural limit of a republic is that distance from the center, which will barely allow the representatives of the people to meet as often as may be necessary for the administration of public affairs. Can it be said, that the limits of the United States exceed this distance? It will not be said by those who recollect that the Atlantic coast is the longest side of the union; that during the term of thirteen years, the representatives of the States have been almost continually assembled; and that the members from the most distant States are not chargeable with greater intermissions of attendance, than those from the States in the neighbourhood of Congress.

That we may form a juster estimate with regard to this interesting subject, let us resort to the actual dimensions of the union. The limits as fixed by the treaty of peace are on the east the Atlantic, on the south the latitude of thirty-one degrees, on the west the Mississippi, and on the north an irregular line running in some instances beyond the forty-fifth degree, in others falling as low as the forty-second. The southern shore of Lake Erie lies below that latitude. Computing the distance between the thirty-one and forty-five degrees, it amounts to nine hundred and seventy-three common miles; computing it from thirty-one to forty-two degrees to seven hundred, sixty four miles and an half. Taking the mean for the distance, the amount will be eight hundred, sixty-eight miles and three-fourths. The mean distance from the Atlantic to the Mississippi does not probably exceed seven hundred and fifty miles. On a comparison of this extent, with that of several countries in Europe, the practicability of rendering our system commensurate to it, appears to be demonstrable. It is not a great deal larger than Germany, where a Diet representing the whole empire is continually assembled; or than Poland before the late dismemberment, where another national Diet was the depository of the supreme power. Passing by France and Spain, we find that in Great Britain, inferior as it may be in size, the representatives of the northern extremity of the island, have as far to travel to the national Council, as will be required of those of the most remote parts of the union.

Favorable as this view of the subject may be, some observations remain which will place it in a light still more satisfactory.

In the first place it is to be remembered, that the general government is not to be charged with the whole power of making and administering laws. Its jurisdiction is limited to certain enumerated objects, which concern all the members of the republic, but which are not to be attained by the separate provisions of any. The subordinate governments which can extend their care to all those other objects, which can be separately provided for, will retain their due authority and activity. Were it proposed by the plan of the Convention to abolish the governments of the particular States, its adversaries would have some ground for their objection, though it would not be difficult to shew that if they were abolished, the general government would be compelled by the principle of self-preservation, to reinstate them in their proper jurisdiction.

A second observation to be made is, that the immediate object of the Fœderal Constitution is to secure the union of the Thirteen Primitive States, which we know to be practicable; and to add to them such other States, as may arise in their own bosoms or in their neighbourhoods, which we cannot doubt to be equally practicable. The arrangements that may be necessary for those angles and fractions of our territory, which lie on our north western frontier, must be left to those whom further discoveries and experience will render more equal to the task.

Let it be remarked in the third place, that the intercourse throughout the union will be daily facilitated by new improvements. Roads will every where be shortened, and kept in better order; accommodations for travellers will be multiplied and meliorated; and interior navigation on our eastern side will be opened throughout, or nearly throughout the whole extent of the Thirteen States. The communication between the western and Atlantic districts, and between different parts of each, will be rendered more and more easy by those numerous canals with which the beneficence of nature has intersected our country, and which art finds it so little difficult to connect and complete.

A fourth and still more important consideration is, that as almost every State will on one side or other, be a frontier, and will thus find in a regard to its safety, an inducement to make some sacrifices for the sake of the general protection; so the States which lie at the greatest distance from the heart of the union, and which of course may partake least of the ordinary circulation of its benefits, will be at the same time immediately contiguous to foreign nations, and will consequently stand on particular occasions, in greatest need of its strength and resources. It may be inconvenient for Georgia or the States forming our western or north eastern borders to send their representatives to the seat of government, but they would find it more so to struggle alone against an invading enemy, or even to support alone the whole expence of those precautions, which may be dictated by the neighbourhood of continual danger. If they should derive less benefit therefore from the union in some respects, than the less distant States, they will derive greater benefit from it in other respects, and thus the proper equilibrium will be maintained throughout.

I submit to you my fellow citizens, these considerations, in full confidence that the good sense which has so often marked your decisions, will allow them their due weight and effect; and that you will never suffer difficulties, however formidable in appearance or however fashionable the error on which they may be founded, to drive you into the gloomy and perilous scene into which the advocates for disunion would conduct you. Hearken not to the unnatural voice which tells you that the people of America, knit together as they are by so many chords of affection, can no longer live together as members of the same family; can no longer continue the mutual guardians of their mutual happiness; can no longer be fellow citizens of one great respectable and flourishing empire. Hearken not to the voice which petulantly tells you that the form of government recommended for your adoption is a novelty in the political world; that it has never yet had a place in the theories of the wildest projectors; that it rashly attempts what it is impossible to accomplish. No my countrymen, shut your ears against this unhallowed language. Shut your hearts against the poison which it conveys; the kindred blood which flows in the veins of American citizens, the mingled blood which they have shed in defence of their sacred rights, consecrate their union, and excite horror at the idea of their becoming aliens, rivals, enemies. And if novelties are to be shunned, believe me the most alarming of all novelties, the most wild of all projects, the most rash of all attempts, is that of rending us in pieces, in order to preserve our liberties and promote our happiness. But why is the experiment of an extended republic to be rejected merely because it may comprise what is new? Is it not the glory of the people of America, that whilst they have paid a decent regard to the opinions of former times and other nations, they have not suffered a blind veneration for antiquity, for custom, or for names, to overrule the suggestions of their own good sense, the knowledge of their own situation, and the lessons of their own experience? To this manly spirit, posterity will be indebted for the possession, and the world for the example of the numerous innovations displayed on the American theatre, in favor of private rights and public happiness. Had no important step been taken by the leaders of the revolution for which a precedent could not be discovered, no government established of which an exact model did not present itself, the people of the United States might, at this moment, have been numbered among the melancholy victims of misguided councils, must at best have been labouring under the weight of some of those forms which have crushed the liberties of the rest of mankind. Happily for America, happily we trust for the whole human race, they pursued a new and more noble course. They accomplished a revolution which has no parallel in the annals of human society: They reared the fabrics of governments which have no model on the face of the globe. They formed the design of a great confederacy, which it is incumbent on their successors to improve and perpetuate. If their works betray imperfections, we wonder at the fewness of them. If they erred most in the structure of the union; this was the work most difficult to be executed; this is the work which has been new modelled by the act of your Convention, and it is that act on which you are now to deliberate and to decide.

PUBLIUS

From President Washington to President Jefferson

NOBLE E. CUNNINGHAM, JR.

EFFECTS OF THE DEVELOPMENT OF PARTIES

WHEN THOMAS JEFFERSON TOOK THE OATH OF OFFICE AS THE third President of the United States on March 4, 1801, many men could remember the time twelve years before when the first president of the new nation had been inaugurated. If they paused to review in their minds the years that had passed, they must have been struck by the changes they had witnessed. They had seen a piece of paper transformed into a workable system of government and a new Union grow stronger and more respected. As they looked back over this eventful period they could well remember the excitement during the early years of the French Revolution and the controversy that was raised over Jay's Treaty. When the French Alliance was dissolved by the Convention of 1800, they must have breathed a sigh of relief as they compared the clearing diplomatic horizon with the dark days when issues of foreign policy had divided the opinions of the people so sharply. They must also have been impressed by the great changes which had taken place in the political life of the country, and although they could not have recognized the historical significance of these developments, they could see that two major parties had grown up within the American political structure and that with them far-reaching changes had been ushered into the political life of the United States.

In less than a decade, the growth of the Republican and Federalist parties significantly changed the character of American politics. At the beginning of the 1790's, elections were, for the most part, decided on a personal basis. A candidate for political office generally had to rely upon his own resources and those of his friends to promote his election. How

Chapter 10 of *The Jeffersonian Republicans: the Formation of Party Organisation*, 1789–1801 (1957). Reprinted by permission of the author, the Institute of Early American History & Culture, Williamsburg, Virginia, and the University of North Carolina Press.

he went about getting elected depended to a large extent on the practices and customs that prevailed in the state in which he sought election. What was considered proper in one state might lose him the election in another. In general, the solicitation of the suffrages of the voters seems to have been considered improper, although the injunction against the practice was not always strictly observed, and in some states it took various subtle forms. In Virginia a candidate could scarcely expect to win the favor of the voters unless he were prepared to treat them to rum punch or other drinks on election day.[1] If he were a member of Congress and found himself unable to be in the district at the time of election, he might send letters, as Madison did in 1790, to influential citizens in each county of the district and entrust his election to their hands; or he might ask his brother or father, as Madison also did, to attend the polls and look out for his interest.[2]

New Englanders took great pride in the absence of electioneering in their choice of representatives. A Connecticut congressman boasted:

In this state, no instance has ever been known where a person has appeared as a public candidate, and solicited the suffrages of the freemen, for a place in the legislature. Should any person have the effrontery or folly to make such an attempt, he may be assured of meeting with the general contempt and indignation of the people, and of throwing an insuperable bar in the way of attaining the object of his pursuit.[3]

But in Maryland no one seemed to disapprove of a candidate's advertising his candidacy in the newspapers or otherwise seeking to forward his own election.[4]

Yet, although campaign practices were locally adapted to the prevailing public opinion concerning the proper conduct for political aspirants, there was a common condition which characterized nearly all political contests at the beginning of the 1790's. This was the fact that it was generally the personal characters of the individual candidates, their public records and private habits, their qualifications for office, and their integrity as citizens which served to commend them to the voters and furnished the issues for the electorate to decide. Men were recommended for office because of their *"diligence, consistency, integrity, and independence."*[5] and a candidate might even be recommended for his *"facetious humor"*

[1] Charles S. Sydnor, *Gentlemen Freeholders: Political Practices in Washington's Virginia* (Chapel Hill, 1952), 51–59.

[2] James Madison to A. Rose and others, August 13, 1790; Madison to James Madison, Sr., August 14, 1790, Hunt, ed., *Madison Writings*, VI, 20–21.

[3] Zephaniah Swift, *A System of the Laws of the State of Connecticut* (Windham, 1795), I, 68.

[4] Annapolis, *Maryland Gazette*, September 22, October 6, 1791.

[5] Philadelphia, *General Advertiser*, October 11, 1791.

or *"modest aversion* to public life," or because he was "a *right up and down* honest man."[6] On election day in Philadelphia in 1791, the editor of the *General Advertiser* pointed out the qualifications required of a political candidate, declaring:

The representative of a free people, should in the first place be a man of strict integrity, upright in his dealings as a man, and steady in his principles as a politician. Joined to a general knowledge of mankind, and of government, he should especially be well acquainted with the interests of his constituents, and with the laws of his country. Sagacity to perceive, activity and industry to pursue, eloquence to promote, and sound judgement to determine on whatever will tend to the good of his country, are among the necessary requisites.[7]

Candidates were frequently assisted in their elections by personal followings of friends and connections, and when contemporaries referred to them as "parties," they usually were thinking in terms of personal followings or political "interests." When William Smith was proposed as a representative from Maryland to the First Congress, for example, it was said that he was set up by a party in Baltimore and the voters were asked: "Does not this *party* consist chiefly of the Smiths, and their connexions and dependents? And may not this *party* with propriety be distinguished hereafter and at the next election, by the appellation of the Smithites."[8] Governor George Clinton's following being drawn from the entire state of New York, was of considerably greater proportions than the groups which gathered around political leaders in most states and had much more the appearance of a political party, but the designation "Clintonians" which was given to Clinton's supporters suggested the basic fact that the "party" in early years was largely a personal following.

By the end of the decade of the nineties, the growth of political parties had wrought fundamental alterations in the political life of the country. The formation of parties was accompanied by a growth of campaigning; elections became more warmly contested, and even the most staid New England towns became infected with what their people had denounced as the "vile practice of electioneering."[9] Just after the election of 1800, a writer in the *Connecticut Courant* declared:

---

[6] Philadelphia, *National Gazette,* September 5, 1792.

[7] Philadelphia, *General Advertiser,* October 11, 1791. The Providence *United States Chronicle* reminded the citizens of Rhode Island that representatives to Congress should be men of "Liberality, Integrity, and Information," August 2, 1792.

[8] *Queries, to the Voters of Baltimore County,* signed "Anti-smithites," January 1789, Broadside, Lib. Cong.

[9] Andrew Lee, *The Origins and Ends of Civil Government . . . A Sermon . . . May 14, 1795* (Hartford, 1795), 37. On electioneering in Massachusetts in 1800 see *The Diary of William Bentley* (Salem, Mass., 1911), II, 346–47, 354, 355.

Elections to office, in New England, have been always, till very lately, *free* beyond any example that can be found elsewhere.... It was not prudent for any man to express a wish for promotion.... Unhappily, however, our democrats have already had some influence in changing this truly republican state of things among us. The detestable practice of electioneering is, by their means, indirectly gaining ground, in these states.[10]

Another writer about the same time commented upon the growing tumult in the conduct of elections in Boston and the "confusion, wrangling and even uproar" on election day. "So loud and so indecently rude, is the noise made by the distribution of ballots for the different candidates," it was observed, "and such the illiberal reflections and uncandid remarks upon their respective characters, as cannot but excite painful sensations in every delicate mind."[11]

With the transcendency of parties over individuals, there was a decline in the feeling that it was improper to campaign for election. A candidate's efforts to win an election could now be viewed not merely as personal ambition but as a contribution to the party cause. Many candidates still did not solicit votes for themselves personally, and, like Nathaniel Macon of North Carolina, they prided themselves in this conduct. After many years in public office, Macon could write: "I have never solicited any man to vote for me or hinted to him that I wished him to do so, nor did I ever solicit any person to make interest, for me to be elected to any place."[12] But such men were not prevented by their political scruples from laboring to advance the party cause and, in so doing, their own elections. Although there were still many who disapproved of campaigning for office, the development of parties was bringing respectability to electioneering.

As campaigning shifted from an individual to a party basis, a candidate's party affiliation often became of more importance than his personal qualifications for office. "It is not the personal good qualities of a candidate that are inquired for," explained one contemporary observer in 1800; "whether he is a Federalist or not, is all the question."[13] After a trip through New Jersey in 1800, a newspaper editor affirmed that "the character of the candidates is sunk in the single question—whether friendly to Adams or Jefferson."[14]

[10] Hartford, *Connecticut Courant,* February 2, 1801.

[11] Boston, *New England Palladium,* February 10, 1801.

[12] Nathaniel Macon, brief autobiographical sketch in Nathaniel Macon Papers, Duke University.

[13] Charles W. Harris to Robert W. Harris, May 1800, Wagstaff, ed., "The Harris Letters," *James Sprunt Historical Publications,* 14 (1916), 71.

[14] Abraham Hodge to John Steele, October 10, 1800, Wagstaff, ed., *Papers of John Steele,* I, 188.

Some voters already were coming to support any candidate who carried the party standard, even when they did not approve of the candidate personally. During the election of 1796 in Maryland, one observer remarked:

In this county, I think I never knew an election so much of *principles*. General Eccleston (the Federal candidate) is obnoxious to about one half the county and is to be opposed next year by them in a sheriff's election, yet the language is, our choice is a party question, not a personal matter—this, for a Southern election, is a pleasing feature of the People's goodness.[15]

Another Maryland voter in 1798 disapproved highly of a Federalist candidate but admitted that even his objectionable conduct "will not prevent me from supporting his election, for the sake of the cause, although I wish we had an abler man."[16]

During the last decade of the eighteenth century, the voters were urged increasingly to subordinate personal considerations to the party cause. "Remember that the election . . . is not a mere contest between favourite individuals," the freeholders of Virginia were told in 1799, "but a contest between principles."[17] And the voters of Massachusetts' Fourth Western District were reminded during the congressional race in 1800 that both candidates were "gentlemen of good moral characters and of respectable abilities; but of different political opinions." One candidate, it was stated, "is a friend to the administration of Washington and of Adams; the other is the advocate of Jefferson and his party. It is therefore a question of principle."[18]

With the introduction of party tickets, the voters were soon being urged to vote the straight party slate. The Newark *Centinel of Freedom* pleaded in 1799:

Electors of New-Jersey, UNITE in support of Republican characters, be unanimous in your ticket and success will attend you. . . . Be firm, be vigilant, be enterprising and you will maintain the ground you have acquired. By your fortitude and your unanimity at this crisis, the rights and freedom of your country may be preserved and handed down to posterity; therefore remember, UNITED YOU STAND, DIVIDED YOU FALL.[19]

[15] William Vans Murray to James McHenry, November 2, 1796, Steiner, *The Life and Correspondence of James McHenry*, 200–1.

[16] F. Thomas to John E. Howard, September 5, 1798, Bayard Papers, Md. Hist. Soc.

[17] Richmond, *Virginia Argus*, March 12, 1799.

[18] Worcester, *Massachusetts Spy*, October 15, 1800.

[19] Newark, *Centinel of Freedom*, October 6, 1799, quoted in Stewart, "Jeffersonian Journalism," 1065.

The Philadelphia *Aurora* exclaimed in 1800 that "every man who is not for the whole Republican Ticket, Regards the Public Good, Less than his Prejudices,"[20] and a federalist campaign leaflet declared: *"Fellow Citizens,* let no slight dislikes or preferences induce you to relax your efforts or *break* the ticket; if you are for President Adams, be *wholly* so; by omissions of any on the *federal* nomination, or *taking up* any of the other, we shall defeat our intentions, and we may (the supposition is not too distant) ruin our Country!"[21] In recommending the ticket of Republican electors to the voters of Virginia in 1800, Republicans declared that "it must be admitted to be extremely probable that a freeholder, weak enough to be solicitous about men [rather] than principle, and who will not vote for the persons thus recommended, will throw away his suffrages. He who will not go with others must go alone."[22]

While formerly it had been a high recommendation for a candidate to be independent of parties, by 1800 it had become a political asset to have the reputation of being a firm party man. A candidate for Congress in New York was opposed because he was

a person of doubtful political gender—his character in public life has hitherto been fluctuating and unsettled—his conduct has been marked with extreme indecision—like a pendulum he has oscilated, now towards one party, and then to another...he has been in the Assembly for two or three years, during all which time he has been in a state of perpetual vibration....A man, who espouses no cause, and commits himself in favor of no particular principles, is never pledged to support the true interests of his constituents, but is always understood to be open to the advances of the highest bidder.[23]

Considerable pains were taken to show that James Ross, the Federalist candidate for Governor of Pennsylvania in 1799, had not been "a *firm supporter* of the administration, and a *steady* man in *federal* politics" while a member of the United States Senate. "It is deceiving their party," a campaign leaflet pointed out, "for his partizans to *pretend* that he is

[20] Philadelphia, *Aurora,* October 11, 1800.

[21] *Address to the Federal Republicans of Burlington County,* by a Committee, appointed at the Court House, on the 30th August, 1800 (Trenton, 1800), 6. For other examples of publications encouraging straight party voting see Morristown, N. J., *Genius of Liberty,* December 18, 1800; [Circular] *In Committee,* Albany, 8th April, 1799, signed Philip S. Van Rensselaer, Chairman, Broadside, Lib. Cong.

[22] *A Vindication of the General Ticket Law,* 12.

[23] *To the Electors of A Representative to Congress, for the First District,* signed "A Republican Elector" [1800], Broadside, N. Y. Pub. Lib. So serious was the charge that the candidate under attack wrote a lengthy refutation of the indictment. See Silas Wood, *Letters addressed to the Electors of Representatives to Congress for the First Election District in the State of New York: . . . in vindication of his public conduct* (New York, 1800), pamphlet, N. Y. Pub. Lib.

firm and *steady.*"[24] By 1800 the idea that a candidate should be a consistent party man—a theory that a decade before would have been scorned as unpatriotic and incompatible with republican government—was widely accepted. In its effect, the acceptance of the virtue of party regularity together with the introduction of the party platform, which placed more of the decisions as to how the government was to be administered in the hands of the voters, tended to restrict the individual initiative and personal discretion of men elected to public office.

Under the pressure of party growth, campaign practices, the conduct of elections, the concept of what public men should be and do, and the general attitude toward the business of politics changed greatly in the brief span of three presidential terms.

PARTY ORGANIZATION IN RETROSPECT

Although historians have generally neglected the practical aspects of party development, the prevailing view of the emergence of the Jeffersonian party pictures Jefferson personally organizing a political party to oppose Hamilton by cementing together local parties in each of the states. Claude Bowers wrote: "As Jefferson's mild eye surveyed the field, he found in almost every State local parties, some long in existence, fighting for popular rights as they understood them. . . . Why not consolidate these local parties into one great national organization, and broaden the issue to include the problems of both State and Nation? . . . The philosopher-politician took up his pen. . . ."[25] More recently, Wilfred E. Binkley has repeated: "Like all our major political parties this earlier one to organize constituted a loose federation of local parties. Without precedents to guide him, Jefferson set out to negotiate the necessary connections and understanding among them."[26] Thus Jefferson is seen traveling to New York to negotiate an understanding between Virginia and New York as a first step in the organization of a party, and one is left to assume that the pattern for subsequent party development was thus established.[27]

Contemporary documents suggest the need to revise this widely ac-

---

[24] *To the Citizens of Pennsylvania,* signed "An Elector" (n. p., [1799]), pamphlet Lib. Cong., 11–15.

[25] Bowers, *Jefferson and Hamilton,* 143; see also Claude G. Bowers, "Jefferson, Master Politician," *Virginia Quarterly Review,* 2 (1926), 324.

[26] Wilfred E. Binkley, *American Political Parties: Their Natural History* (New York, 2d ed., 1947), 78. Another recent work showing the acceptance of the same point of view is Herbert Agar, *The Price of Union* (New York, 1950), 88.

[27] William Goodman, *The Two-Party System in the United States* (Princeton, 1956), 165; Morison and Commager, *The Growth of the American Republic,* I, 343.

cepted view. The mass of evidence points to the conclusion that the Republican party was not the outgrowth of persisting state parties. Indeed, one does not find the type of ready-made state party that needed only to affiliate with a national headquarters set up by Jefferson. In some instances (e.g., New York) the new party built upon existing state factions, and elsewhere it attracted various of the old elements of political power in the several states. But the Republican party was a new growth that sprang from the divisions in Congress and the national government; it was a product of national rather than state politics.[28] Nor did major parties appear so suddenly as the theory of the confederation of existing parties suggests; party growth rather was a process of gradual development.

It was in Congress and in national politics that the early signs of party development were most noticeable. As parties developed, major party lines generally became clear in national politics and elections sooner than in state political life. As the Republican party gained strength and began presenting party tickets in the several states, it commonly started, as in Pennsylvania, by endorsing candidates for Congress and for presidential electors. Gaining popular support, the party extended its activities in state politics and initiated tickets for the legislature and other state offices. By 1800, Philadelphia Republicans added to the party ticket for the first time a candidate for the office of sheriff.[29] More and more, men came to be nominated and elected to state offices wholly on the basis of the stand which they took on national politics.

The role of members of Congress in the development of parties also should be more fully recognized. Congressmen, exposed to the growing partisan conflict in the national legislature, came to be party men before parties had reached very deeply into the political life of the country, and they played a significant role in spreading party growth. As parties developed, the members of Congress finally came to form, in essence, a national party organization and increasingly exercised a vital role in party control. Meetings of Congress, with members frequently grouped in

[28] Several recent studies of the development of parties on the state level have recognized the importance of national politics in the growth of state parties and have concluded that federal politics gave rise to political parties in the individual states studied. Harry M. Tinkcom, *The Republicans and Federalists in Pennsylvania, 1790–1801: A Study in National Stimulus and Local Response* (Harrisburg, 1950), 73, 153, 199, 211; Norman L. Stamps, "Political Parties in Connecticut, 1789–1819" (unpublished Ph.D thesis, Yale University, 1950), 2; Richard P. McCormick, *The History of Voting in New Jersey: A Study of the Development of Election Machinery, 1664–1911* (New Brunswick, N. J., 1953), 87.

[29] Philadelphia, *Aurora,* October 13, 1800; a defense of the innovation appears in the *Aurora,* August 16, 1800.

politically-oriented boarding houses, had certain aspects of party "conventions." Through the congressional caucus, the party leaders in Congress decided upon presidential nominations, and by 1800 the caucus had become strong enough to enforce its decision. As Republicans organized party machinery on a state level, as they were doing in Virginia and elsewhere in 1800, party centralization gradually lessened. But the Republican party had grown up as a national party in response to the stimulus of national politics, and this fact was still strongly reflected in the party which elected Jefferson to the presidency in 1801.

The role of Jefferson in the formation of the Republican party must be viewed in relation to the developments in Congress and to the important place of Madison's leadership in that body. Before Jefferson retired as Secretary of State at the end of 1793, he had come to be looked upon as the leader of the Republican interest. This circumstance was due both to his opposition to the Hamiltonian program and to the fact that the friends of Hamilton singled him out for their most concentrated attack. Though Jefferson's role does not correspond to the view so widely circulated in the Federalist press—that the Virginian was avidly organizing opposition to the government and constantly intriguing with members of Congress to defeat the measures of the Secretary of the Treasury—he did cooperate with Madison in bringing Freneau to Philadelphia to establish the *National Gazette* (here again the important role of Madison must be recognized), and by 1793 he was no longer maintaining that official aloofness from the proceedings of Congress to which he previously had undertaken to adhere. During 1793, the Secretary of State assisted friends in Congress in preparing resolutions designed to drive Hamilton from office, and he seemed to be thinking in terms of party when he drew up a line of policy for Republicans to follow during the controversy created by Genet and the French issue. He appeared also to be working for party purposes when he urged Madison to prepare some replies to Hamiltonian doctrines in the press.

Although Jefferson had become something of a party leader before he retired from Washington's cabinet on the last day of December 1793, that role was abdicated when he returned to Monticello. For the next three years it was Madison who assumed the Republican leadership. By the time he left the House at the end of the Fourth Congress, the Republican party in Congress was no longer the loose and indefinite association it had been when Jefferson had retired, but a well-defined party with some measure of organization, although its members did not always display unity or follow party leadership. By 1796, party lines had tightened throughout the country, and when Jefferson returned to active political life, with his election to the vice presidency, he clearly accepted the role of party leader. His efforts in mobilizing the party for the battle with the Federalists in 1800 displayed political shrewdness and finesse.

With Vice President Jefferson its active head, the Republican party grew to maturity, and the struggle with the Federalists for political dominance was accompanied by great strides in party organization and in the introduction of party machinery. The present study has sought to display the gradual evolution of party organization and machinery and the development of the "art of electioneering." It is clear that party methods and techniques were well advanced by 1800. Although Federalists not uncommonly duplicated Republican improvements in their party organization, Republicans generally appear to have taken the initiative in introducing party machinery and new methods of winning elections. The attention which Republicans gave to these matters was in a large measure inspired by the need for an aggressive campaign and superior organization to overcome the political advantage which the Federalists enjoyed as the party in power.

Effective organization and aggressive campaigning were the keys to Republican success in the election of 1800. In their attention to party organization and machinery, the Republicans remained constantly aware of the necessity of maintaining popular support. Party spokesmen therefore exploited every available agency of mass communication: official papers such as petitions against governmental measures, public circular letters from congressmen to their constituents, newspapers, pamphlets, handbills, private letters which circulated among leading figures, and personal contacts and word-of-mouth communications. The nature of democracy made it imperative that the people should play a prominent part in party activities, and political machinery was geared to win their votes.

But popular participation in politics should not be confused with popular initiative in the introduction of party machinery. In the 1790's one rarely finds effective party organization springing from the so-called "grass roots." Instead, the organization of the Republican party and the introduction of smoothly functioning party machinery were due largely to the leadership of a few dedicated and influential political leaders, such as Jefferson, Madison, members of Congress, John Beckley, and others. The newspapers report numerous popular party gatherings, but this more abundant source of information has often obscured the fact that the archives hold not a few confidential letters revealing the careful preparation that commonly preceded such meetings.

The press might announce, as the New York *Daily Advertiser* did in 1795, that "a numerous and respectable meeting of the freeholders of the town of Kingston. . . . Resolved, That in the opinion of a large majority of this meeting, Aaron Burr be nominated and recommended as a fit person for Governor at the ensuing election; and that we will support him with our votes and interest."[30] This notice might easily leave the impression that the nomination was a spontaneous expression of popular wishes, but an unpublicized letter written ten days before this meeting by the district's congressman, Peter Van Gaasbeck, to a leading political figure of his district suggests otherwise:

I presume you will have seen the Publication of the Governor and Lieut. Governor, declining being candidates at the ensuing Election—in my opinion no time ought to be lost to arrange and Publish the candidates to be supported—if we take the lead, all is secure, therefore immediately have a meeting, and announce our worthy friend Aaron Burr for Governor.... After this is published,—prepare your slay and Horses and meet me at Easton on Saturday the 7th February—where I have also requested some of our Kingston Friends to meet me.... When you go to Kingston, assure our Friends that every expense they are at will be cordially refunded from him who is not to be seen in that act; now my worthy fellow put the wheel in Motion....[31]

Though it is not always possible to delve behind the newspaper reports, it seems clear that public political participation was not infrequently guided. At the same time it is important to notice that political leaders recognized the importance of public sentiment and the necessity of popular participation in politics, for, after all, the people cast the votes.

Between the inaugurations of Washington and Jefferson, the two-party system became rooted in American politics. So important had the role of parties become in the political life of the nation that the Constitution itself was soon to be amended to recognize the place of parties, whose rise had made the constitutional provisions for the election of the president and the vice president outdated and unrealistic and had led to the troublesome tie between Jefferson and Burr. In 1804, the Twelfth Amendment was added to the Constitution to provide for separate balloting for president and vice president.

With the Federalist defeat in 1800, there were many who hoped that political parties might now be set at rest. But the Federalists were not yet ready to surrender, as one New York Federalist intimated when he wrote:

[30] New York, *Daily Advertiser*, February 28, 1795, extra.
[31] Peter Van Gaasbeck to Ebenezer Foote, January 26, 1795, Annie Burr Jennings Collection, Yale. See also Van Gaasbeck to Foote, February 12, 1795, *ibid*. For similar preparations for another county meeting reported in the New York *Daily Advertiser*, April 2, 1795, see Van Gaasbeck to Foote, March 17, 1795, *ibid.*, Foote to Van Gaasbeck, March 18, 1795, Katherine A. Foote, ed., *Ebenezer Foote the Founder, being an Epistolary Light on his Time as shed by Letters from his Files* (Delhi, N. Y., 1927), 54.

It has been vainly boasted that the Sun of Federalism was about to Set and that we were about to die but Surely we are not dead yet and if it must be so let it not be without a Struggle—let us pray as Sampson did on a former Occasion that we may be avenged on our political enemies once more and that those men who are Stigmatizing us with the name of Tory and every other opprobrious Epithet might be once more Disappointed.[32]

Federalists and Republicans appeared in unaccustomed roles as the new administration began on March 4, 1801, but the party conflict had not ended.

═══════════════════════════

Suffrage in the New West

CHILTON WILLIAMSON

IN SEVERAL OF HIS MORE FAMOUS WRITINGS, FREDERICK JACKSON Turner developed the theory that the growth of American democracy, as it was known in the nineteenth century, was due to the influence of the frontier. Discussing this growth with reference to the suffrage, he said in his *Rise of the New West*, "It was only as the interior of the country developed that suffrage restrictions gradually gave way in the direction of manhood suffrage."[1] *The Frontier in American History* restated this theme: "The wind of Democracy blew so strongly from the west, that even in the older states of New York, Massachusetts, Connecticut and Virginia, conventions were called which liberalized the constitutions by strengthening the democratic basis of the state."[2]

Turner implied that a major motive for suffrage reform in the east was the prevention of a drain of population to the west. Nevertheless,

---

[32] Francis Crawford to Ebenezer Foote, March 7, 1801, Papers of Ebenezer Foote, Lib. Cong.

Chapter 11 of *American Suffrage from Property to Democracy 1760–1860* (Princeton, 1960). Reprinted by permission of the author and Princeton University Press.

ED'S. NOTE: In this chapter Professor Williamson refers to 'Blackstonianism,' which is the doctrine, stated by Sir William Blackstone in his *Commentaries on the Laws of England* (1770), that the suffrage should be conferred only on men who owned enough property to make them independent of the will of others. Blackstone drew this from the republican thinkers of the English Civil War period.

[1] Turner, F. J., *The Rise of the New West* (New York, 1906), p. 175.

[2] Turner, F. J., *The Frontier in American History* (New York, 1920), p. 250.

the facts of seaboard suffrage reform do not support this thesis; although this argument was used, as in Connecticut, it was never a major issue there or anywhere. By 1812, the states of Vermont, Maryland, and South Carolina had divorced property from the suffrage as a result of movements which owed very little, if anything, to the frontier spirit. A freehold qualification survived along the seaboard only in Rhode Island and in Virginia in all state elections, and in New York and North Carolina in some but not all. The remaining seaboard states, with the exception of Connecticut and Massachusetts (in law, at least), based their adult male electorate upon a taxpaying qualification which amounted almost to universal manhood suffrage wherever all adult males were subject to the payment of a poll tax. It must be borne in mind also that, except perhaps in times of high political excitement, adult male suffrage prevailed wherever there was laxity in or indifference to strict enforcement of the suffrage laws. Furthermore, the extent of suffrage democracy in the west has been exaggerated. Ohio and Louisiana confined the suffrage to taxpayers, Tennessee to freeholders unless the voter had been resident in the county for six months.[3] As late as 1812, only one state of the New West, Kentucky, had eliminated all property or taxpaying qualifications. If this analysis is correct, Turner had the western cart before the eastern horse.

By no means all contemporary observers endeavored, like Turner, to draw a distinction between eastern and western developments or attributed to the west the decisive role in democratic reform. In 1806, Benjamin H. Latrobe, the great architect, acknowledged that eastern suffrage reform was sweeping the country. "After the adoption of the Federal Constitution," he wrote, "the extension of the right of suffrage in the States to a majority of all the adult male citizens, planted a germ which had [sic] gradually evolved and has spread actual and practical democracy and political equality over the whole union."[4] Three years later, a Massachusetts pamphleteer, while discussing the merits of a contested election for the United States House of Representatives, asserted that in the eastern states "elections are so popular as to amount almost to universal suffrage."[5]

It would be difficult to show that easterners believed that western constitutions before or after the War of 1812 offered any novelties worth incorporating into their own constitutions. Regarding the constitution of Mississippi of 1817, a Massachusetts newspaper made a revealing comment. "It is . . . so similar," it said, "to the constitutions of many of the

---

[3] See Thorpe, *op. cit.*, III, pp. 1,264–1,277; V, pp. 2,897–2,913; III, pp. 1,380–1,392; VI, pp. 3,414–3,425.

[4] Maryland Historical Society, *Latrobe Letterbook*, 1806, p. 623.

[5] Baylies, William, *A View of the Proceedings of the House of Representatives of the United States in the Case of the Plymouth Election* (Boston, 1809), p. 18.

other states, that its perusal does not excite much interest."[6] As might be expected, eastern reformers and conservatives alike found their principles reflected in the various constitutions of the New West. Connecticut conservatives, for example, praised the taxpaying suffrage requirement of the Ohio constitution because it excluded from voting men who were not property owners. When reformers urged the east to borrow from the west, as they sometimes did, western principles were often rejected as being appropriate to a frontier society but unsuited to an older, more sophisticated seaboard society. Judge Van Ness of the New York constitutional convention of 1821 rejected arguments that New York should pattern its institutions upon the democratic precedents of the west, saying that the state of New York did not stand in need of being instructed by every petty new state beyond the Alleghenies.[7] On their part, eastern reformers took comfort from the fact that Missouri had voted for universal manhood suffrage when it was admitted to the Union in 1822. Obviously, western precedents could be used to underwrite either position taken in the east.

In one particular, however, circumstances of frontier life did render inexpedient property tests for voting. In a new country, the process of surveying land and granting titles is likely to be laborious and long-drawn out, and to lag behind the more urgent demands and needs of the settlers. Such was the case when the British created the Province of West Florida after the Seven Years' War. In this colony, the freehold qualification for voting proved impractical because there were too few freeholders to sustain a genuinely representative government. As a result, the British were obliged to choose between abandoning self-government entirely or admitting all householders to the suffrage.[8] They chose the latter.

Virginia faced a comparable problem in dealing with the elections by which Kentucky was set off as a separate state in 1792. When Virginia had created Kentucky County in 1776, it had extended to it its own freehold qualification for voting. This qualification had to be abandoned if there were to be more than a small number of voters, because the enormous amount of litigation over land titles made it difficult for settlers to secure deeds.[9] Moreover, at this time the only really effective organs of government were the militia companies. For this reason, the Danville Convention of 1785, designed to treat with Virginia for statehood, was elected by the militia men on the basis of one delegate per

[6] *Worcester Spy,* quoted in *Albany Gazette,* October 11, 1817.

[7] Carter, Stone and Gould, *op. cit.,* p. 270.

[8] Howard, C. N., *British Development of West Florida 1763–1769* (Berkeley, 1947), pp. 43–44.

[9] Hening, *Statutes,* XII, p. 37.

militia company.[10] This breach of the freehold qualification in Virginia elections led to still another, whereby free white male inhabitants were allowed to vote in subsequent elections for constitutional conventions. The connection between these changes and the fact that Kentucky entered the union with a constitution conceding universal manhood suffrage is undoubtedly very close. Not all Kentuckians were happy over these developments. The Political Club of Danville, a group composed of a number of lawyers and others who had come from Virginia, opposed universal suffrage at a club meeting in 1787. The members voted that "some other qualification besides freedom ought to be required."[11] The debate had no effect, however, upon opinion at large or even upon the constitutional convention. Virginia had permitted the breach of the freehold qualification for very practical reasons. Here, as elsewhere, a return to the past was impossible.

Equally pragmatic considerations caused the federal government to abandon the 50-acre freehold qualification for voting in the western territories, a qualification inherited from the old Continental Congress. Some territorial officials, including the governor of Ohio Territory, Arthur St. Clair, favored its retention. St. Clair was a strong believer in Blackstonianism. "I do not count independence and wealth always together," he said, "but I pronounce poverty and dependence to be inseparable." For this reason, he heartily disapproved of the Pennsylvania constitution because it did not require a property test for voting.[12]

When the time came to hold elections for the first legislature of Ohio territory, however, it was found that few persons were qualified under the 50-acre freehold clause because their titles to lands, particularly in the Symnes Purchase, had not yet been granted. The majority of freeholders were owners of relatively small town lots. In order to create enough voters so that genuine elections could be held, the federal government in 1798 enfranchised owners of town lots which were worth as much as 50-acre freeholds.[13] St. Clair was opposed to giving the vote to buyers of Symnes Purchase lands on the grounds that until they secured title they would not act as free agents. The only reason he upheld a freehold qualification, and ballot rather than viva voce elections, he said, was to prevent undue representation for the landlord interest.

[10] Brown, John M., "The Political Beginnings of Kentucky," *Filson Club Publications,* no. 6 (Louisville, 1889), p. 61, passim.

[11] Speed, Thomas, "The Political Club, Danville, Ky., 1786–90," *Filson Club Publications,* IX (Louisville, 1894), p. 125.

[12] Smith, W. H., "A Familiar Talk about Monarchists and Jacobins," *Ohio Archaeological and Historical Publications,* II, pp. 187–215.

[13] Smith, W. H. (ed.), *St. Clair Papers* (Cincinnati, 1882, 2 vols.), II, pp. 436–438.

Similar problems beset the inhabitants of Mississippi Territory about this time. The legislature complained to the Congress in 1804 that the 50-acre qualification deprived persons of considerable property of the right to vote, and requested that all persons, otherwise qualified, who had paid a tax six months previous to the election be allowed to vote. The legitimacy of the request was unchallengeable in the light of a situation in which, it was convincingly stated, only 236 persons out of 4,444 could vote in the territory, a source of chagrin to the Federalist governor, Winthrop Sargent.[14] As a temporary expedient, pre-emptioners were enfranchised in 1807. The inhabitants of Indiana Territory were in a similar predicament and joined the Mississippians in requesting Congress to reconsider the 50-acre qualification.

At this time, Congress was unwilling to abandon the freehold concept. Instead, it passed two acts early in 1808 by which all free adult males in Indiana and all free adult white males in Mississippi who had a 50-acre freehold or an equitable freehold or who owned a town lot worth $100 could vote.[15] Dissatisfied with the small extent of reform, partly because some hoped that a democratic suffrage would attract settlers to their territory, residents of Indiana renewed their efforts to secure a broader franchise. Despite their gratitude, they said, for the concession already made, they hoped that Congress would extend the vote to all taxpayers or militia men.[16] In response to these requests, Congress, having defeated an effort to prohibit squatters from voting, abandoned the freehold qualification in 1811 and substituted for it a tax-paying one-year residency requirement.

A comparable situation prevailed in Illinois, where a number of residents asserted that only 200 or 300 persons were bona fide freeholders of the territory. Governor Ninian Edwards corroborated their statements.[17] In 1812, Congress recognized the impracticability of a freehold qualification under these circumstances and abandoned it. Two years later, Congress gave up the freehold qualification in Mississippi, following an analysis of the electoral situation which purported to show that many well-to-do individuals, owners of slaves and large numbers of cattle, were unable to meet the property test and that it had been debased by the dishonesty and corruption involved in the creation of a number of fagot voters.

Suffrage change was a product also of the democratic convictions of the residents of the territories at a time when these convictions were

[14] Sydnor, C. S., *A Gentleman of the Old Natchez Region* (Durham, 1938), p. 27.

[15] Carter, Clarence E., *The Territorial Papers of the United States* (Washington, D.C., 1934–58, 20 vols.), VII, p. 526; I, pp. 411n, 616–618.

[16] Carter, *op. cit.*, VII, pp. 690–691; VIII, pp. 111–112, 112n.

[17] Carter, *op. cit.*, XVI, pp. 199–202.

becoming more widespread. For example, a number of southerners living in Vincennes petitioned Governor William Henry Harrison in 1802 that they be permitted to bring slaves into the territory, that public education be provided, and that the suffrage qualifications be changed because, as they existed in freehold form, they were "subversive of the liberties" of the citizens and tended to give too much weight to wealth.[18] Nevertheless, neither they nor other petitioners from the territories requested, at this time, as did seaboard reformers in Maryland and South Carolina, adult male suffrage. Previous to 1814, they were content to ask for a taxpaying and militia qualification. Mississippi reformers in 1814 requested in the language of Jefferson, "general suffrage," that is, a taxpaying and militia qualification. In 1817, William Lattimore, the territorial delegate to Congress, secured the passage of an act to establish a taxpaying electorate, which he trusted would be popular with Mississippians.[19]

The real import of the democratic direction of the suffrage change in the New West is hard to determine. In the first place, suffrage laws, as in the east, could very well be ignored by all parties. In Alabama Territory, universal white suffrage was practiced in at least one election in 1818, when the candidates consented to allowing all adult males to vote. Secondly, it may be questioned whether a genuine democracy was possible in relatively primitive communities on the frontier, where the situation can be likened to that prevailing before the Revolution in Georgia and South Carolina. At that time, neither of these colonies had been welded into a cohesive or organic whole. In practice, power was exercised by small groups in and around Charleston or Savannah, the franchise was neglected because it was not highly valued, and election to office was either avoided or refused. Whether in pre-Revolutionary Nova Scotia or in post-Revolutionary Vermont or Tennessee, the frontier did not provide an environment conducive to a responsible, and to that extent, democratic government for a new region inhabited by a scattering of people. A newspaper attack on territorial government quoted Rousseau on this score. "Countries thinly inhabited," Rousseau had written in his *Social Contract,* "are the most proper places for tyrants; wild beasts reign only in deserts."[20] Governor St. Clair had already come to this conclusion and feared oligarchical government. He hoped that the secret ballot might prove a partial corrective in the Northwest Territory.

An argument against a free land policy which would have shocked Jefferson was advanced by a westerner to the Secretary of the Treasury in 1810. In his opinion, free land was an undesirable policy because it

[18] Indiana Historical Society, *Collections,* VII (1922), pp. 62–67.
[19] *The Washington Republican and Natchez Intelligencer,* April 9, 1817.
[20] Carter, *op. cit.,* VII, pp. 135–140.

would cause a rush of the poor to the territories where their votes would be garnered by cheap politicians.[21] Such fears were not totally groundless. Territorial governors were denounced as being as tyrannical as royal governors of the British North American colonies and were even accused of attempting to control elections, as were other territorial officials. In an election in Missouri Territory in 1817, timid males were herded to the polls in the presence of troops, in the familiar atmosphere of liquor fumes and glinting daggers and pistols. The election was branded more despotic than those in England.[22] As in the east, sheriffs proved capricious in enforcing the voting qualifications, interpreting them one way here and another there. Viva voce elections denied voters protection against those who would intimidate them. Popular participation in territorial elections was lessened by the use of the county as the electoral unit.

Indiana reformers, like those of the seaboard, saw clearly that suffrage reform, *per se,* was not enough, that reform of electoral procedures was of equal importance. For this reason, when they achieved a taxpaying militia qualification in 1811, they sought also, and with success, to curb the abuses of sheriffal authority by turning over the supervision of elections to judges of the County Courts of Common Pleas, as well as to increase voter participation by abandoning the county in favor of the township as the polling unit. This last reform was possibly a greater factor in enfranchising the population of Indiana than the abandonment of the freehold qualification.[23]

While the rapid withering of the freehold qualification was effecting an approximation of suffrage democracy in the New West, the prospect of further reform developed as the time came for each of the territories to emerge from the tutelage of the federal government as a full-fledged state of the union. The speed with which some of them earned the right to statehood was the result of partisan politics. Tennessee was admitted hastily in 1796 against Federalist wishes to delay statehood and thus cut down the size of the Republican vote. The admission of Ohio when its population was less than the 60,000 required to qualify as a state is the best illustration of the purely political considerations underlying the movement for statehood in some parts of the country. Republicans wanted more votes.[24]

Whatever the immediate reason, the territorial voters were given eight

[21] *Ibid.,* VIII, pp. 59–60.

[22] *Missouri Gazette,* Aug. 9, 1817.

[23] Barnhart, J. D., "The Democratization of Indiana Territory," *Indiana Magazine of History* (XLIII, March 1947), pp. 1–21.

[24] *The Visitor* (New Haven), Jan. 25, 1803; *St. Clair Papers,* I, pp. 228–230; Combs, W. H., and Cole, W. E., *Tennessee: A Political Study* (Knoxville, 1940), p. 11.

different opportunities between 1796 and 1821 to elect delegates to conventions for the writing of state constitutions prior to admission to the union. Suffrage questions were bound to be discussed and determined in these conventions because it had been the practice since the Revolution to incorporate state and county electoral qualifications in constitutions. Like those who framed the seaboard documents, the men responsible for writing those of the New West came to their conventions with considerable knowledge of the existing constitutions of the various states. If it is true, as the president of the Florida Convention of 1838 asserted, that the members of that body were without books on constitutional law, without knowledge of history, near or remote, and unfamiliar with the opinions of the great lawyers, this convention was indeed unique.[25]

Actually, western conventions drew liberally upon the institutions and practices of the seaboard. Westerners appeared to be most satisfied when their fundamental instruments of government were as much as possible like those with which they had been familiar. The inhabitants of Wayne County in Michigan Territory, for example, requested of Lewis Cass that they be governed by the laws of New York, Massachusetts, Virginia, Ohio, and Vermont.[26] On the occasion of the meeting of the first territorial legislature of Iowa, members were said to be collecting copies of the statutes of as many states as they could, each trying to secure the incorporation of as many of the laws of his home state as possible.[27] Western constitution makers borrowed from the eastern states and from each other. Tennessee relied heavily upon Pennsylvania and North Carolina; Ohio on Tennessee, Pennsylvania, and Kentucky; Illinois and Indiana on Ohio and Kentucky. Alabama borrowed from her neighbor Mississippi.

The new constitutions borrowed not only from other documents, but also from the various schools of political thought which these documents represented. Western newspapers helped to familiarize their readers with the ideas or even with fragments of the writings of Thomas Paine, Algernon Sidney, James Harrington, John Locke, Jean Jacques Rousseau, Voltaire, and William Cobbett. They also published reports of the reformist activities of Sir Francis Burdett and Major John Cartwright in Britain.[28] The more conservative suffrage thought of the seaboard was represented as well. William C. C. Claiborne, future governor of Mis-

---

[25] Hoskins, F. W., "The St. Joseph Constitution," *Florida Historical Society Quarterly Proceedings* (XVI, April 1938), pp. 242–250.

[26] Rowland, D. (ed.), *The Mississippi Territorial Archives: 1799–1803* (Nashville, 1905), p. 338; *Detroit Gazette*, April 24, 1818.

[27] *The Annals of Iowa: A Historical Quarterly* (III, 3rd Series, 1897–1899), pp. 337, 337n.

[28] *The Orleans Gazette*, April 30, 1806; *Kentucky Gazette*, Sept. 1, 1787; *Missouri Gazette*, Aug. 1, 1812, Dec. 30, 1815; *The Mississippi Republican*, April 29, May 30, 1812.

sissippi Territory, left Richmond for Tennessee with his copies of the *Revised Statutes of Virginia* and the writings of Blackstone. As late as the 1830's in Illinois and the 1840's in Louisiana, Blackstonianism had its supporters.

Nevertheless, the suffrage qualifications of the states admitted to the union between 1796 and 1821 incorporated the democratic ideas which had been the conscious inheritance of the American people since the Revolution. Of the eight states admitted during this period, three required the payment of taxes for voting. The remainder conceded adult manhood suffrage to whites only because, as a resident of Michigan said, Indians and Negroes were excluded from the "great North American Family."[29]

The Congress, in exercising its power over the territories, followed the same trend. It permitted taxpayers to elect members of the various state conventions until the passage of the Enabling Act under which Alabama wrote its constitution in 1819. With this act, the federal government abandoned even this slight concession to the property concept in voting. So long as many western territories levied poll taxes, either permanently or for short periods, a shift from taxpaying to manhood suffrage probably had less real significance than the prior abandonment by Congress of the freehold qualification. Perhaps this situation accounts for the failure of even Republicans in Ohio to be interested in universal suffrage, even for whites, early in the nineteenth century. Yet western suffrage reform was not devoid of meaning for the future. The marked rise of tenantry in the midwest from the 1830's forward would have brought about a reversal of the long-term trend toward a democratic suffrage if the freehold and tax-paying tests, in their original form, had not been eliminated.[30]

As along the seaboard, the issue of elections based upon the level of county, township, or district and the question of the secret ballot were matters of great importance in the New West. In Indiana written ballots were used from 1811 forward, and in Illinois from 1813. In Illinois, however, a sharp struggle over this issue lasted from 1813 to 1829. Defenders of open voting stated frankly that it enabled candidates to pledge a man before election. Critics attacked the practice on the grounds that it was a survival of British tyranny. Advocates of the secret ballot were defeated and in 1829 Illinois returned to public voting. This state was thus in the exceptional position on an issue of which the merits and justice had been proved in the popular mind elsewhere.[31]

[29] Carter, *op. cit.*, XI, p. 730.

[30] Gates, P. W., "Land Policy and Tenancy in the Prairie States," *The Journal of Economic History* (I, May 1941), pp. 60–82.

[31] Carter, *op. cit.*, VI, pp. 36–39; Pease, T. C., *The Frontier State, 1818–1848* (Springfield, 1918), p. 39.

Western constitutions reflected those of the east also in the distinctions between the suffrage qualifications for state and local elections, distinctions which survived in some western and southern states as late as the Civil War. Even Alabama, with universal white manhood suffrage, occasionally refused, as in the case of the act incorporating Dadeville in 1837, to allow any but householders and freeholders to vote in town elections.[32] Kentucky in similar acts often required that voters in town elections be payers of taxes either on their polls or on their property. Louisville, when incorporated in 1828, extended the vote in local elections to persons qualified to vote for members of the legislature. Four years later, however, the act was amended in such a way as to eliminate all who did not pay taxes.[33] Similarly, Tennessee frequently refused to create as liberal suffrage provisions for local as for state elections. Ashport, under its charter of 1839, allowed only freeholders and taxpaying residents to vote in local elections. Memphis required by an act of 1853 that only city taxpayers could vote in city elections.[34] When St. Louis, Missouri, was incorporated in 1822, only taxpayers, otherwise qualified, were allowed to vote. As late as 1835, towns were being incorporated in the state which confined town elections to persons who had paid local taxes.[35]

States lying north of the Ohio were no different from those to the south. Indiana, for example, required that voters in the borough of Vincennes be householders or freeholders and in the city of Jeffersonville that they be taxpayers.[36] As late as 1837 in Illinois, a taxpaying qualification in local elections was still popular.[37] When Chicago was given city status in 1837, the electorate was confined to the taxpayers in order to identify the suffrage with sound fiscal policies. Blackstone was the authority cited.[38]

The philosophy underlying a state's denial of the suffrage in local elections to all those qualified to vote in state elections was never better expressed than by Albert Gallatin when he wrote Lafayette in 1833 that he had never known any evil to arise from universal suffrage in Pennsylvania

[32] *Acts Passed at the Called Session of the General Assembly of the State of Alabama* (Tuscaloosa, 1837), p. 35.

[33] *Acts Passed at the First Session of the 40th General Assembly for the Commonwealth of Kentucky* (Frankfort, 1832), pp. 199–200.

[34] *Acts of the State of Tennessee, Passed at the 1st Session of the 30th General Assembly* . . . (Nashville, 1854), p. 297.

[35] *The Revised Statutes of the State of Missouri* (St. Louis, 1835), p. 603.

[36] *Laws of a Local Nature* . . . (Indianapolis, 1836), pp. 32–33; *Laws of a Local Nature* . . . (Indianapolis, 1839), p. 18.

[37] *Laws of the State of Illinois* . . . (Vandalia, 1837), pp. 18–19.

[38] Sparling, S. E., *Municipal History and Present Organization of the City of Chicago* (Madison, 1898), p. 29; Pierce, Bessie L., *A History of Chicago, 1673–1848* (New York, 1937), pp. 333–335.

state elections. In elections for municipal officers who had no power over persons, but great power over taxation and expenditures, however, Gallatin maintained that only those who made a financial contribution to the community should be allowed to vote.[39] The last stand of the principle of "no representation without taxation" was in the sphere of local elections. A late variant of this principle was Iowa's requirement that only city taxpayers could vote in those town affairs which concerned taxation or the borrowing of money.

In view of the extent to which western suffrage history was a recapitulation of the suffrage history of the eastern seaboard, it is difficult to believe that the New West was unique or that it made any new contribution to the growth of suffrage democracy. The *Iowa Capitol Republican,* in reporting suffrage developments in Iowa, recognized that the issue of suffrage democracy was not sectional but national, and an expression of the philosophy of the natural rights of man. During the sessions of the constitutional convention of 1846, the *Republican* wrote, "The friends of equal rights throughout the country will rejoice to learn of the progress that the principles of universal suffrage have made in Iowa."[40]

[39] Adams, Henry, *The Life of Albert Gallatin* (New York, 1943), pp. 654–655.
[40] Shambaugh, B. F. (ed.), *Fragments of the Debates of the Iowa Constitutional Conventions of 1844 and 1846* (Iowa City, 1900), p. 341.

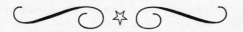

SOCIAL AND ECONOMIC
ASPIRATIONS IN THE
DEMOCRATIC ETHOS

The emphasis of the preceding sections has been mainly political. Democracy itself is a political concept. It is often used loosely, and can be applied to various institutions; but we are speaking figuratively or by extension when we call a social atmosphere "democratic" or use the word to describe economic conditions or even personal relations. Long before the birth of an American republic, political philosophers had seen that a certain distribution of property would be conducive to the stability of a democratic form of government; but it was in the United States that the great task of fitting the political concept to a social and economic reality was undertaken and to a very large extent successfully carried out.

For any mobile or expanding society, democracy would inevitably be closely connected with economic opportunity. Even before the War of Independence, the growing diversification of the economies of most of the colonies had led to an opening out of opportunity for returns on different kinds of investment. Both in land tenure and in commerce, economic conditions militated against the growth of a consolidated privileged class, bent on strengthening its own privileges and preventing the rise of outsiders; it is certainly significant that where, as in the Hudson River Valley, the Connecticut River Valley of Massachusetts, and in the Tidewater area of the southern states, the conditions favored the consolidation of large and superior properties, the great land and slave-owners were able to dominate politics, exercizing an easy, unhurried power over the assemblies and courts. Even these positions, however, were in danger of erosion as a result of westward movements of population, of new areas of economic opportunity and consequently of social and economic mobility.

After a severe setback in the mid–1780s, the American economy continued to make advances in most areas of productivity and standards of living. This progress depended on a combination of skills, energies, and fortunes, some of which were the result of American initiatives, others not. The general advance of the economy was sustained by American exports in a rising international market, which in turn supplied capital for further investment in American development. Much investment was due to a large number of relatively small savings in a great variety of small, or family-sized business enterprises. The expansion of a busy and productive populace meant an expanding market for domestically produced consumer goods. Business enterprise became almost the only general American passion, and visitors such as Alexis de Tocqueville, whose comments appear here, were constantly struck by the incessant hard work and the absorption of almost all classes of Americans in business and its demands on them.

Nowhere is our literature weaker than in the working out of the connections between this phase of economic activity and politics. We see—or seem to see—the outlines clearly enough, but we have comparatively little research-based information about the details. Some of the most informative work has been done on local banks and the history of banking, both at a state and national level.[1] It is inescapable that the history of the particular democracy with which we are here concerned is closely linked to the rise of an economy dominated by small entrepreneurs; Professor Richard Hofstadter, in an essay which after nearly twenty years remains one of the most impressive single interpretations, pointed out that, in addition to being a phase in the expansion of democracy, the Jackson movement was also "a phase in the expansion of liberated capitalism."[2]

This ferment of activity had social as well as economic implications, and the significance of mobility is very clearly demonstrated by Miss King's article on the rise and role of what was called the "First-Class Hotel." This essay may be noted by readers as a particularly useful example of the way in which the perceptive study of a specific type of institution can throw light over several segments of society.

In giving Americans the confidence and skills they needed, nothing was more important than education. The better educated the population, the more rapid its advance. We are able to include two short extracts from Professor Rush Welter's book, *Popular Education and Democratic Thought in America,* which differentiates among 1) the purposes of the colonial system of education, 2) those of the "Republicans" who afterwards dominated society and politics, and 3) the Democrats. These distinctions are clear from his text and need not be elaborated here; they do much to explain one of the themes underlying this selection: the change in the American social order between the Revolutionary era and that of equalitarian democracy.

[1] In particular, see Bray Hammond's *Banks and Politics in America from the Revolution to the Civil War* (Princeton, 1957).

[2] Richard Hofstadter, *The American Political Tradition and the Men who Made It* (New York, 1948), p. 55.

The Social Functions of Education

RUSH WELTER

THE SOCIAL FUNCTIONS OF REPUBLICAN EDUCATION

WHAT ITS REPUBLICAN ADVOCATES EXPECTED OF EDUCATION, THEN, was remarkably the same, early and late, right wing and left. So far as individual human beings were concerned, they hoped that the general diffusion of knowledge would both maximize happiness and help to elevate deserving youths to the highest places in society and government. But even here they had in view at least as much as the individuals' gains the benefits that such a policy would confer on the state as a whole, and for the most part the state or the community was more important in their eyes than the individual. Thus, they hoped for contributions to American scholarship and American technology. They hoped for encouragement of national loyalty, of loyalty to republican institutions, of loyalty to what they identified in a single word as "freedom." During the early years, as their interest in universities suggests, most of them were only moderately concerned over education of the mass of the electorate for participation in politics. As time passed, and with varying degrees of anxiety they saw the suffrage broadened to include propertyless workingmen as well as independent yeomen-farmers, they came to be increasingly interested in elementary education for all. Early and late, however, they sought to employ education to support government by those who were best qualified to govern.

There was a fairly sharp difference between their views and those of the democratic era to come, while the opinions of even the most liberal figures among them betrayed significant links to the past. It would be foolish to maintain that no changes took place in American politics and American social theory during the fifty years that began with the Declaration of Independence, but the argument that there was a radical revolution may also be overworked. Important changes occurred: disestablishment of particular churches and separation of church and state; broadening of the suffrage and reduction of the influence of property in the state legislatures; a tentative liberalizing of the traditional gloomy view of

Reprinted from *Popular Education and Democratic Thought in America* (1962), by permission of Columbia University Press, New York, pp. 36–41, 56–58.

human nature. Possibly this last development was the most important of all innovations for the long run, yet the conception of human nature employed in American political thought remained remarkably constant from 1630 through 1826.[1] On the whole, and allowing for the drastic break with the past that disestablishment of the churches represented, it would seem that the most characteristic elements of federal and republican thought made it more nearly a liberalization of colonial attitudes than an adumbration of democratic beliefs.

The new perspective that (roughly speaking) Jackson's election symbolized has been obscured by the fact that republican terminology was adapted to democratic needs, by the survival of republican political leaders into the succeeding era, and by the deliberate retrospective appeal of Jacksonian democrats to the plastic image of Jefferson. Presumably the clamor of republicans for a general diffusion of knowledge, coming as it did historically just before the common school awakening, has also served to minimize the change. But it need only be pointed out that to the extent republican education departed from disorganized eighteenth-century practice it came close to reviving seventeenth-century precedents in secular terms, or that when Virginia and other states began to adopt democratic educational systems shortly before the Civil War they did not follow Thomas Jefferson's views. Indeed, Jefferson was wiser than many of his recent worshipers have acknowledged when he requested that his tombstone identify him as "author of the Declaration of American Independence, of the Statute of Virginia for religious freedom, & Father of the University of Virginia."[2] National independence, religious liberty, and public support for the most elevated education possible—these were the typical objectives of the American as republican.

How valid this general interpretation is may appear more clearly if we apply to republican attitudes the conceptual framework we used to characterize colonial educational theory and practice. The resemblances are close. Colonial education was thoroughly instrumental, and clearly republican was also. Its novelty lay not in diminishing its utilitarian purposes—certainly Jefferson and other heirs of the Enlightenment, advocates of the education of the people, were in their way even more instrumental in their thinking than their predecessors—but in shifting its uses from religion to politics and economics. Moreover, republican education was unmistakably hierarchical, unless every pronouncement of the radical Jefferson concerning a natural aristocracy and the proper gradations of education be ignored. Even educational plans that described an academic continuum rather than a bipolar scheme like Jefferson's for educating com-

---

[1] See in particular Kenyon, "Conceptions of Human Nature in American Political Thought, 1630–1826," unpublished doctoral dissertation, Radcliffe College, 1949.

[2] Jefferson, *Writings*, X, 396.

mon people and *aristoi* were decidedly selective, as James G. Carter pointed out.

Republican education was by the same token authority-oriented, in the terminology I have already applied to colonial practice. Despite miscellaneous innovations in pedagogy and curriculum (and these are often exaggerated), it was intended to function as an instrument supporting the existing arrangement of society and social authority. Still further, it was limited in scope. Those who believed with Jefferson that education is the "most legitimate engine of government" conceived of it as only one among several engines, and most of them were not so optimistic as to accord it that influence Jefferson proclaimed. More often it seemed a useful auxiliary in an over-all design for the constructive use of the state's powers, rather than the essential definition of the state's role in society. Of course too much may be made of an analytical scheme, but this proposition provides us with an important criterion for distinguishing democratic theories of the role of education from republican theories. We shall find that when Americans fully embraced democracy, education achieved a new status in their thought. At least in the theory of its advocates it was to seem more than a democratic instrument of democratic politics; it was in many ways to absorb politics and political structure, and in effect to be identified with them. In a real sense this identification was precisely what neither colonial nor republican education was capable of achieving.

There is another way of characterizing the republican commitment to popular education, which may be equally helpful in distinguishing it from the democratic commitment that was to succeed it. This is the extent to which republican theory and practice alike imitated or anticipated educational developments in England, which was slow to adopt either democratic suffrage or public education. For example, education under the auspices of the Public School Society in New York was almost identical with that in England immediately after the Great Reform Bill and until the extension of the suffrage in 1867. After 1832 Parliament annually appropriated sums in aid of two private religious societies that undertook to provide an elementary education, by the monitorial method, in all the towns of England. These societies monopolized the parliamentary grants, using them for teaching not only the three R's but also the Protestant religion. What made two societies necessary was the fact that there were both an established church and a large body of dissenters. In New York City, which in other respects adopted the plan the English government was to follow, there was no establishment and hence need for only one society.[3]

[3] In England in 1847 Catholic groups were given a share of public funds, but in New York all religious education under state auspices was barred when the Catholic vote became powerful. On English developments see in particular chapter II of J. L.

More significantly still, the doctrines many republican leaders subscribed to virtually paralleled those of England's Philosophical Radicals, who advocated reform in the British constitution but who cherished the interests of the middle classes rather more than those of factory workers and the urban poor. In his famous review-article on the education of the poor for the *Edinburgh Review,* for example, James Mill justified pauper education at public expense on the grounds of social necessity but not of individual right, and he advocated a plan for state aid to education very much like that proposed by Nicholas Biddle two years before. Other advocates of popular education in Great Britain tended to visualize a hierarchy of schools and voluntary institutes adapted to the needs of a rising middle class rather than the exigencies of the poor. Even Francis Place—"the radical tailor of Charing Cross"—believed that the poor should be expected to contribute something to the cost of their own education, while he particularly urged the proper education of the middle class because it would "necessarily, and at once, elevate the condition of the class below, and raise the standard of knowledge and virtue in the class above." In America his reference to three distinct classes would have seemed strange, but his belief in an education geared to different social roles would not.[4]

Perhaps the most significant difference between British and American advocates of popular education during our republican era, therefore, rested on the fact that in Britain male suffrage was restricted to householders well past the time at which it became virtually universal in the United States. Consequently, British spokesmen had less reason than their American counterparts to urge the political education of the people. Yet even in this respect their theories were remarkably similar. On the one hand, the British tended to believe that a free press was more important than free schools to good government. While few American writers would have subscribed to this proposition in literal terms, much of their thought clearly suggested that gaps in the formal education of the elec-

---

and Barbara Hammond, *The Age of the Chartists;* also E. L. Woodward, *The Age of Reform, 1815–1870* (Oxford: Clarendon Press, 1938), passim; G. D. H. Cole and Raymond Postgate, *The British Common People, 1746–1938* (New York: Knopf, 1939), passim; and Raymond G. Cowherd, *The Politics of English Dissent* (New York: New York University Press, 1956), ch. 9.

[4] [James Mill], "Education of the Poor," *Edinburgh Review,* XXI, No. 41 (February, 1813), 207–219; Graham Wallas, *The Life of Francis Place,* 1771–1854 rev. ed., London: George Allen & Unwin, 1925), ch. 4; [Francis Place] "Education," *Westminister Review,* I, No. 1 (January, 1824), 43–79. See also Elie Halévy, *The Growth of Philosophic Radicalism,* trans. Mary Morris (Boston: Beacon, 1955), pp. 282–296, and Thistlethwaite, *The Anglo-American Connection,* ch. 5.

torate might be made up by informal means, among which they listed a free press. "Where the press is free, and every man able to read," Thomas Jefferson wrote Colonel Charles Yancey in 1816, "all is safe." On the other hand, when the suffrage was finally extended to most town dwellers in 1867, British leaders pressed the demand for formal education at public expense. "We must educate our masters," Robert Lowe was to insist then, much as Charles Stewart Daveis had insisted at Fryeburg, Maine, in 1825.[5]

In other words, republican advocates of popular education in the United States often shared the perspectives of middle-class reformers in England, who saw themselves exercising social and political authority between an idle and often dissolute aristocracy and an idle and often dissolute working class. We need not press this transatlantic comparison, but it may help to point up the ultimate weakness of our republican schemes for popular education. Not only were they inadequate in fact to meet the demands of the rising generation; they were also inadequate in theory.[6] In republican thought, the common man was not given enough cause for supporting education with public funds. He ignored exhortations that gave primary emphasis to the social utility of education and skimped on the individual advantages; he resisted a social theory that manifestly fixed him in a status even while it gave him opportunity to work his way out of it through education. Indeed, he resisted the very conception of a "general diffusion of knowledge," which in most republican writings smacked of *noblesse oblige* and of a suggestion that what mattered most to every man would be trickled down to him from above. Republican education aimed both too high and too low for the democrats whose day was beginning to dawn.

THE SOCIAL FUNCTIONS OF DEMOCRATIC EDUCATION

Like the workingmen's agitation of the 1820s, the agitation of the 1830s ultimately focused in education. Moreover, it embraced democratic

---

[5] Jefferson to Yancey, January 6, 1816, *Writings,* X, 4. Lowe's remark is a staple of British social history; his actual words were "I believe it will be absolutely necessary that you should prevail on our future masters to learn their letters." (*Oxford Dictionary of Quotations* [London: Oxford University Press, 1941], p. 572.)

[6] Strikingly, British liberals continued to hold up American republican achievements in public education as a model to their countrymen during the 1830s even after American liberals had begun to criticize them for their inadequacy. Even if American advocates of educational reform exaggerated the deficiencies in republican provisions for popular education it is significant that they repudiated what the British hailed.

rather than republican concepts of the diffusion of knowledge: education must be formal, public, and equal—not an uncertain mixture of formal and informal institutions, public and private responsibilities, "aristocratic" and pauper training. The nature of the educational commitment working-men and reformers expressed during both the 1820s and the 1830s takes on added significance if we apply to it the same analytical scheme that we employed in evaluating colonial and republican commitments to popular education. Those commitments, we remember, were instrumental, hierarchical, authority-oriented, and limited in scope. By contrast, although the workingmen advocated public schools for clearly instrumental reasons, in other respects their educational doctrine constituted a stunning departure from republican precedent.

In the first place, the workingmen obviously repudiated a hierarchically oriented education. Not only did they denounce private schools and colleges for their "aristocratic" pretensions, but they also focused their constructive efforts on building up a genuinely democratic educational system. It is true that they made relatively little effort to extend this democracy to higher levels of education, but only because they were sure that elementary schooling would serve their political and social ends.

By the same token, their definition of the relationship between authority and education drastically modified the traditional sense of that relationship. On the one hand, their theory called for a popular education that would abridge—not enhance—the authority of established leaders of the society. They proposed both to eliminate encroachments on popular liberty and to protect the electorate against new political impositions. On the other hand, in educating that electorate against contemporary evils, they also proposed to make schools serve a new authority, that of the people. Whereas republican educational institutions had been intended to serve the *needs* of the people, democratic institutions were much more likely to respond to their *wants*. Common schools were only the first of many educational innovations that democratic authority would produce.

Still, it was schools rather than other kinds of innovation that the workingmen sought to impose on their country. Far from enlarging the scope and authority of government, they intended to reduce it, save only for committing it to vastly increased expenditures on public education. Here too they tended to reverse republican precedents, until in the final analysis their social theory assigned to education and to education alone almost all of the responsibilities for social welfare that state governments had previously exercised. In the long run, whereas colonial and republican education had been limited in scope, education was the one function of democratic government that might continue to expand even when political evils had been dealt with by limiting the scope of government. A good many republicans had hoped to diminish the activity of government, but none had really contemplated substituting education for it.

Abandoning republican precedents, the workingmen also modified the social and political perspectives of the British liberals from whom many of their doctrines were derived. For example, the workingmen's attack on chartered institutions closely followed Adam Smith's analysis of monopolies in *The Wealth of Nations,* while their thought also echoed most of his other economic principles. Yet in two major respects they transformed his thought. In the first place, they advocated democracy, whereas Smith and the English liberals who succeeded him were slow to adopt it. Secondly, while Smith proposed that the modern state educate the "laboring poor" in order to protect mankind against degradation and the state against disorder, he also criticized all forms of education that depended for their support upon either private or public charity.[7] In other words, he advocated laissez faire in education as well as in other realms, although he would modify it out of necessity, whereas in America the workingmen who adopted his liberal economics also demanded public schooling as the very source and definition of free government.

Hence the American workingman may remind us instead of the English Chartists, who began during the 1830s to form workingmen's political associations and to press for universal education as a way of securing democratic privileges. Nevertheless, transatlantic differences in the agitation of workingmen were almost as striking as transatlantic differences in Liberalism. Chartist spokesmen increasingly repudiated mechanics' institutes and lyceums as a vehicle of reform because they were sponsored by middle-class reformers who wished to discourage aggressive political action by the working classes. By contrast, American workingmen enthusiastically imitated these English devices; they were insensitive to the political implications of self-help as a vehicle of social reform, and complained only that such institutes could not be effective unless they were grounded upon universal public schooling. In the long run, moreover, Chartist extremists grew skeptical of schools themselves, and even a moderate Chartist like William Lovett was apprehensive of state control over public education. In America, extremists and moderates alike insisted upon public schools under state control.[8]

[7] Adam Smith, *An Enquiry into the Nature and Causes of the Wealth of Nations,* ed. Edwin Cannan (New York: Modern Library, 1937), pp. 716–740.

[8] See Hovell, *The Chartist Movement,* passim, especially pp. 52–63, 68–69, 200–207; A. E. Dobbs, *Education and Social Movements, 1700–1850* (London: Longmans, Green, 1919), chs. 5–8; and Thistlethwaite, *The Anglo-American Connection,* pp. 134–140; also R. K. Webb, *The British Working Class Reader, 1790–1848: Literary and Social Tension* (London: Allen & Unwin, 1955).

We can understand why the American workingmen's movement was so much less radical, so much more confident of the power of education, than its British counterpart. Most American workingmen already exercised the suffrage; American society was neither so stratified nor so impoverished as Great Britain's; American workingmen had not yet despaired of achieving middle-class status. But the reasons are less important than the fact: American workingmen pressed for public education while British workingmen came increasingly to distrust it as an agency of the status quo. When monopoly had been eradicated, the Americans' thought suggested, they would be content with liberty and schools—with what I have called "anarchy with a schoolmaster" in extension of Thomas Carlyle's gibe at British liberals for believing only in "anarchy plus a constable."

It followed that the American workingmen would speak to a wider public than their British counterparts. The political history of the 1830s and 1840s, to which we now turn, is in large part a history of the impact of their liberal principles upon other areas of American social thought.

The First-Class Hotel and the Age of the Common Man

DORIS ELIZABETH KING

THE DAY PRESIDENT-ELECT ANDREW JACKSON ARRIVED IN WASHINGton for his inauguration, a select committee headed by his friend Senator John Eaton went out to meet the hero of the "common man" and escorted him to lodgings in the new National Hotel. Later, after the jubilant populace had wrecked the White House during the inaugural reception, the new President hurried back to the National to take refuge.[1] It was no mere coincidence that the first President to represent the "people's choice"

Reprinted from the *Journal of Southern History* XXIII, 2, May 1957, by permission of the Managing Editor. Copyright 1957 by the Southern Historical Association.

[1] Wilhelmus B. Bryan, *A History of the National Capital* (2 vols., New York, 1914–1916), II, 212–15.

found waiting for him the first first-class hotel ever erected in the nation's capital; for the story of the development of the first-class hotel is part of the story of the Rise of the Common Man.

As early as 1793, when the city of Washington had been little more than a dream, there had been an attempt to build a great public hotel, one splendid enough to lend dignity to the officials of the proud new republic. The city commissioners, failing in their various attempts to stimulate interest in the district's development, had finally gone so far as to authorize a Federal Lottery, the first prize of which was to be a "superb hotel" worth "$50,000." Designed by the supervising architect for the Capitol, the Union Public Hotel was to provide every comfort and luxury imaginable, including bathing rooms. But the lottery failed, and the hotel was never completed. Years later the shell of the building was purchased by the government from the lottery winner and served as the United States patent and post offices. After the War of 1812 it served temporarily as the national Capitol.[2]

Yet, for several reasons, this early project deserves a prominent place in hotel history. First, it established once and forever the "public character" of the American hotel. It had had the word "public" in its name and had received wide publicity as a government project. Moreover, the city's freemasons laid its cornerstone with parade and ceremony on "the memorable 4th day of July, 1793," a public holiday.[3] And finally, by its design and size, the building was obviously meant to resemble a public structure.[4] All this was significant.

Throughout the following century British travelers were to note time and again that American hotels assumed "the character of public buildings," even in their architecture.[5] One Englishman was to exclaim in surprise because "With us hotels are regarded as purely private property,

[2] A brief history of the Union Public Hotel, often called Blodget's Hotel, can be written by using the following sources: *Gazette of the United States,* January 19, July 17, 1793; Washington *Gazette,* September 28, 1796; *National Intelligencer,* December 17, 1836; Samuel Blodget, *Economica* (Washington, 1806), Appendix; Tobias Lear, *Observations on the River Potomack* (A reprint of the 1793 edition, Baltimore, 1940); Patent Office Society, *Outline History of the Patent Office.* Reprinted from the Patent Office Society *Journal* (Washington, 1918–   ), XVIII (1936), 124; and Bryan, *History of the National Capital,* I, 184–94, 205–30. Also see Prints and Photographs Division of the Library of Congress.

[3] A photograph of the copper plate which was attached to the original cornerstone can be seen in the Washingtonia Division of the Public Library of the District of Columbia.

[4] Isaac Weld, *Travels Through the States of North America . . . during the Years 1795, 1796, and 1797* (4th ed., 2 vols., London, 1807), I, 84.

[5] Alexander Mackay, *The Western World* (3 vols., London, 1850), II, 83.

and it is seldom that, in their appearance, they stand out from the mass of private houses around them."[6] Americans traveling in France noticed that the European hotel had "nothing to distinguish it from the houses on either side except the portal. . . ."[7] Furthermore, many American hotels were to have their cornerstones laid on some day memorable in American history, usually with speeches which interwove praise of republican government and of American enterprise, and drew attention to the dignity of labor and laborer.

In 1790 the word "hotel" could hardly be found in a city directory. The great majority of public houses in the United States were listed under the word "tavern" and actually carried that word in their names. By 1800 "hotel" was an almost common title, but the careful reader would notice that a house listed as *such and such tavern* in 1790 was listed as *such and such hotel* in 1800. Owners, moved by the growing popularity of things French, had merely rechristened the old houses. Webster's *American Dictionary* explains that the French name was then meant to denote a "house for genteel strangers or lodgers," but newspaper advertisements made it clear that any citizen of the republic was welcome.

Even during the early years of the nineteenth century the traveler could tell little or no difference between a tavern and a tavern-turned-hotel.[8] Either was likely to be a remodeled private dwelling house, operated by a keeper who considered the place as much home as business. He was generally described as a "topping man" in his community, one who also held a militia title, a judgeship, or a seat in the state legislature. In the country he was usually a landowner who kept tavern in self-defense, rather than squander his all in the name of hospitality.[9]

[6] *Ibid.* Also see William E. Baxter, *America and the Americans* (London, 1855), 32.

[7] Nathaniel S. Wheaton, *A Journal of a Residence during Several Months in London . . . and a Short Tour in France and Scotland in the Years 1823 and 1824* (Boston, 1830), 386.

[8] Thomas Twining, *Travels in India a Hundred Years Ago, With a Visit to the United States* (London, 1893), 392, 403. Also see John C. Fitzpatrick (ed.), *The Diaries of George Washington, 1748–1799* (4 vols., Boston, 1925); Adam Hodgson, *Letters from North America . . .* (2 vols., London, 1824), I, 20, 30–32; and Henry B. Fearon, *Sketches of America* (London, 1819), 246–47.

[9] American tavern and hotelkeepers of the early nineteenth century are described in Priscilla Wakefield, *Excursions in North America . . .* (London, 1806), 39; Lt. Francis Hall, *Travels in Canada, and the United States in 1816 and 1817* (London, 1819), 317; Hodgson, *Letters,* I, 20–22; William Tell Harris, *Remarks Made during a Tour through the United States of America, in the Years 1817, 1818, and 1819* (London, 1821), 66–67; Whitman Mead, *Travels in North America* (New York, 1820), 15; James K. Paulding, *Letters from the South . . .* (2 vols. New York, 1817), II, 63–64; John M. Duncan, *Travels Through Part of*

Yet be it called tavern or hotel, the public house in the United States was a peculiarly American institution. Historians have often declared that the American tavern was nothing more or less than a carbon copy of the English inn, not "differing from it in any special way,"[10] but nothing could be further from the truth. The Englishman traveling in America in the late eighteenth and early nineteenth centuries was often in a state of confusion.

First of all, what an Englishman called an inn, an American called a tavern. In the English mind one could eat or drink but not find lodging in a tavern.[11] Still more confusing was the system under which these American houses were operated, a system which by 1830 was known as the American Plan. Britishers often complained bitterly that they were required to register when they entered a house and to pay for both room and board. Worse yet, charges for both were set daily prices. At a stagecoach stop the traveler could purchase a single meal, but the price, the menu, and the time of eating were all predetermined. As Britishers were not accustomed to such dining arrangements in their inns,[12] they often used the term table d'hôte in their descriptions, mentioning a similarity with French inns. However, observers in France were already noting that the table d'hôte was dying out in French cities, except for houses which catered particularly to Americans.[13]

---

the United States and Canada in 1818 and 1819 (2 vols., Glasgow, 1823), II, 230, 247; Edward S. Abdy, Journal of a Residence and Tour in the United States . . . (3 vols., London, 1835), II, 310; Thomas Hamilton, Men and Manners in America (2 vols., London and Edinburgh, 1833), II, 276–77; and James Fenimore Cooper, Notions of the Americans . . . (2 vols., Philadelphia, 1828), I, 64–65.

[10] Jefferson Williamson, The American Hotel: An Anecdotal History (New York, 1930), 8. Also see Seymour Dunbar, A History of Travel in America (4 vols., Indianapolis, 1915), I, 212.

[11] John F. D. Smyth, Tour in the United States of America . . . (2 vols., London, 1784), I, 49; Weld, Travels, I, 27, 41; Wakefield, Excursions, 39; Hodgson, Letters, I, 20, 30–32; Isaac Holmes, An Account of the United States of America . . . (London, 1823), 355. Also see John Walker, A Critical Pronouncing Dictionary and Expositor of the English Language . . . (Dublin, 1791).

[12] The English used the word "ordinary" to designate an eating place at which prices were fixed. See Walker, Dictionary and Expositor. However, as ordinaries were not usually found in connection with English inns the English were surprised to find that in the southern part of the United States the words "tavern" and "ordinary" were used as synonyms. See Smyth, Tour, I, 70, for example. The word "ordinary," as applied to public houses, became uncommon by 1820, but after that date the dining rooms in the hotels were often called "ordinaries."

[13] "There are few if any . . . in Paris at present." [Richard Twiss], A Trip to Paris in July and August, 1792 (London, 1793), 114. Emma Willard, in Journal and Letters, from France and Great-Britain (Troy, N. Y., 1833), 19, states that her city hotel in France had the table d'hôte, "more after the American fashion

But what surprised and disturbed the English most of all was the public and democratic nature of these houses. The English were accustomed to obsequious hosts who came bowing and smiling to the door, and to servants who groveled in expectation of generous tips. American keepers seldom paid them any attention, and American "help" was insulted by the proferring of a tip.[14] Moreover, the privacy so dear to the heart of the Englishman seldom existed in an American house. Taverns and hotels were frequently crowded by Americans "on the move," and the best accommodations were often occupied by permanent boarders—judges, lawyers, storekeepers, and others who brought their families to live in these houses.

The mere idea of making a home in a hotel seemed "little short of profanation" to the Britisher. But even worse was the notorious table d'hôte at which the Englishman was expected to dine with farmer, teamster, and his own manservant. Only with the most earnest pleading could he occasionally spare himself from having to share bed as well as board. The discontented foreigners spent considerable time contemplating the reasons Americans tolerated, even seemed fond of, such houses. They generally concluded that it was because the United States was literally a nation on the move, because the lack of traveling salesmen gave upcountry merchants reason to travel, and because house-rent and servants' wages were high—which meant that the table d'hôte and the lack of tipping made hotel living relatively inexpensive. The chief explanation seemed to be that Americans were by nature a gregarious people who loved to live in public, to see and be seen, to hear and be heard, and to participate "on a level." The young American ambitious to get ahead would not dare to ask for a private room even if he wanted it; for this act would lead to the "serious charge" that he was "aristocratic."[15]

---

than the French," but James Paul Cobbett reported in 1823 that there were striking similarities between French and American houses. See his *A Ride of Eight Hundred Miles in France* (3rd ed., London, 1827), entry for October 22, 1823. Whereas Willard was writing of a city hotel, Cobbett probably meant the rural houses.

[14] For a description of the hotelkeeper see footnote 9. For testimony concerning the lack of tipping see Richard Parkinson, *A Tour in America in 1798, 1799, and 1800* (2 vols., London, 1805), I, 254; Holmes, *An Account,* 355; Weld, *Travels,* 27, 41; and William Cobbett, *A Year's Residence in the United States of America* (3rd ed., London, 1828), 201. Also see footnote 15.

[15] American hotels and taverns, 1790–1825, are discussed in great detail in the travel accounts of the period. For information concerning the keeper, the "help," the table d'hôte, the lack of privacy, the popularity, the democratic nature, and the probable *raison d'être* of these houses see the following works: Parkinson, *A Tour,* I, 49, 254; Cobbett, *A Year's Residence,* 201; Wakefield, *Excursions,* 39; Weld, *Travels,* I, 27, 41; Fearon, *Sketches,* 246–47; Hodgson, *Letters,* I, 20, 30–

Between 1793 and 1825, while British visitors filled volumes with their complaints, the word "hotel" grew increasingly popular, and the word "tavern" declined in both popularity and reputation. During those years a few ambitious speculators erected or tried to erect new hotels, buildings designed especially for public use, so costly and large that newspaper editors wrote of them in detail and with discernible pride. Most of these projects failed, thanks to war, or threat of war, or depression.

The most significant and prophetic of the houses completed between 1793 and 1825 was the Boston Exchange Hotel, often called the Exchange Coffee House Hotel.[16] The work of a lawyer-promoter named Andrew Dexter, the eight-story Exchange was described as the largest and handsomest building in America.[17] The hotel portion was opened to the public in 1809, but the economic troubles engendered by the Napoleonic wars brought it to immediate ruin. Dexter fled the country and the $400,000 building was put up for auction. Boston's leading merchants, some of whom had offices in the Exchange, showed pride in the new house and

---

32; Twining, *Travels,* 393; Harris, *Remarks,* 66; Holmes, *An Account,* 342, 355; John Palmer, *Journal of Travels in the United States of North America* . . . (London, 1818), 26; Duncan, *Travels,* II, 247, 320; John Bernard, *Retrospections of America, 1797–1811* (New York, 1887), 153, 203–204; John Davis, *Travels of Four Years and a Half in the United States of America during 1798, 1799, 1800, 1801, and 1802* (London, 1803), 222; Morris Birkbeck, *Notes on a Journey in America* . . . (London, 1818), 11; Benjamin Henry Latrobe, *The Journal of Latrobe* . . . (New York, 1905), 86; Hamilton, *Men and Manners,* II, 4, 6; Frederick Marryat, *Second Series of a Diary in America* . . . (Philadelphia, 1840), 33.

[16] Williamson, in *The American Hotel,* 13, refers to the New York City Hotel, erected in 1794, as the "first building erected for hotel purposes in America," and states that it was the first hotel erected by a joint-stock company. However, a few small hotels had been constructed before the New York City Hotel opened. Moreover, the house was the product of a tontine association and not a modern joint-stock company. Even had it been all that Williamson claims, the hotel was by no means as influential or impressive as the Boston Exchange. In 1828 the City Hotel was still the "chief place of resort" in New York, but travelers often condemned it as a "wretched place" in which one could not secure "hot baths" or other comforts. See *The Picture of New-York, and Stranger's Guide* . . . (New York, 1828), 397; Frederick de Roos, *Personal Narrative of Travels in the United States and Canada in 1826* . . . (London, 1827), 34; Peter Neilson, *Recollections of a Six Years' Residence in the United States* (2 vols., Glasgow, 1830), I, 30, 249; James Stuart, *Three Years in North America* (2 vols., New York, 1833), I, 30; Merle E. Evans, "Knickerbocker Hotels and Restaurants, 1800–1850," in the *New-York Historical Society Quarterly* (New York, 1917–), XXXVI (1952), 377–409; and William Harrison Bayles, *Old Taverns of New York* (New York, 1915).

[17] Avrahm Yarmolinsky, *Picturesque United States of America, 1811, 1812, 1813, Being a Memoir on Paul Svinin* (New York, 1930), 40.

immediately organized a stock company which purchased it. Under their supervision the whole building became known as the Exchange Hotel and as the "most elegant hotel in the United States."[18]

Certainly it was the largest house of its day, "containing nearly 300 rooms," including immense assembly rooms, ballrooms, lounges, card and billiard rooms, banquet halls, private and public dining rooms, numbered private bedrooms, a hairdressers' room, and a "large number" of "bathing rooms." The ground floor had offices and shops, and a gigantic rotunda topped by an impressive dome served as the Exchange Room.[19] Boston newspaper editors gave most of the credit for its excellent reputation to the hotelkeeper, a Connecticut Yankee named David Barnum. When the hotel burned to the ground in November 1818 great and public was the mourning. Local editors reported a great desire among the citizenry that the house be replaced "for the honor of the town," but the panic of 1819 prevented its restoration.[20]

Despite its short life the Boston Exchange Hotel served as a bold and daring precursor. In plan and facilities its close resemblance to the twentieth century hotel is striking. Moreover, it was the most famous exchange hotel of its day and served as a model for many later ones. Eventually the words "hotel" and "exchange" came to be synonymous in several American cities, and more than one such house held or used banking privileges.[21] The typical exchange hotel rotunda gradually became

18, 19 Suffolk County (Mass.) Registry of Deeds, 1806, liber. 231, no. 14; liber. 227, no. 259; liber. 229, no. 290; Boston *City Directory,* 1800–1820; *New England Palladium,* August, 7, 1807; December 20, 1808; November 6, 1818; *Boston Gazette,* May 15, June 12, July 13, November 16, December 28, 1809; *Niles' Weekly Register* (Baltimore, 1811–1849), November 14, 1818; Justin Winsor, *The Memorial History of the City of Boston* . . . (4 vols., Boston, 1881–1883), IV, 55.

20 *New England Palladium,* November 6, 1818; *Niles' Weekly Register,* November 14, 1818. Also see other Boston papers for November 1818.

21 Dunbar, in his *History of Travel,* I, 112, points out that the first merchants' exchanges in America grew out of informal meetings held in colonial taverns. For examples of hotel company charters which show the dual exchange-hotel nature of their founding organizations see the statutes of the state of Louisiana for the period 1830–1840. The rivalry between French and American merchants in New Orleans produced several exchanges and led a local editor to conclude that "in truth, we have too many exchanges." The three which he mentioned were the French Exchange (St. Louis Hotel), the American Exchange (St. Charles Hotel), and the Merchants Exchange. As a result of the general confusion the French and American exchanges gradually became known as hotels, each acquiring the name of the street on which it was located. See the New Orleans *True American,* September 18, 1838. Although the American Exchange never used the banking privileges granted to it, many hotels engaged in banking or exchange activities without proper authorization, a situation which caused some state legislatures to threaten to cancel their charters. Dunbar's *History of Travel,* III, 1106, contains

the typical hotel lobby, and when the rotunda became crowded with travelers and baggage, the barroom became the place of business. Foreigners were to note that drinking in hotel barrooms was "strictly part of a business transaction."[22] By 1840 the typical American hotel was one owned by a chartered company of civic-minded merchants who considered a show-place hotel necessary for prosperity and for "the honor of the town."

It was not until about 1825, when the effects of the depression began to wear away, that the American hotel again made noteworthy progress. In that year there began to appear widely spread new hotels, so "palatial," so "luxurious," and so "modern"—to use their own words—that newspapermen began to search for a new name to call them. The term they adopted, "first-class hotel," is with us yet. Perhaps the earliest use of the term was in the *National Intelligencer* of June 19, 1827. The splendor of these new and "modern" houses, the editor explained, "has obtained for them the appellation of the 'palaces of the public.'"

Although the phrase "first-class hotel" did not make its way into Webster's *Dictionary,* it soon came to have a universally understood, and eventually a legal, meaning. Soon after 1830 state legislatures began to charter hotel companies with the condition that they erect "first-class" houses, and during the 1860's a Baltimore circuit judge went so far as to rule that a certain hotel could not be closed, because as a "first-class hotel, with a reputation as such," it was a public necessity.[23]

Newspapermen and travelers of all varieties generally agreed as to which hotels were "first-class" establishments. Careful study of their comments shows that a first-class hotel (1825-1860) had to possess all or most of the following characteristics: (1) it was an imposing, monumental, public-looking building, a building which had been designed by a professional architect especially for hotel purposes and which contained well over 100 rooms—including private suites; (2) it was so costly and so luxurious that it was obvious some bold and awe-inspiring financial maneuvering had been necessary on the part of some one or some company; (3) it was kept by an experienced, professional hotelkeeper whose "system" of management required "no ordinary powers of government

---

a picture of a $5.00 note issued by a hotel. Also see Doris E. King, "Early Hotel Entrepreneurs and Promoters, 1793–1860," in *Explorations in Entrepreneurial History* (Harvard University, 1956), VIII, no. 3, 148–60.

[22] Louis F. Tasistro, *Random Shots and Southern Breezes* (2 vols., New York, 1842), I, 69–70.

[23] For example of charters requiring erection of a "first-class hotel" see *Acts of Kentucky, 1854,* Charter of Falls City Hotel Company, Louisville, Kentucky. For ruling of Baltimore circuit judge concerning Barnum's Hotel see printed *Reports of Cases* filed in Barnum Hotel Papers in the Maryland Historical Society Library.

and administration"; (4) it was operated by a staff of well-trained, free servants, even in Southern communities; and (5) its accommodations served both local and "Travelling Public" with food, liquor, and lodging, and inspired the awe of polished Europeans as well as of backwoodsmen Americans. It should be noted also that the hotelkeepers were generally New England Yankees, even in the South.[24]

Writing in 1826, a New Yorker expressed the opinion that among all the great improvements then occurring in the country, none were more important than those being made in hotel accommodations. The explanation for this he gave as the "increase in travelling," fostered by the "great improvement in steamboat and canal navigation. . . ."[25] The particular house which had caused the New Yorker to make his judgment was the new Baltimore City Hotel, the first house in American history to win fame as the possessor of all the five characteristics listed above. Moreover, it was the largest and best known of all the hotels when the editor of the *National Intelligencer* first used the term "first-class hotel."

On May 7, 1825, *Niles' Weekly Register* had reported that a plan was underway to build a "grand new hotel" in Baltimore, a house which undoubtedly would be superior, because it was to be operated by hotelkeeper David Barnum. Barnum had migrated to the old Baltimore Indian Queen soon after the Boston Exchange fire, bringing his staff of free servants and the contents of his wine cellar with him. By 1825 he had won the respect of that city and the financial support of its leading merchants. Thanks primarily to the backing of the great merchant princes his dream of building a great new hotel was realized. On November 19, 1825, boasting that the "hardtimes" had been defeated, the *Register's* editor pointed with particular pride to the hotel and to a projected steamship line. The house was to be "second to none other in the Union." Notice should be taken that the *Register* mentioned a steamship rather than a railroad line; for it was not until after the hotel had begun operation that a group of merchants met to plan the formation of the Baltimore and Ohio Railroad Company.[26]

---

[24] The federal census returns for 1840, 1850, and 1860 provide a great deal of information concerning the birthplaces of hotelworkers, including the hotelkeepers themselves.

[25] Letter to the editor of a New York newspaper, quoted in the Baltimore *Gazette and Daily Advertiser*, October 25, 1826. Also see Boston *Courier*, August 25, 1828, and *American Traveller*, February 16, 1836. Also see quotation from writings of Timothy Dwight in Dunbar, *History of Travel*, I, 217.

[26] *Federal Gazette and Baltimore Daily Advertiser*, October 15, 1819; January 1, 1820; *National Intelligencer*, November 17, 24, 1825; Baltimore *Sun*, May 11, 1844; January 30, 1863; Baltimore Land Records, liber. W. G. 177, folios, 612–28, 631, 637 ff.; and *Baltimore: Past and Present* (Baltimore, 1871), 92, 97.

The new City Hotel, better known as Barnum's, opened its doors in September 1826 and the public responded with enthusiastic praise. Visitors were deeply impressed by its imposing six-story, block-size mass, by its "200 apartments," its elegant private and public drawing rooms, its enormous ballroom and dining room, its basement lunchroom, its ornate barroom, its barbershop and ground-level stores, its great variety of bedrooms with their numbered keys, its family suites, curtained beds, rich velvet carpets, costly draperies, rosewood pianos, hot and cold baths, and by the gaslight which lighted "the whole." But most of all guests were delighted by the superb food, which might be enjoyed in the bedroom or at the fashionable table d' hôte, and by the dignity and impressive *savoir faire* of the man whose magic touch had seemingly made something new and wonderful of the American hotel.[27]

The New Yorker, writing about his stay in the very new house, proclaimed it a "model for all I have seen . . . in this or any other country," and expressed the hope that his native city might soon be blessed with a hotel equal to it.[28] Soon newspapers throughout the country were referring to Barnum as "the Metternich of all hosts" and the "emperor of American landlords."[29] European visitors were equally impressed. Frances Trollope, Charles Dickens, and George W. Featherstonhaugh, among the most caustic critics of all things American, were only a few of the foreigners who pronounced Barnum's "excellent" and "by far" the best house in the United States.[30] Not without reason did hotels along New York's Broadway lower their flags to half-mast upon receiving the news of Barnum's death.[31]

By the time the editor of the *National Intelligencer* wrote his editorial

[27] Baltimore *Gazette and Daily Advertiser,* November 4, 9, 1826; September 30, 1826; January 1, 1827; October 25, 1826; Baltimore *Sun,* May 11, 1844; January 30, 1863; Thomas W. Griffith, *Annals of Baltimore* (Baltimore, 1826), 252; Barnum Hotel Papers and Account Books, located in the Maryland Historical Society Library. Also see de Roos, *Personal Narrative,* 34; Stuart, *Three Years in North America,* I, 249; Journals of the Reverend Samuel Greenleaf Bullfinch (1827), located in the Bullfinch Papers of the Massachusetts Historical Society; and Baltimore Inventories, 1844, liber. D. M. P., no. 54, folio 260.

[28] Letter to the editor of a New York newspaper, quoted in the Baltimore *Gazette and Daily Advertiser,* October 25, 1826.

[29] Editorial from the Philadelphia *Enquirer,* reprinted in the Baltimore *Sun,* August 3, 1843. Also see Baltimore *Sun,* May 13–18, 1844, and *National Intelligencer,* May 18, 1844.

[30] Frances Trollope, *Domestic Manners of the Americans* (2 vols. in one, New York, 1901), I, 303; Charles Dickens, *American Notes for General Circulation* (2 vols., London, 1842), II, 25, and George W. Featherstonhaugh, *Excursion Through the Slave States . . .* (2 vols., London, 1844), I, 1, 2.

[31] *National Intelligencer,* May 18, 1844.

concerning "first-class" establishments in June 1827 the city of Washington could also look with pride to its own, even newer house, Gadsby's National Hotel. The story of Washington's earliest first-class house, significantly enough, is entwined with that of both David Barnum and Andrew Jackson.

John Gadsby, an Englishman who started in the hotel business in Alexandria, had moved into the Baltimore Indian Queen about 1809. In 1819 he had moved out, leaving the house to Barnum, but Barnum retained Gadsby's nephew and assistant, one Andrew McLaughlin. In later years McLaughlin married Barnum's daughter, and the two keepers remained friendly rivals until both died in 1844.[32]

From Baltimore Gadsby moved into the Franklin House in Washington, a house better known as "O'Neale's." The house had been patronized by such notables as Senator Eaton and Senator Jackson, and when O'Neale was forced into bankruptcy Eaton purchased the place, probably because he had become enamored of the keeper's pretty daughter Peggy. Gadsby immediately won and profited by the friendship of the powerful Jacksonian element, but when he sought to build a new hotel to rival Barnum's he had to seek the help of some of the city's leading realtors, especially the famous Calvert family.[33] The city celebrated the opening of the National with an elaborate Washington's birthday ball in 1827, an event at which every distinguished person in the capital had made an appearance.[34] Though Washingtonians had to admit that the house was not quite so large or so elegant as Barnum's, they and their visitors thought it fully deserving of the title "first-class hotel."

In the years following the American Revolution all the various socioeconomic and political forces which had brought the "common man" into the limelight had also worked together to produce bigger and better hotels, hotels so obviously better that a new classification had to be found for them. Like the old taverns, the new hotels were so obviously "public" and "democratic" in their character that foreigners were often to describe

[32] Parkinson, A Tour, I, 277; Davis, Travels, 222; Baltimore American, September 7, 1808; Federal Gazette and Baltimore Daily Advertiser, September 2, 1819; National Intelligencer, April 23, May 23, 1823; August 21, September 24, 1826; June 19, 1827; September 23, 1828; May 18, 1844; Washington Post, January 3, 1932; Washington Star, July 12, 1942; Bryan, A History of the National Capital, II, 60.

[33] Ibid. Also see Clifford Lewis, "Hotels of Washington Past and Present," in John C. Proctor (ed.), Washington, Past and Present (4 vols., New York, 1930), II, 780–85; Francis J. Grund, Aristocracy in America (2 vols., London, 1839), II, 183; and engraving of National Hotel on bill (1836) filed under Armitage and Defize in Vertical Files of the Maryland Historical Society Library.

[34] National Intelligencer, February 24, 1827.

them as a true reflection of the nature of American society.[35] In addition, thanks to the influence of the exchange idea, the new houses were more "business" than "home," and provided far more than "all the comforts of home." In writing about one exchange hotel a New Orleans editor stated that the workers moved about so quietly and politely "that each guest may easily fancy himself a prince surrounded by a flock of courtiers."[36] In these words, knowingly or otherwise, he had stated the highest achievement of the first-class hotel.

Considering that one might justifiably link the story of the "rise of the public palace" to the story of the "rise of the common man," it is surprising that historians have not generally emphasized the connection. Instead, they have generally stated that the first-class hotel sprang into being full grown, and quite suddenly, with the erection of the Tremont House, which opened in Boston in 1829,[37] or that it was a "triumph of the thirties,"[38] intimating at least that it was a by-product of railroad construction.

Histories which describe the Tremont House as the earliest of the first-class houses usually do so simply because it is described as such in Jefferson Williamson's *The American Hotel: An Anecdotal History,* published in 1930. This is the only volume on the early history of the hotel now available. Therefore it should be explained that Williamson's reason for labeling the house was that "by virtue of numerous superi-

---

[35] James Silk Buckingham, *The Slave States of America* (2 vols., London, 1842), I, 336; Baxter, *America and the Americans,* 29–34; John Milton Mackie, *From Cape Cod to Dixie and the Tropics* (New York, 1864), 160.

[36] New Orleans *Picayune,* November 16, 1841. Be it noted, however, that these "courtiers," like the tavern "help" of old, were fully aware of their status as citizens of the Republic. Europeans noticed that native-born workers were "uppity" and expected no tips, and that Americanized immigrants were the same. However, with the use of immigrant labor in the 1830's and 1840's tipping became more nearly common. See Charles Mackay, *Life and Liberty in America* (London, 1859), 343; Tyrone Power, *Impressions of America during the Years 1833, 1834, and 1835* (2 vols., Philadelphia, 1836), I, 79; Michel Chevalier, *Society, Manners and Politics in the United States . . . ,* Translated by Thomas G. Bradford (Boston, 1839), 433; Stuart, *Three Years in North America,* I, 32; II, 147; Hamilton, *Men and Manners,* II, 4, 6.

[37] For example see Williamson, *The American Hotel,* 8, 13–17; and Talbot F. Hamlin, *Greek Revival Architecture in America* (New York, 1944), 112. For a more accurate account of the Tremont's history see Suffolk County (Mass.) Registry of Deeds, liber. 335, folio 258; liber. 336, folio 169; Boston *Courier,* June 12, July 3, July 7, 1828; Boston *Statesman,* April 9, 1828; Boston *Weekly Messenger,* December 8, 1831; *New England Palladium,* September 24, October 23, 1829; William Havard Eliot, *A Description of Tremont House . . .* (Boston, 1830).

[38] Oliver W. Larkin, *Art and Life in America* (New York, 1949), 158.

orities, it was indisputably the first definitely recognized example of the modern first-class hotel."[39] Yet, though he claimed that the Tremont was then the world's largest hotel, Barnum's was not only larger but had displayed the enumerated "superiorities" and so-called innovations at an earlier date. In fact many of them had appeared in the old Boston Exchange, and it is significant that the promoter of the Tremont never claimed anything more than that he hoped to provide Boston with the excellent accommodations it had not known since the Exchange fire.[40] Perhaps it is enough to say that the terms "modern," "palatial," and "first-class" were all in use and in print at least two years before the Tremont came into being.

As for the possible influence of railroad construction, it is obvious that the earliest first-class houses were in operation before the advent of the passenger railroad, and a study of newspapers and travel accounts shows that the great hotels erected between 1830 and 1860 were not the products of railroad companies. Such companies built few hotels before 1860, and these were generally no more than rough dormitories erected at rural junctions. Moreover, railroad companies usually found it unprofitable to operate hotels and generally sold those they had built at the earliest opportunity. In no respect does it seem possible to think of the development of the first-class hotel as a "triumph of the thirties."

However, the years between 1830 and 1840 do constitute an important phase in the history of the American hotel, for during these years first-class hotels grew in number and in popularity, a fact which the new railroads and the new national political conventions both help to explain. Moreover, as the people moved westward the palatial hotel moved with them, and the "boom-time" speculation of the early thirties led rival cities to erect rival houses.

As might be expected, living in first-class hotels proved even more popular than tavern living had been, so popular in fact that foreign visitors often viewed the practice as a serious defect in American society.[41] In fact, a few American writers described it as a serious threat

---

[39] Williamson, The American Hotel, 13.

[40] Eliot, A Description of Tremont House, preface.

[41] The popularity of hotel living is described in many travel accounts, including the following: Hamilton, Men and Manners, II, 37; Marryat, Second Series of A Diary, 33; John W. Oldmixon, Transatlantic Wanderings... (London, 1855), 2, 27; Baxter, America and the Americans, 32; Thomas C. Grattan, Civilized America (2 vols., London, 1859), I, 110–13; Francis J. Grund, Americans in their Moral, Social, and Political Relations (Boston, 1837), 327, and Henry Benjamin Whipple, Bishop Whipple's Southern Diary, 1843–1844 (Minneapolis, 1937), 196. The following accounts describe the practice as a menace to family life and to the morals of American womanhood: Fredrika Bremer, The Homes of the New

to marriage and family life.[42] But most Americans agreed with the magazine editor who boasted that these houses constituted one of the "advancements of civilization and refinement in our growing country."[43]

With the evidence on hand one might well suggest that the first-class hotels actually precipitated such advances. One writer described a convention crowd at Barnum's thus: "What a crowd! All sorts, kinds, sizes, and complexions, sober and drunk, noisy and clean, loafers, busters, gentlemen, Yankees. Oh, never did I see such an assembly."[44] Yet this crowd in convention assembled did not forget to thank the city of Baltimore for the excellent accommodations it had provided.[45] A New Yorker described the ballroom of a New Orleans hotel as a microcosmos of American society which included a "dashing belle," the "bewildered milliner-martyred daughter of an interior planter," and a "male representative of Western trade, or Eastern manufactures."[46]

Whether he was a provincial planter, an untutored backwoodsman, or an upcountry merchant, the American who made his way for the first time into a first-class hotel was not likely to go away unimpressed. Once he had eaten the famous canvasback duck at Barnum's, drunk of the wine cellar at the Astor, strolled into the marble-tiled baths at the St. Charles, or been waited on hand and foot by a corps of faultless servants, he was apt to turn homeward slowly, firmly resolved that his own town,

---

World (2 vols., New York, 1854), II, 195; Trollope, *Domestic Manners,* II, 111; Buckingham, *Slave States,* I, 350; Marryat, *Second Series of a Diary,* 44; and John R. Godley, *Letters from America* (2 vols., London, 1844), II, 38.

[42] New Orleans *Commercial Bulletin,* August 1, 1836; New Orleans *Picayune,* January 19, 1851; *Harper's Weekly* (New York, 1857–1916). I (1857), 274. Most critics of hotel life stated that the table d'hôte, with its fixed price, was the strongest attraction the hotel offered. "Destroy that," exclaimed the editor of *Harper's Weekly,* and women "will have homes." The table d'hôte system continued to be very popular in first-class hotels until 1860, despite the fact that the term "European plan" had been used in newspaper advertising as early as the 1830's. See advertisements in *American Traveller,* September 3, 1833; July 31, 1835; January 5, 1836; and New Orleans *Bee,* November 19, 1835.

[43] *Gleason's Pictorial Drawing-Room Companion* (Boston, 1851–1859), II (1852), 265.

[44] Whipple, *Bishop Whipple's Southern Diary,* 154.

[45] *Niles' Weekly Register,* September 26, October 8, December 24, 1831; May 26, 1832. Also see *National Intelligencer,* October 1, December 17, 1831. A study of the newspapers of 1831 has led to the conviction that the presence of Barnum's Hotel was a major factor in determining the location of many of the early national political conventions in Baltimore.

[46] Abraham Oakey Hall, *The Manhattaner in New Orleans* (New York, 1851), 12–14. Also see Mackie, *Cape Cod to Dixie,* 10, and Mackay, *Western World,* I, 107, 117.

and perhaps his own home, would some day afford such pleasures. And, after all, was not the "rise of the common man" the result of just such dreams, multiplied a millionfold? And would it not be difficult to draw a more accurate picture of the "risen" common man than to depict him wearing a delegate's badge at his party's first national convention, and standing ankle-deep in the velvet rugs of Barnum's?

The Spirit in Which Americans Cultivate the Arts: Why Nearly All Americans Prefer Business Activities

ALEXIS de TOCQUEVILLE

IT WOULD BE TO WASTE THE TIME OF MY READERS AND MY OWN IF I strove to demonstrate how the general mediocrity of fortunes, the absence of superfluous wealth, the universal desire of comfort, and the constant efforts by which every one attempts to procure it, make the taste for the useful predominate over the love of the beautiful in the heart of man. Democratic nations, among which all these things exist, will therefore cultivate the arts which serve to render life easy, in preference to those whose object is to adorn it. They will habitually prefer the useful to the beautiful, and they will require that the beautiful should be useful. But I propose to go further; and after having pointed out this first feature, to sketch several others.

It commonly happens that in the ages of privilege the practice of almost all the arts becomes a privilege; and that every profession is a separate walk, upon which it is not allowable for every one to enter. Even when productive industry is free, the fixed character which belongs to aristocratic nations gradually segregates all the persons who practise the same art, till they form a distinct class, always composed of the same families, whose members are all known to each other, and among whom a public

Democracy in America (first published 1835), from the translation by Henry Reeve.

opinion of their own and a species of corporate pride soon spring up. In a class or guild of this kind, each artisan has not only his fortune to make, but his reputation to preserve. He is not exclusively swayed by his own interest, or even by that of his customer, but by that of the body to which he belongs; and the interest of that body is, that each artisan should produce the best possible workmanship. In aristocratic ages, the object of the arts is therefore to manufacture as well as possible—not with the greatest despatch, or at the lowest rate.

When, on the contrary, every profession is open to all—when a multitude of persons are constantly embracing and abandoning it—and when its several members are strangers to each other, indifferent, and from their numbers hardly seen among themselves; the social tie is destroyed, and each workman, standing alone, endeavours simply to gain the greatest possible quantity of money at the least possible cost. The will of the customer is then his only limit. But at the same time a corresponding revolution takes place in the customer also. In countries in which riches as well as power are concentrated, and retained in the hands of the few, the use of the greater part of this world's goods belongs to a small number of individuals, who are always the same. Necessity, public opinion, or moderate desires exclude all others from the enjoyment of them. As this aristocratic class remains fixed at the pinnacle of greatness on which it stands, without diminution or increase, it is always acted upon by the same wants and affected by them in the same manner. The men of whom it is composed naturally derive from their superior and hereditary position a taste for what is extremely well made and lasting. This affects the general way of thinking of the nation in relation to the arts. It often occurs, among such a people, that even the peasant will rather go without the objects he covets than procure them in a state of imperfection. In aristocracies, then, the handicraftsmen work for only a limited number of very fastidious customers: the profit they hope to make depends principally on the perfection of their workmanship.

Such is no longer the case when, all privileges being abolished, ranks are intermingled, and men are for ever rising or sinking upon the ladder of society. Among a democratic people a number of citizens always exist whose patrimony is divided and decreasing. They have contracted, under more prosperous circumstances, certain wants, which remain after the means of satisfying such wants are gone; and they are anxiously looking out for some surreptitious methods of providing for them. On the other hand, there are always in democracies a large number of men whose fortune is upon the increase, but whose desires grow much faster than their fortunes: and who gloat upon the gifts of wealth in anticipation, long before they have means to command them. Such men are eager to find some short cut to these gratifications, already almost within their reach. From the combination of these two causes the result is, that in democracies there is always a multitude of individuals whose wants are above their means, and who are very willing to take up with imperfect satisfaction rather than abandon the object of their desires.

The artisan readily understands these passions, for he himself partakes in them: in an aristocracy he would seek to sell his workmanship at a high price to the few; he now conceives that the more expeditious way of getting rich is to sell them at a low price to all. But there are only two ways of lowering the price of commodities. The first is to discover some better, shorter, and more ingenious method of producing them: the second is to manufacture a larger quantity of goods, nearly similar, but of less value. Among a democratic population, all the intellectual faculties of the workman are directed to these two objects: he strives to invent methods which may enable him not only to work better, but quicker and cheaper; or, if he cannot succeed in that, to diminish the intrinsic qualities of the thing he makes, without rendering it wholly unfit for the use for which it is intended. When none but the wealthy had watches, they were almost all very good ones: few are now made which are worth much, but everybody has one in his pocket. Thus the democratic principle not only tends to direct the human mind to the useful arts, but it induces the artisan to produce with greater rapidity a quantity of imperfect commodities, and the consumer to content himself with these commodities. . . .

The handicraftsmen of democratic ages endeavour not only to bring their useful productions within the reach of the whole community, but they strive to give to all their commodities attractive qualities which they do not in reality possess. In the confusion of all ranks every one hopes to appear what he is not, and makes great exertions to succeed in this object. This sentiment, indeed, which is but too natural to the heart of man, does not originate in the democratic principle; but that principle applies it to material objects. To mimic virtue is of every age; but the hypocrisy of luxury belongs more particularly to the ages of democracy.

To satisfy these new cravings of human vanity the arts have recourse to every species of imposture: and these devices sometimes go so far as to defeat their own purpose. Imitation diamonds are now made which easily may be mistaken for real ones; as soon as the art of fabricating false diamonds shall have reached so high a degree of perfection that they cannot be distinguished from real ones, it is probable that both one and the other will be abandoned, and become mere pebbles again.

This leads me to speak of those arts which are called the fine arts, by way of distinction. I do not believe that it is a necessary effect of a democratic social condition and of democratic institutions to diminish the number of men who cultivate the fine arts; but these causes exert a very powerful influence on the manner in which these arts are cultivated. Many of those who had already contracted a taste for the fine arts are impoverished: on the other hand, many of those who are not yet rich begin to conceive that taste, at least by imitation; and the number of consumers increases, but opulent and fastidious consumers become more scarce. Something analogous to what I have already pointed out in the useful arts then takes place in the fine arts; the productions of artists are more numerous, but the merit of each production is diminished. No longer able to soar to what is great, they cultivate what is pretty and elegant; and appearance is more attended to than reality. In aristocracies a few great pictures are produced; in democratic countries, a vast number of insignificant ones. In the former, statues are raised of bronze; in the latter, they are modelled in plaster.

When I arrived for the first time at New York, by that part of the Atlantic Ocean which is called the Sound, I was surprised to perceive along the shore, at some distance from the city, a considerable number of little palaces of white marble, several of which were built after the models of ancient architecture. When I went the next day to inspect more closely the building which had particularly attracted my notice, I found that its walls were of white-washed brick, and its columns of painted wood. All the edifices which I had admired the night before were of the same kind.

The social condition and the institutions of democracy impart, moreover, certain peculiar tendencies to all the imitative arts, which it is easy to point out. They frequently withdraw them from the delineation of the soul to fix them exclusively on that of the body: and they substitute the representation of motion and sensation for that of sentiment and thought: in a word, they put the Real in the place of the Ideal. I doubt whether Raphael studied the minutest intricacies of the mechanism of the human body as thoroughly as the draughtsmen of our own time. He did not attach the same importance to rigorous accuracy on this point as they do, because he aspired to surpass Nature. He sought to make of man something which should be superior to man, and to embellish beauty's self. . . . The painters of the Middle Ages generally sought far above themselves, and away from their own time, for mighty subjects, which left to their imagination an unbounded range. Our painters frequently employ their talents in the exact imitation of the details of private life, which they have always before their eyes; and they are for ever copying trivial objects, the originals of which are only too abundant in Nature.

I have just observed that in democratic ages monuments of the arts tend to become more numerous and less important. I now hasten to point out the exception to this rule. In a democratic community individuals are very powerless; but the State which represents them all, and contains them all in its grasp, is very powerful. Nowhere do citizens appear so insignificant as in a democratic nation; nowhere does the nation itself appear greater, or does the mind more easily take in a wide general survey of it. In democratic communities the imagination is compressed when men consider themselves; it expands indefinitely when they think of the State. Hence it is that the same men who live on a small scale in narrow dwellings frequently aspire to gigantic splendour in the erection of their public monuments.

The Americans traced out the circuit of an immense city on the site which they intended to make their capital, but which, up to the present time, is hardly more densely peopled than Pontoise, though, according to them, it will one day contain a million inhabitants. They have already rooted up trees for ten miles round, lest they should interfere with the future citizens of this imaginary metropolis. They have erected a magnificent palace for Congress in the centre of the city, and have given it the pompous name of the Capitol. The several States of the Union are every day planning and erecting for themselves prodigious undertakings, which would astonish the engineers of the great European nations. Thus democracy not only leads men to a vast number of inconsiderable productions; it also leads them to raise some monuments on the largest scale: but between these two extremes there is a blank. A few scattered remains of enormous buildings can therefore teach us nothing of the social condition and the institutions of the people by whom they were raised. I may add, though the remark leads me to step out of my subject, that they do not make us better acquainted with its greatness, its civilization, and its real prosperity. Whensoever a power of any kind shall be able to make a whole people co-operate in a single undertaking, that power, with a little knowledge and a great deal of time, will succeed in obtaining something enormous from the co-operation of efforts so multiplied. But this does not lead to the conclusion that the people was very happy, very enlightened, or even very strong. . . .

OCCUPATIONS AND BUSINESS CALLINGS

Among a democratic people, where there is no hereditary wealth, every man works to earn a living, or has worked, or is born of parents who have worked. The notion of labour is therefore presented to the mind on every side as the necessary, natural, and honest condition of human existence. Not only is labour not dishonourable among such a people, but it is held in honour: the prejudice is not against it, but in its favour. In the United States a wealthy man thinks that he owes it to public opinion to devote his leisure to some kind of industrial or commercial pursuit, or to public business. He would think himself in bad repute if he employed his life solely in living. It is for the purpose of escaping this obligation to work that so many rich Americans come to Europe, where they find some scattered remains of aristocratic society, among which idleness is still held in honour.

Equality of conditions not only ennobles the notion of labour in men's estimation, but it raises the notion of labour as a source of profit. In aristocracies it is not exactly labour that is despised, but labour with a view to profit. Labour is honorific in itself, when it is undertaken at the sole bidding of ambition or of virtue. Yet in aristocratic society it constantly happens that he who works for honour is not insensible to the attractions of profit. But these two desires only intermingle in the innermost depths of his soul: he carefully hides from every eye the point at which they join; he would fain conceal it from himself. In aristocratic countries there are few public officers who do not affect to serve their country without interested motives. Their salary is an incident of which they think but little, and of which they always affect not to think at all. Thus the notion of profit is kept distinct from that of labour; however they may be united in point of fact, they are not thought of together.

In democratic communities these two notions are, on the contrary, always palpably united. As the desire of well-being is universal—as fortunes are slender or fluctuating—as every one wants either to increase his own resources, or to provide fresh ones for his progeny, men clearly see that it is profit which, if not wholly at least partially, leads them to work. Even those who are principally actuated by the love of fame are necessarily made familiar with the thought that they are not exclusively actuated by that motive; and they discover that the desire of getting a living is mingled in their minds with the desire of making life illustrious.

As soon as, on the one hand, labour is held by the whole community to be an honourable necessity of man's condition, and, on the other, as soon as labour is always ostensibly performed, wholly or in part, for the purpose of earning remuneration, the immense interval which separated different callings in aristocratic societies disappears. If all are not alike, all at least have one feature in common. No profession exists in which men do not work for money; and the remuneration which is common to them all gives them all an air of resemblance. This serves to explain the opinions which the Americans entertain with respect to different callings. In America no one is degraded because he works, for every one about him works also; nor is any one humiliated by the notion of receiving pay, for the President of the United States also works for pay. He is paid for commanding, other men for obeying orders. In the United States professions are more or less laborious, more or less profitable; but they are never either high or low: every honest calling is honourable.

Agriculture is, perhaps, of all the useful arts that which improves most slowly among democratic nations. Frequently, indeed, it would seem to be stationary, because other arts are making rapid strides toward perfection. On the other hand, almost all the tastes and habits which the equality of condition engenders naturally lead men to commercial and industrial occupations.

Suppose an active, enlightened, and free man, enjoying a competency, but full of desires: he is too poor to live in idleness; he is rich enough to feel himself protected from the immediate fear of want, and he thinks how he can better his condition. This man has conceived a taste for physical gratifications, which thousands of his fellow-men indulge in around him; he has himself begun to enjoy these pleasures, and he is eager to increase his means of satisfying these tastes more completely. But life is slipping away, time is urgent—to what is he to turn? The cultivation of the ground promises an almost certain result to his exertions, but a slow one; men are not enriched by it without patience and toil. Agriculture is therefore only suited to those who have already large superfluous wealth, or to those whose penury bids them only seek a bare subsistence. The choice of such a man as we have sup   ed is soon made; he sells his plot of ground, leaves his dwelling, an embarks in some hazardous but lucrative calling. Democratic communities abound in men of this kind; and in proportion as the equality of conditions becomes greater, their multitude increases. Thus democracy not only swells the number of workingmen, but it leads men to prefer one kind of labour to another; and while it diverts them from agriculture, it encourages their taste for commerce and manufactures.

This spirit may be observed even among the richest members of the community. In democratic countries, however opulent a man is supposed to be, he is almost always discontented with his fortune, because he finds that he is less rich than his father was, and he fears that his sons will be less rich than himself. Most rich men in democracies are therefore constantly haunted by the desire of obtaining wealth, and they naturally turn their attention to trade and manufactures, which appear to offer the readiest and most powerful means of success. In this respect they share the instincts of the poor, without feeling the same necessities; say rather, they feel the most imperious of all necessities, that of not sinking in the world.

In aristocracies the rich are at the same time those who govern. The attention which they unceasingly devote to important public affairs diverts them from the lesser cares which trade and manufactures demand. If the will of an individual happens nevertheless to turn his attention to business, the will of the body to which he belongs will immediately debar him from pursuing it; for however men may declaim against the rule of numbers, they cannot wholly escape their sway; and even among those aristocratic bodies which most obstinately refuse to acknowledge the rights of the majority of the nation, a private majority is formed which governs the rest.

In democratic countries, where money does not lead those who possess it to political power, but often removes them from it, the rich do not know how to spend their leisure. They are driven into active life by the inquietude and the greatness of their desires, by the extent of their resources, and by the taste for what is extraordinary, which is almost always felt by those who rise, by whatsoever means, above the crowd. Trade is the only road open to them. In democracies nothing is greater or more brilliant than commerce: it attracts the attention of the public, and fills the imagination of the multitude; all energetic passions are directed toward it. Neither their own prejudices, nor those of anybody else, can prevent the rich from devoting themselves to it. The wealthy members of democracies never form a body which has manners and regulations of its own; the opinions peculiar to their class do not restrain them, and the common opinions of their country urge them on. Moreover, as all the large fortunes which are to be met with in a democratic community are of commercial growth, many generations must succeed each other before their possessors can have entirely laid aside their habits of business.

Circumscribed within the narrow space which politics leave them, rich men in democracies eagerly embark in commercial enterprise: there they can extend and employ their natural advantages; and indeed it is even by the boldness and the magnitude of their industrial speculations that we may measure the slight esteem in which productive industry would have been held by them if they had been born amid an aristocracy.

A similar observation is likewise applicable to all men living in democracies, whether they be poor or rich. Those who live in the midst of democratic fluctuations have always before their eyes the phantom of chance; and they end by liking all undertakings in which chance plays a part. They are, therefore, all led to engage in commerce, not only for the sake of the profit it holds out to them, but for the love of the constant excitement occasioned by that pursuit.

The United States of America have only been emancipated for half a century from the state of colonial dependence in which they stood to Great Britain; the number of large fortunes there is small, and capital is still scarce. Yet no people in the world has made such rapid progress in trade and manufactures as the Americans: they constitute at the present day the second maritime nation in the world; and although their manufactures have to struggle with almost insurmountable natural impediments, they are not prevented from making great and daily advances. In the

United States the greatest undertakings and speculations are executed without difficulty, because the whole population is engaged in productive industry, and because the poorest as well as the most opulent members of the commonwealth are ready to combine their efforts for these purposes. The consequence is, that a stranger is constantly amazed by the immense public works executed by a nation which contains, so to speak, no rich men. The Americans arrived but as yesterday on the territory which they inhabit, and they have already changed the whole order of Nature for their own advantage. They have joined the Hudson to the Mississippi, and made the Atlantic Ocean communicate with the Gulf of Mexico, across a continent of more than five hundred leagues in extent which separates the two seas. The longest railroads which have been constructed up to the present time are in America. But what most astonishes me in the United States is not so much the marvellous grandeur of some undertakings, as the innumerable multitude of small ones. Almost all the farmers of the United States combine some trade with agriculture; most of them make agriculture itself a trade. It seldom happens that an American farmer settles for good upon the land which he occupies: especially in the districts of the far West he brings land into tillage in order to sell it again, and not to farm it: he builds a farmhouse on the speculation that, as the state of the country will soon be changed by the increase of population, a good price will be gotten for it. Every year a swarm of the inhabitants of the North arrive in the Southern States, and settle in the parts where the cotton-plant and the sugar-cane grow. These men cultivate the soil in order to make it produce in a few years enough to enrich them; and they already look forward to the time when they may return home to enjoy the competency thus acquired. Thus the Americans carry their business-like qualities into agriculture; and their trading passions are displayed in that as in their other pursuits.

The Americans make immense progress in productive industry, because they all devote themselves to it at once; and for this same reason they are exposed to very unexpected and formidable embarrassments. As they are all engaged in commerce, their commercial affairs are affected by such various and complex causes that it is impossible to foresee what difficulties may arise. As they are all more or less engaged in productive industry, at the least shock given to business all private fortunes are put in jeopardy at the same time, and the State is shaken. I believe that the return of these commercial panics is an endemic disease of the democratic nations of our age. It may be rendered less dangerous, but it cannot be cured; because it does not originate in accidental circumstances, but in the temperament of these nations.

THE PROCESS AND CONSEQUENCES
OF DEMOCRATIC ADVANCE

Democracy did not sweep over America in waves: it crept in by a thousand streams. But in a very real sense, democracy in America was a direct product of sheer necessity, and its results have been of enduring importance. American settlers from the beginning were out to develop the country, and the problems which the land itself presented to people in their situation, with their historical background and their intense ambitions, could be solved only by active association and by a widespread sharing, or distribution, of public duties. This system was adopted very early in the history of the New England towns, and the habits so formed came to the aid of numerous transient communities and new settlements in other parts of the country.

The process has been brilliantly illustrated by Professor Daniel J. Boorstin,[1] who shows how the method of voluntary association and voluntary acceptance of majority decisions enabled Americans to cope with problems of government, of defence, and of doing every kind of necessary job. Boorstin's history is far more subtle in its appreciation of complexities than ever Turner's was, but all the same it is reminiscent of Turner and owes something to his school. Turner's teaching was more deliberately invoked by Stanley Elkins and Eric McKitrick in a long essay published in the form of two successive

[1] Daniel J. Boorstin, *The Americans: The National Experience* (New York, 1965), esp. pp. 65–112.

articles under the title "A Meaning for Turner's Frontier,"[2] the first of which is reproduced in this section.

Readers will notice that Elkins and McKitrick round off their argument by coming back to early New England and emphasizing the elementary fact that a large number of jobs had to be done, so that many humble and simple people had to be called on to help in the service of their communities. In the interim they have shown how conditions in the old Northwest discouraged the engrossment of vast estates and how the settlers were too much for either the absent landlord-speculator or even for the restraining hand of the federal government. But in the Southwest different conditions prevailed, and here they develop an argument that should be contrasted with that of Hartz.[3]

The Southern colonies had all been governed on the county court system, which had in its main features been transplanted from England. It was government by an oligarchy of the gentry, who succeeded themselves on the bench and who invariably represented their counties in the legislature. This system moved into the Southwest, and although constitutions became more democratic in form, planter magistracies continued to wield the substance of power. The basic reasons lay in their early engrossment of the substance of economic power under conditions where it was possible to build from strength. Elections were often hotly contested—yet the contests were usually a form of popular entertainment, and the issues were soon forgotten.

In principle, Elkins and McKitrick differ deeply from Hartz, and the serious student will want to go back to their articles, and to Hartz' *The Liberal Tradition,* and work out his own ideas by comparing the arguments.

Turner made it an important theme of his argument that democratic institutions and reforms spread from new western states back into the older eastern ones. But Professor Williamson's basic study of American suffrage has shown the chronological fallibility of this thesis; eastern states moved in pace with, sometimes ahead of, the West. This analysis constitutes a most important modification to the earlier interpretation; it does not, however, seriously impair the Elkins–McKitrick argument, since they would maintain that the American tradition of associated political action had already been planted in the East. It was brought to life by vital issues.

Issues—political competition over questions of policy—played an important part in keeping popular interest alive in the North. As we know, democracy in our sense of the term neither sprang from the soil nor prevailed over colonial America. But wherever issues of real importance faced the voters, as they sometimes did in the colonial period, the electorates showed themselves surprisingly vocal and independent. The issues frequently divided the people on questions of interest—religious, economic or local; but these interests very seldom faced each other across the barriers of the

[2] Part I, "Democracy in the Old Northwest" and Part II, "The Southwest Frontier and New England," *Political Science Quarterly,* Vol. LXIX, no. 3 and 4, 1954.
[3] See pp. 15–27.

suffrage. (They did occasionally, as in Virginia in 1829.) In general, state constitutional arrangements could accommodate conflicts of interest and were not required to defend the interests of one class by depriving another of all political power. This is one of the salient findings of Professor McCormick, whose article on the relationship of suffrage to party alignments falls into this section.

At the same time, however, issues did arise; they were not mere play-things of political leaders, and they could be of vital importance, especially in state politics. It seems right to conclude with a reference to Andrew Jackson, the symbol, albeit the somewhat dubious and ambiguous symbol, of the common man risen to power. Professor Sellers shows how it happened in Jackson's own state of Tennessee. A very powerful merchant oligarchy effectively ruled this partly western state, admitted to the Union in 1796. Yet this oligarchy, attempting to manipulate the candidacy of Jackson for purely tactical reasons, was unseated by forces that it had formerly controlled with ease. Things were getting out of hand; the voters were no longer willing to accept government as a gift from their social superiors—if they had any. In Tennessee after a hard campaign, James K. Polk, a committed reformer, was elected to Congress in 1825; the gentry did not like the drift, and a former justice of the Supreme Court of that state expressed this feeling of alarm: "Had I the power," he said, "no exertion of which I was capable would be wanting to arrest the progress of that wild and furious democracy which has long threatened to overwhelm our country at no distant date in the Vortex of Anarchy."[4]

The phenomenon he described was in part a cultural force that had been undermining the older set of social and political relationships since the days of the Revolution. In one sense at least this great transition *was* the American Revolution. Political democracy was both an instrument of this phenomenon and an expression of its moral force.

---

[4] Charles G. Sellers, Jr., *James K. Polk, Jacksonian, 1795–1843* (Princeton, 1957), p. 99.

A Meaning for Turner's Frontier

STANLEY ELKINS
AND
ERIC McKITRICK

DEMOCRACY IN THE OLD NORTHWEST

1

IT WOULD BE DIFFICULT TODAY, NOW THAT SIXTY YEARS HAVE PASSED, to revive the sense of intellectual ardor with which Frederick Jackson Turner's paper on the American frontier was greeted so soon after its first inauspicious reading.[1] So full of promise did the remarkable theory then appear, so charged with import, that its present status as an academic curiosity seems to symbolize some profound intervening disillusionment. A crucial motif of American spiritual experience seemed at one time to have found its fittest expression in Turner's inspired essay, and with his ceremonial "closing" of our frontier in 1893 a generation of publicists began finding the terms, products of convictions already deeply felt, whereby great stretches of American history might at last be given meaning. Persistent echoes of these convictions are heard even today.[2] And yet by now nearly every attempt to impose conceptual structure upon the lyricism of Turner and his followers has been abandoned. Intuition and cool reason appear to have succeeded in baffling each other.

It needs little prompting to recall the "frontier thesis," with its message that the presence of cheap land and an ever-receding frontier "explain" American development; its arguments, indeed, could be assorted under three rough headings. Turner's first claim for American culture was one of "uniqueness"; in mutiny against the Johns Hopkins "germ theorists" of the 1880s and their genealogical accounts of American political institutions traced back to England, back even to the gloomy

Reprinted with permission from the *Political Science Quarterly*, Vol. LXIX, No. 3, September, 1954, pp. 321–353.

[1] "The Significance of the Frontier in American History," read at the annual meeting of the American Historical Association at Chicago in July 1893.

[2] See Henry Nash Smith, *Virgin Land: The American West as Symbol and Myth* (Cambridge, 1950) for proof that on a poetic level the frontier idea still has its fascinations. See also Walter Prescott Webb's *The Great Frontier* (Boston, 1952).

forests of central Europe, Turner felt that these institutions and their character were to be accounted for most plausibly in terms purely American. Next, he produced a metaphor: the open frontier with its easily available land was a "safety valve" for underprivileged Easterners, its promise serving as a minimizer of urban unrest. The third claim, an extension of the first, was a report, again metaphoric, of the origins of true democracy. As settlers pushed out beyond the mountains, ties with the East and with Europe were steadily weakened, ancestral memories grew dim, and a "shearing-off" process took place: "layers" of civilization were removed until the pioneer stood in native worth, self-reliant, individualistic, a democrat of Jacksonian model. "American democracy was born of no theorist's dream; it was not carried in the *Susan Constant* to Virginia nor in the *Mayflower* to Plymouth. It came out of the American forest, and it gained new strength each time it touched a new frontier."[3]

A new phalanx of critics has now demolished the Turner conception. His vagueness, his abstraction, his hopeless imprecision, his poverty of concrete example, have each been held up to the scientific eye. Turner, in all but ignoring the English origins of our institutions, gains nothing but misunderstanding by his "ungracious exclusion of Locke and Milton."[4] The "safety valve," moreover, is at best a misleading poetic figure. How could the Eastern worker, poverty-stricken and ignorant of agriculture, think seriously of so staggering a project as removing to the West? The new Western farmer was most typically a recent Eastern farmer who had emigrated with at least a little money in his pocket, and the cities themselves, ironically indeed, eventually came to serve as safety valves for all farmers embittered with the agrarian life. But the deadliest criticisms of all are reserved for the Turneresque vision of the frontier's rôle in the birth of American democracy. Turner's state of nature, his shearing-off of civilized corruption, hints at a pastoral anarchy neither realized nor remotely desired by the bands of settlers in their wilderness outposts. The first efforts of these pioneers were to set up and to stabilize those very political institutions, parallel in as many ways as might be, which they had left behind them in the East. A kind of primitive geopolitics is brusquely challenged by a riddle which Turner could not have answered: why the *American* forest—why didn't democracy come out of other "forests"—why not the Siberian frontier?[5] The few remaining defenders

[3] *The Frontier in American History* (New York, 1920), p. 293.

[4] Benjamin F. Wright, Jr., "Political Institutions and the Frontier," in D.R. Fox, ed., *Sources of Culture in the Middle West* (New York, 1934), p. 36.

[5] An excellent symposium of these critical views, containing all the subtleties denied them here, may be found in *The Turner Thesis*, Number 2 of the Amherst

of Frederick Jackson Turner have been able to produce very little in the way of rejoinder.

And yet, though conviction now burns so low, it remains to be noted that even the unkindest of Turner's critics have conceded, with a kind of bedeviled monotony, that *some* relation most likely does exist between our history and our frontier. The fact thus stands that, in this direction at least, no advance has yet been made beyond Turner's own dazzling abstraction. The problem is still there, its vitality unextinguished. It is no further resolved than ever.

If we examine with suspicion the body of critical work, we discover an interesting paradox. Turner and his teachings have been approached with deadly seriousness on their own terms—no other—and handled with what turns out to be *textual* criticism: a method which is illuminating but whose value for the analysis and correction of theoretical material is acutely limited.[6] The result has been to demonstrate the absurdities of Turner's internal logic—which is an undoubted contribution to perspective. Yet it should still be recognized that no concrete attempt to restate Turner's idea has ever actually been undertaken. Now might there not, after all, be a way of rescuing Turner? Is it possible to ask the great question itself in a form permitting a concrete answer?

Turner's critics may be allowed the most sweeping of concessions. Nearly everything[7] could be sacrificed—everything, that is except the one thing that matters: the development of political democracy as a habit and the American as a unique political creature. This was the supreme fact which overwhelmed Tocqueville in the 1830s; every American still knows in his heart that the frontier had something to do with it.

Problems in American Civilization, George R. Taylor, ed. (Boston, 1949). The criticism is well summarized in Richard Hofstadter, "Turner and the Frontier Myth," *American Scholar*, XVIII, 433–43 (Oct. 1949).

6 The "textual" approach has been used with more success in the analysis of modern poetry and is the principal tool of the "New Criticism." There are indications, however, that even here the method's shortcomings are beginning to be felt. See "The New Criticism," a forum discussion by William Barrett, Kenneth Burke, Malcolm Cowley, Robert Gorham Davis, Allen Tate, and Hiram Haydn, *American Scholar*, XX, 86–104, 218–31 (Jan.-Apr. 1951).

7 This would involve principally the claim for institutional "novelty" (which puts an extra burden on the theory) and the "safety valve" (which isn't necessary). For that matter, although the frontier assuredly had little to say to the "underprivileged," its *real* "safety valve" aspect is all too seldom stressed. To the part-time real estate operator, whether tobacco planter of the early Tidewater or wheat farmer of the pre-World War Middle Border, the frontier as a safety valve against agricultural bankruptcy has always made perfect sense.

"What?" is, of course, the crucial question. It has always been difficult to ask it, if only because it has never seemed very important to discover a working, functional definition of "political democracy." "Democracy" is alluded to, invoked, celebrated, its collapse predicted daily. Democracy, in our traditions, has rich connections with the yeoman farmer (involving, as it were, "grass roots" and freedom from the urban banker); it is at once individualistic and coöperative, equalitarian and fraternal; hand in hand with stout self-reliance goes the civic exercise of universal suffrage. For most of our daily purposes democracy is a synonym for all that is virtuous in our social traditions and on the public scene.

Yet it still appears that we need a *working* definition of political democracy. It should in some way account for concepts central to most traditional notions, but it should also be functional, in the sense that its terms may be tested. Its focus should undoubtedly be upon participation—participation by large numbers of people in decisions which affect their lives. But it should be real, not ceremonial, participation. The extent of the suffrage would not be its most dependable measure, any more than the casting of one man's vote is the quickest way of influencing a political decision. Awareness of the community's affairs should have something to do with it, but only to the extent that individuals themselves feel capable of interfering in those affairs. Would this be to the community's best interest? Often, but not always; yet here we are not required to think of democracy as a community virtue. Some have, indeed, called it a national vice.

Suppose that political democracy be regarded as a manipulative attitude toward government, shared by large numbers of people. Let it be thought of as a wide participation in public affairs, a diffusion of leadership, a widespread sense of personal competence to make a difference. Under what conditions have such things typically occurred? When have the energies of the people been most engaged? What pushes a man into public activity? It appears that nothing accomplishes this more quickly than the formation of a settlement.

Our national experience, indeed, furnishes us much material for a hypothesis. Political democracy evolves most quickly during the initial stages of setting up a new community; it is seen most dramatically while the process of organization and the solving of basic problems are still crucial; it is observed to best advantage when this flow of basic problems is met by a homogeneous population. Now "homogeneity" should here involve two parallel sorts of facts: not only a similar level of social and economic status and aspirations among the people, but most particularly a lack of, or failure of, a traditional, ready-made structure of leadership in the community. A simple test of the effectiveness of structured leadership is its ability to command acceptance and respect.[8]

With a heavy flow of community problems, in short, and without such a structure of natural leadership, democracy presents itself much less as a bright possibility than as a brutal necessity. The very incomprehensibility of alternatives has always made it most unlikely that an American should see this. But Tocqueville saw it instantly. "In aristocratic societies," he wrote, "men do not need to combine in order to act, because they are strongly held together."

... Among democratic nations, on the contrary, all the citizens are independent and feeble; they can hardly do anything by themselves and none of them can oblige his fellow men to lend him their assistance. They all, therefore, fall into a state of incapacity, if they do not learn voluntarily to help each other.[9]

Before turning to history for a trial of this so simple yet interesting idea, let us set it in yet another dimension by examining a series of extremely important findings in contemporary sociology. Robert K. Merton has conducted a study, whose results are soon to be made public, of social behavior in public housing communities.[10] A theory of political democracy which would meet all our criteria may be derived from Mr. Merton's work; there is little that we shall say from a historical viewpoint which has not already, in a present-day setting, been thoroughly documented by him.

He and his associates have observed two public housing projects, one being designated as "Craftown" and the other as "Hilltown." Craftown, located in southern New Jersey, administered by the Federal Public Housing Authority, and set up originally to house warworkers, was much the more active and interesting of the two. The key to the activity there was a "time of troubles" in the initial stages of the community's existence. The people who settled in Craftown ("homogeneous" in the

8 "Not only is leadership limited objectively by given patterns of authority but the will to lead of the leader is vitiated if what he stands for cannot command a following.... [The leader's] effectiveness in no small measure derives from how much loyalty he can count upon." Jeremiah F. Wolpert, "Toward a Sociology of Authority," in Alvin W. Gouldner, ed., *Studies in Leadership* (New York, 1950), p. 681. This is the point made by Guglielmo Ferrero in his discussion of "legitimacy"; see *The Principles of Power,* trans. by Theodore Jaeckel (New York, 1942), p. 23.

9 *Democracy in America* (Oxford Galaxy Ed., New York, 1946), p. 320.

10 The study's working title is *Patterns of Social Life: Explorations in the Sociology of Housing,* by Robert K. Merton, Patricia S. West and Marie Jahoda. We are greatly indebted to Mr. Merton for his generosity in allowing us to examine the material in manuscript.

sense that a majority were employed in nearby shipyards and defense plants) were immediately faced by a staggering series of problems of a fundamental sort, affecting the entire community. These bore on law and order, government, public health, housing, education, religion, municipal services, transportation, and markets. Slovenly construction had resulted in leaky roofs, flooded cellars, and warped floors. There were no school, no churches, no electricity, no community hall, no grocery stores. Bus service was irregular and the nearest depot was a mile away. There were no hard-surfaced roads or sidewalks and much of the area was flooded during the rainy season. There was a wave of vandalism and no organization for its suppression. There was an epidemic of poliomyelitis. There were no municipal services of any kind; the environing township did not want to assume the cost of such services and by legislative action Craftown was gerrymandered into an independent township—which meant that it had to set up its own institutions for government and for the maintenance of law and order.

Craftown did have a ready-made structure, as it were, of leadership; its affairs were under the administration of a federal bureau, the Federal Public Housing Authority, and handled by a resident manager and staff. Under stable conditions such a structure would have been adequate for most of the community's basic concerns. Yet the problems in Craftown were so overwhelming, so immediate, so pressing, that the residents could not afford to wait upon the government for action. They were therefore forced to behave in that same pattern which so fascinated Tocqueville: they were driven to "the forming of associations." Mass meetings, committees and subcommittees were organized, a township board was set up, officials of great variety were elected; a volunteer police force, fire department and local court were established, with residents serving as constables, firemen and judges. A coöperative store soon came into existence. An ambulance squad, a nursery and child care center, and a great variety of organizations devoted to community needs made their appearance during this critical period. Pressures brought upon the bus company and the government agencies resulted in the improvement of transportation, the paving of streets, repair of houses, drainage of swamps, and the erection of buildings for education, worship and other functions of the community.

This experience resulted in an extraordinary level of public participation by people who for the most part had never had previous political experience; and it produced a political life charged with the utmost energy. Many jobs were created by the crisis—by the flow of problems—and they had to be handled by someone; many rôles were created, someone had to fill them. The key was necessity. Persons who had previously never needed to be concerned with politics[11] now found themselves developing a familiarity with institutions, acquiring a sense of personal competence to manipulate them, to make things happen, to make a difference. Thus the coin of necessity had its other side: there were compensations for the individual. With many offices to be filled, large numbers of people found themselves contending for them; the prestige connected with officeholding, the sense of energy and power involved in decision-making, became for the first time a possibility, a reality, an exploitable form of self-expression.[12]

Now Hilltown, in contrast to Craftown, may be regarded as something of a control case. Many factors present in Craftown were present here—but a crucial one was missing. Hilltown, like Craftown, was a public housing project in an industrial area; it too was managed by the Federal Public Housing Authority; its population was likewise characterized by "homogeneity"—insofar as that involved a similar level of social and economic status among the residents. What Hilltown did not experience was a "time of troubles." Unlike Craftown, it was well planned and operated, it was not faced with a failure of municipal services, it was not confronted by lack of transportation, stores, electricity, or facilities for education and religion. The residents, to be sure, had their individual problems—occasional badly fitting doors and the like—but they were not of a community nature, not of a sort that made community organization seem indispensable. Widespread public participation in community affairs was never needed there, and it never took place. Sporadic efforts toward the establishment of a council, the election of officers, and the setting up of community activities aroused little interest and met with failure. The original structure of leadership—the federal agency and its local office—proved quite adequate for the handling of Hilltown's concerns, it was never seriously challenged, and it required no supplementation by resident activity.[13] "Democracy," in short, was unnecessary there.

[11] Mr. Merton offers various graphs and tables to establish this. In one of them, 88 per cent of the early comers were found to be more highly active in Craftown organizations than in their former communities; only 8 per cent had had the same degree of participation in both communities.

[12] Two other communities, each of which underwent a similar experience in similar circumstances, were Park Forest, Illinois, and Shanks Village, New York, described in William H. Whyte, Jr., "The Future, c/o Park Forest," *Fortune,* June 1953, pp. 126–31, 186–96; and Bernard Horn, "Collegetown: A Study of Transient Student Veteran Families in a Temporary Housing Community" (unpub. M.A. thesis, Columbia University, 1948).

[13] Thus "homogeneity"—in the total sense which we have given that concept—did not exist in Hilltown. There was a clear distinction—to extend the analogy—between "the rulers and the ruled."

One more reference to the Craftown episode should be made, in order to note two interesting subsidiary consequences of this problem-solving experience, this wide participation, this sense of individual competence spread among such great numbers. One was a close supervision of the officialdom which the Craftowners themselves had created—and a lesser degree of respect for it[14] than had apparently been the case in their previous communities. The other was a body of shared "traditions," with a common vocabulary, rich with meaning, whereby the experience might be relived and reshared. Although the level of activity was never as high in later times as it was in the beginning—the problems by then had been solved—the intensity of the "time of troubles" served to link the "pioneers" and the later-comers together by a kind of verbal bond. Talking about it was important: once this experience had been undergone, it was not lost. In such a usable fund of tradition, resources for meeting a new crisis, should one appear, would remain always available.[15]

How might such a contemporary model square with the pioneer frontier? No sorcery of forest or prairie could materialize the democrat, yet it should be safe to guess that the periods of wholesale migration to the West forced a setting in which such an experience as that just outlined had to be enacted a thousand times over: an experience crucial in the careers of millions of Americans. Frederick Jackson Turner has stated the undeniable fact—that an organic connection exists between American democracy and the American frontier. The insight is his. But

---

[14] These facts seem to go together. An illuminating Craftown anecdote concerns a woman who was fined $5 by one of the locally elected judges for letting her dog run loose. "Well, that's just like working men," she declared. "A rich man wouldn't be so interested in money.... I don't think any working man should mix in politics. I think a man that has money is better able to rule." It is at the same time quite possible to imagine the same woman making *this* statement (also recorded at Craftown): "I never voted in the city for mayor or things like that. I just didn't have the interest. In the city they get in anyhow and there's nothing you can do about it. Here they're more connected with people."

[15] Mr. Merton points out that this phenomenon was taken as a concrete cultural fact by Malinowski, who called it "phatic communion." "Each utterance is an act serving the direct aim of binding hearer to speaker by a tie of some social sentiment or other... language appears to us in this function not as an instrument of reflection but as a mode of action." Bronislaw Malinowski, in C. K. Ogden and I. A. Richards, *The Meaning of Meaning* (New York, 1923), pp. 478–79. The connection between this kind of thing and the folklore of democracy is seldom appreciated: consider, for example, the typical American reaction to disaster—the ease with which the traditions of the frontier are converted into spontaneous organizational techniques for coping with the emergency. The community response to the tornado which struck Flint, Michigan, in 1953 provides a perfect case in point; examples like it are numberless.

Turner never offered a conceptual framework by which it might be tested. We are proposing such a model; it involves the establishment of new communities. Its variables are a period of problem-solving and a homogeneous population whose key factor is the lack of a structure of leadership. We shall test these terms in various ways by the examination of three frontiers, each of which should illustrate a special dimension of the argument. They are the Old Northwest, the Southwest frontier of Alabama and Mississippi, and the Puritan frontier of Massachusetts Bay.

2

"The frontier," to Turner and his followers, as well as to most others, seemed almost automatically to mean the Old Northwest—the "valley of democracy"—whose settlement took place during the first third of the nineteenth century. To discover why the connection should be made so naturally, let us select this region, with its key states Ohio, Indiana and Illinois, as the first frontier to be observed.

The chronicles of these states abound with reminiscences of the pioneer; close upon them in the county histories came haphazard statistics which proudly mark progress from howling wilderness to fat countryside and prosperous burgs. Between these points come many a crisis, many a relished success. We should consider not the solitary drifters, the Daniel Boones, but the thousand isolated communities each of which in its own way must have undergone its "time of troubles." There, the basic problems of organization were intimately connected with matters of life and death. They were problems to be met only by the united forces of the community. Think of the basic question of housing itself, and how its solution was elevated by necessity, throughout the Old Northwest, to the status of institution and legend: the cabin-raising.[16] The clearing of the forest and the manner in which this was accomplished gave an idiom to our politics: the logrolling.[17] Defense against the Indians required that the experience of the Marietta settlers, forced to raise their own militia

16 "When the time comes, and the forces collect together, a captain is appointed, and the men divide into proper sections, and [are] assigned to their several duties." Henry B. Curtis, "Pioneer Days in Central Ohio," *O. State Arch. and Hist. Pubs.,* I, 245 (1887). Almost any state or county history or pioneer memoir will refer to or describe this familiar social function; see, e.g., William T. Utter, *The Frontier State* (Columbus, 1942), pp. 138, 139–41; W. C. Howells, *Recollections of Life in Ohio* (Cincinnati, 1895), pp. 144–51; etc., etc.

17 There is a vivid contemporary description of a combined logrolling and political rally in Baynard Rush Hall, *The New Purchase,* James A. Woodburn, ed. (Princeton, 1916), pp. 202–205. See also Logan Esarey, *History of Indiana* (Indianapolis, 1915), pp. 421, 425–26.

in the 1790s, be repeated elsewhere many times over at least until after the War of 1812.[18] And there was the question of law and order: the traveler Elias Fordham, stopping one night in 1818 at a cabin near Paoli, Indiana, found himself in the midst of preparations by the citizenry for apprehending a gang of brigands. How often must such a scene—the formation of *ad hoc* constabularies, the administration of emergency justice—have been enacted in those days?[19]

Close behind such supreme needs came that of educating the young, which claimed an early order of concern throughout the Northwest. Traveling instructors were often employed to go from house to house; later, when the children could pass through the forest without danger, they might gather for a time at one of the settlers' houses until community labor could be assembled to put up a school.[20] The demand for religion was little less urgent; first came the circuit rider to a house or barn designated for worship; denominational differences might then have to be submerged in the erection of a common chapel until each sect could build its own meeting house.[21] Even problems of public health, with no hospitals and few doctors, had to be solved occasionally under heroic

[18] Beverly W. Bond, Jr., *The Civilization of the Old Northwest* (New York, 1934), pp. 249, 268, 351, 357. "The shrill whistle of the fife and the beat of the drum, calling to arms for the defense of their countrymen, was answered by many a gray-haired sire and many a youthful pioneer." H. W. Chadwick, comp., *Early History of Jackson County* (Brownstown, Ind., 1943), p. 14. The War of 1812 in the Northwest, particularly in Ohio, had as much or more to do with hostile Indians as with the British, and defense was typically handled by the raising of local militia. See "Ohio and the War of 1812," ch. iv in Utter, *op. cit.*, pp. 88–119.

[19] Elias P. Fordham, *Personal Narrative,* ed. by Frederic Ogg (Cleveland, 1906), pp. 154–55; Hall, *op. cit.*, p. 196; Charles Francis Ingals, "A Pioneer in Lee County, Illinois," ed. by Lydia Colby, *Ill. State Hist. Soc. Jour.*, XXVI, 281 (Oct. 1933).

[20] "As soon as conditions were favorable the pioneers of the neighborhood constructed a rude cabin schoolhouse.... There was no school revenue to be distributed, so each voter himself had to play the part of the builder. The neighbors divided themselves into choppers, hewers, carpenters, and masons. Those who found it impossible to report for duty might pay an equivalent in nails, boards, or other materials. The man who neither worked nor paid was fined thirty-seven and one-half cents a day." William F. Vogel, "Home Life in Early Indiana," *Ind. Mag. of Hist.,* X, 297 (Sept. 1914).

[21] The "interfaith chapel" was invariably the early solution to this problem (there was one in Craftown, also in Park Forest and Shanks Village). "The first church ... was free to all denominations, and here, for miles and miles came the pioneer and family on the Sabbath day to worship God." Chadwick, *op. cit.*, p. 35. See also Vogel, *loc. cit.*, p. 291; Morris Birkbeck, *Letters from Illinois* (London, 1818), p. 23; John D. Barnhardt, Jr., "The Rise of the Methodist Episcopal Church in Illinois from the Beginning to the Year 1832," *Ill. State Hist. Soc. Jour.,* XII, 149–217 (July 1919).

circumstances. When cholera struck Jacksonville, Illinois, in 1833, the cabinetmaker John Henry boarded thirteen persons at his house for three weeks, supervised a crew of assistants in the building of coffins for each of the fifty-five dead, personally visited each house of sickness, took fifty-three corpses to the burying ground, and, assisted by two farmers, a blacksmith, a shoemaker, a brickmaker and a carpenter, dug the graves and interred the dead—a series of functions quite above the line of normal business.[22]

Now as these communities toiled through the process of stabilizing their affairs, what effect must such an experience have had upon the individuals themselves, exposed as they were to the sudden necessity of making great numbers of basic and vital decisions, private and public? With thousands of ambitious men, predominantly young men[23] looking for careers, pouring into vast unsettled tracts, setting up new communities, and being met with all the complex hazards of such an adventure, the scope and variety of new political experience was surely tremendous. A staggering number of public rôles was thrust forward during such an enterprise, far too many to wait upon the appearance of seasoned leaders. With the organization of each wilderness county and pioneer township, the roster of offices to be filled and operated was naturally a perfect blank (how long had it been since this was so in Philadelphia?); somebody, willing or unwilling, must be found to fill each one.

Whether farmers, lawyers, merchants, artisans, or even men of means, the "leading citizens" in county after county were typically men of no previous political experience.[24] For example, there was Morgan County, Illinois. Its first settler was Seymour Kellogg, who brought his wife and seven children from New York State, was made a commissioner at the first election and shortly afterward became justice of the peace. Murray McConnel, who read law on his farm at odd hours and became Jackson-

[22] C. H. Rammelkamp, ed., "The Memoirs of John Henry: A Pioneer of Morgan County," *Ill. State Hist. Soc. Jour.*, XVIII, 55 (Apr. 1925).

[23] In a history of the town of Lancaster, Ohio, which was founded in 1800, there is a longish series of biographical sketches of its "leading pioneers." Twenty-seven of these sketches concern settlers who arrived within the first ten years of the town's existence and who held office, and of these 27, age data are given for 15. For what such a haphazard sample is worth, the average age of this group at the date of the town's founding was twenty-four. C. M. L. Wiseman, *Centennial History of Lancaster* (Lancaster, 1898).

[24] The county histories make every effort to secure the immortality of their leading citizens by reciting as many of their accomplishments as are known. Thus if the biographical sketches make no mention of public office held elsewhere, it should be safe to assume that at least in most of the cases their civic careers began in the new settlement.

ville's first lawyer, was forthwith sent to the legislature (though unwillingly) and later served the community in various other capacities. Jacksonville's first cabinetmaker, the aforementioned John Henry (scarcely literate), was drawn into politics immediately, and before his career was over had been an assemblyman, state senator and member of Congress, not to say superintendent of the local insane asylum and patron of learning to the Female Academy. The first printer there was Josiah Lucas, who had arrived from Maryland ("without friends") and established a paper with local support. Championing Henry Clay, he was shortly in a maelstrom of politics, and the experience thus gained netted him a postmastership to the House of Representatives and "many offices both civil and military," culminating in a minister's post in Europe.[25] Variations on this typical pattern are to be found in county after county in the Old Northwest.[26]

What we exhibit here are the elements of a simple syllogism; the first settlers anywhere, no matter who they were or how scanty their prior political experience, were the men who had to be the first officeholders. This meant that the pioneers, in the very process of establishing and organizing their settlements, were faced with a burden of decision-making disproportionate to that exacted of the later-comers. The political lore, the manipulative skills, which must have been acquired in that process should somehow be kept in the foreground when judging the ferocious vitality, the extravagant energy, of early political life in the Old Northwest.

Inasmuch as many new political rôles were being created by the needs of this new society, both necessity and opportunities for political careers might more and more be seen reflected in the long lists of candidates and high level of participation. In Hamilton County, Ohio, there was an election of delegates to the constitutional convention of 1802, and for ten openings there were ninety-four candidates—twenty-six of them re-

---

[25] Frank S. Heinl, "The First Settlers in Morgan County," *Ill. State Hist. Soc. Jour.*, XVIII, 76–87 (Apr. 1925); Rammelkamp, *loc. cit.*, pp. 39–40 and *passim;* George Murray McConnel, "Some Reminiscences of My Father, Murray McConnel," *Ill. State Hist. Soc. Jour.*, XVIII, 89–100 (Apr. 1925).

[26] The seemingly fabulous Wesley Park—who was the first settler at Auburn, Indiana, and DeKalb County's first sheriff, road commissioner, road supervisor, jail commissioner, and clerk of the first county board—was actually a figure quite typical. We see blacksmith-judges and carpenter-sheriffs everywhere. See S. W. Widney, "Pioneer Sketches of DeKalb County," *Ind. Mag. of Hist.*, XXV, 116, 125–26, 128 (June 1929). "Few of the officials prior to 1850 [in Parke County, Indiana] were men of education. For years it was the custom to elect a coroner from among the stalwart blacksmiths. . . ." Maurice Murphy, "Some Features of the History of Parke County," *Ind. Mag. of Hist.*, XII, 151 (June 1916).

ceiving from 121 to 1,635 votes apiece.[27] The personal canvass, the practice of hawking one's political appeal from door to door, not generally assumed to have entered American politics until the Jacksonian era, was familiar in the Northwest well before 1824. A cabin-dweller's effusion in the *Illinois Intelligencer* of July 1, 1818, describes how hosts of candidates, at the approach of an election, would descend upon him with whisky, trinkets for the children, compliments, and grand promises.

> But what most rarely does my good wife please,
> Is that the snot nos'd baby gets a buss![28]

"And every body," wrote Baynard Rush Hall of Indiana's New Purchase, "expected at some time to be a candidate for something; or that his uncle would be; or his cousin, or his cousin's wife's cousin's friend would be; so that every body and every body's relations, and every body's relation's friends, were for ever electioneering." Even boys verging on manhood were "feared, petted, courted and cajoled."[29] Such arts of cajolery could be appropriate and necessary only to a society in which officials were watched far more closely and respected far less than was the magistrate of Boston or the justice of the peace in Fairfax County, Virginia. Hall, an Easterner of refinement, reflected with deep distaste that if "eternal vigilance" were the price of liberty it was well paid in the New Purchase, the "sovereign people" there being "the most uncompromising task masters": "Our officers all, from Governor down to a deputy constable's deputy and fence-viewer's clerk's first assistant, were in the direct gift of the people. We even elected magistrates, clerks of court, and the judges presiding and associate!"[30]

Thus the extraordinary animation with which the people of Craftown flung themselves into political activity may be seen richly paralleled in the life of the Old Northwest. Every militia muster, every cabin-raising, scow-launching, shooting match, and logrolling was in itself a political assembly where leading figures of the neighborhood made speeches, read certificates, and contended for votes. Sometimes at logrollings rival candidates would take charge of opposing sections of workers, fitness for office having much to do with whose group disposed of its logs first. The enterprising farmer understood, it is said, that this political energy could

---

[27] Bond, *op. cit.*, pp. 102, 124.

[28] Quoted in Solon J. Buck, *Illinois in 1818* (Springfield, 1917), p. 260. Consider again the power of "phatic communion": in the 1952 presidential election the governor of that same great state of Illinois might have been seen blandly kissing babies.

[29] Hall, *New Purchase*, p. 178.

[30] *Ibid.*, pp. 177, 200–201.

be exploited at its height about a month before election time, and tried to schedule his logrolling accordingly.[31]

Our concept of political democracy, it may be remembered, involved a homogeneous population. Can it be asserted that these early Northwest communities were characterized by such a population? There is striking evidence that both attributes of "homogeneity"—a similar level of aspiration and status, and conditions rendering impossible a prior structure of leadership—were widely present here, just as they were in Craftown. A leading symptom of this may be found in the land arrangements. Beverly Bond has made calculations, based on lists of lands advertised for delinquent taxes, as to typical holdings in the Northwest about 1812, and concludes that the "average farm" at that time was probably less than 250 acres.[32] Though such tentative statistics are embarrassing in themselves, the limiting conditions which make them plausible are clear enough—uniform conditions not only permitting but forcing a reduced scale of holdings. Much has been made of large engrossments of land by speculators in the Northwest Territory, yet before the admission of Ohio in 1803, and many years before that of Indiana and Illinois, it was apparent to all that the day of the great land magnate was at an end. His operations were doomed by the very techniques of settlement and by the measures taken by the settlers themselves to thwart his designs.

Despite large quantities of government land on the market, much of which was bought by speculators, the attraction of choice locations led regularly to settlement in advance of purchase—squatting, in short— especially when sales were delayed, as they often were. Thousands of such petty *faits accomplis* all over the Northwest frontier could hardly be reversed,[33] no matter how powerful the petitioners, and the terms of sale, reflected in a series of land laws ever more generous,[34] were but one indication of such a state of things. An even more formidable token of

[31] Vogel, *loc. cit.*, p. 309. "Our candidates certainly sweat for their expected honours," Hall remarks. ". . . Nay, a very few hundreds of rival and zealous candidates would, in a year or so, if judiciously driven under proper task masters, clear a considerable territory." *Op. cit.*, p. 205.

[32] *Civilization of the Old Northwest*, pp. 331–32.

[33] Buck, *op. cit.*, pp. 47, 54–55. "The situation was so serious that the matter was taken up with the secretary of state, and the president issued a proclamation directing that after a certain day in March, 1816, all squatters on the public lands should be removed. Against the execution of this proclamation, Benjamin Stephenson, the delegate from Illinois territory, protested vigorously. . . . The marshal of the Illinois territory actually made preparations to remove the intruders; but the secretary of the treasury wrote him on May 11, 1816, recommending 'a prudent and conciliatory course'; and nothing seems to have been accomplished." *Ibid.*, p. 54.

[34] Notably the Congressional legislation of 1796, 1800 and 1804.

doom to the great absentee holder was revealed in the tax rates levied on unimproved land by the early legislatures. While all these future states were still under one territorial assembly, that body at its first session passed a law taxing three grades of land—a law which was only the first of several, each more severe than its predecessor, consecrated to the mission of breaking up large unimproved tracts held by nonresidents. Increasing powers were given to local sheriffs presiding over the sales of delinquent holdings.[35] This meant that in practice the large speculator, forced as he was to pay cash for these tracts, must effect relatively quick turnovers in a buyer's market: there was really plenty of land to be had and the costs of holding it for a rise were becoming higher year by year.[36] For the rest, with labor costs uniformly high and with a population whose average resources, either in land or in liquid wealth, must initially be moderate, the great farm on the Southern model could never be a widespread reality. What this particularly indicates is that a land-holding élite—with all the traditional functions, social and political, that such an élite would certainly exercise—was rendered quite out of the question. The leadership of *this* society would have to be recruited on manifestly different terms.

Who was it, then, that organized the pressure for these land acts; who goaded the federal Congress into passing them; who connived in the legislature; who wrote the tax laws? Who indeed but the frontier politician who kissed the "snot nos'd baby" in that lonely cabin? He well understood how his majorities depended upon the zeal with which he and his friends could manipulate the government on their constituents' behalf. Their problems were concrete; the guaranteeing of preëmption rights was an urgency of the topmost order; this was the primary stimulus which forced the tax laws, the universal suffrage clauses in the state constitutions, and the Congressional land legislation. The "sovereign people" of the Old Northwest was a "most uncompromising task master" to its servants. Symbolic of the future was the case of William Henry Harrison, to whom fell the unhappy office of mediating, so to speak, between "the people" and the Northwest's greatest land speculator, John Cleves Symmes. Harrison, as territorial delegate to Congress, was successful in bringing about the Land Act of 1800 in the interests of the settlers but a dismal failure in his efforts to get justice for Symmes, his father-in-law, whose vast holdings in Ohio were crumbling away in an avalanche of claims and judgments. The unfortunate Symmes was no match for

[35] Bond, *op. cit.*, pp. 337–38.

[36] A special situation in Illinois added to the difficulty of amassing large absentee holdings; actual sales of public land could not begin there until 1814 owing to the perplexity of the French claims, and the result was a growing population of squatters and slim pickings for speculators. Buck, *op. cit.*, p. 44.

a thousand ruthless frontier manipulators.[37] The democracy of the Northwest would be that of the squatter, the frontier business man, and, no doubt, that of the *small* speculator.

Granted that a structure of *landed* political leadership was impossible, might not a different species of élite appear, say an élite of lawyers? It is true that admission to the bar in the early days was a virtual guarantee of political advancement. But the stability of any such structure must be certified by some recognized assurance of self-perpetuation. The very recruitment patterns, the conditions under which political preferment had to be gained and held in the Northwest, should make us think twice before considering the great majority of lawyers in politics there as constituting such a structure. Every lawyer was literally on his own. It was the desperate need for wits and talent on the frontier that gave him his chance, a chance renewed by the community as long as he continued to deliver. Here the rôles of patron and client are reversed; it is difficult for a "ruling class" to establish and guarantee tenure under such conditions. Murray McConnel, the self-made lawyer of Jacksonville, was once warned that his politically ambitious young clerk—Stephen Douglas—was using him as a steppingstone. "No matter," he replied, "his ambition will probably prove of more worth to the nation than all our modesty."[38] This was about the only kind of laying on of hands possible in the Northwest: the embodiment of success, of frontier virtue, was the self-made man.

What we have done so far is to discover a kind of "primitive" level of the frontier experience, a level at which a vast flow of problems forced a high degree of participation in the making of decisions, an acute pitch of political awareness among the settlers. The traditions of the pioneers remind us that this experience was not lost. An egalitarian tone was set, and ceremonial observances by which the experience was reinvoked and reshared made their way into the social habits of the people. Stephen Douglas, for one, understood its obligations, and by stopping at Geneva on one of his county canvasses to assist at a logrolling he was performing a symbolic act.[39]

[37] Symmes had sold, in advance, a number of tracts outside his 1792 patent, expecting to take them up at 66⅔ cents an acre. Subsequently the price rose to $2.00, on which Symmes could not possibly make good. An original contract for 1,000,000 acres had been partly paid for in Continental certificates, and the patent of 1792 gave him title to those lands for which he had paid. Neither his influence nor that of Harrison was ever able to guarantee the entire claim of 1,000,000 acres. Meanwhile the Scioto Company had completely collapsed, and the representations of the Illinois and Wabash companies met with even less success than did those of Symmes.

[38] McConnel, *loc. cit.*, p. 95.

[39] Heinl, *loc. cit.*, p. 84. See also *supra*, note 15.

Now another frontier was being developed at this same period in the Southwest, the frontier of Alabama and Mississippi, where scenes more or less similar were enacted. Yet we are unable to speak of "democracy" there with quite the same lack of ambiguity as we may with the Northwest. One reason for this is that throughout the Northwest the "problem-solving" experience did not generally stop with the taming of the savages and the establishment of law and order, but was continued, and indeed more or less perpetuated, on another level.

This second level of experience may be called that of town life. Let us remember that our focus has been fixed upon the *community* character of political democracy, involving a setting in which the people are close enough together to make common efforts possible, and a social texture thick enough to make it not only feasible but crucial to organize for a variety of objects. It is true enough that the basis of most such settlements was rural agriculture. But it is undoubtedly true as well that the ease with which the basic agrarian experience flowed into that of commercial small-urban enterprise was much greater and more natural in the Northwest than in the Southwest. The primitive, "agrarian" level of democracy is the one from which we have drawn democracy's folklore, a folklore still appropriate enough for our ceremonial. But it has been chronically difficult for our serious thought to go very far beyond it. The very vision of "grass roots democracy," with its herbivorous overtones, is itself a reproach to an urban culture to which it no longer seems to apply.[40]

Yet we should not feel that there is actually any paradox. Indeed; there are formidable reasons for concluding that the development of American small-town enterprise (and by extension, of urban capitalism) is most centrally—organically—connected with that of American political democracy.[41]

[40] Thurman Arnold in his *Folklore of Capitalism* (New Haven and London, 1937) makes a parallel point in suggesting that the "traditions" of American business have been derived from a primitive phase in its development; Richard Hofstadter, in a forthcoming work on Populism and Progressivism, notes the same interesting fact with respect to our agriculture. These writers in each case stress the conceptual difficulties which the "myths" of an earlier stage impose upon the realities of a later, much-advanced one. Mr. Hofstadter metaphorically characterizes this polarity as "soft" and "hard." It might be added that a humane view of American culture would recognize a need, on the part of both the business man and the farmer, for "folklore": the need of each for dramatizing to himself his own rôle, for maintaining his self-respect.

[41] For years the late Professor Schumpeter maintained a theory of this sort. "History," he wrote, "clearly confirms this suggestion: historically, the modern democracy rose along with capitalism, and in actual connection with it. But the same holds true for democratic practice: democracy in the sense of our theory of competitive leadership presided over the process of political and institutional

Watching the organization of the Old Northwest, county by county, we are struck by something which is not duplicated on our Southern frontier: the appearance of teeming numbers of *small towns*. By this we mean, not the post-office hamlet with its fifty souls, but rather the market center which had two hundred or more people and was struggling to become bigger. It was a development quite automatic and logical in the Northwest. Cheap land and dear labor set fatal limits on wide-scale land engrossment for purposes other than speculation (and we have already seen the limits set on speculation), so that, for agriculture, subsistence and market farming, rather than extensive raising of staples, would largely be the rule in the '30s and '40s. It was toward the town that an increasingly market-conscious population was orienting itself, not toward the plantation, nor to the cosmopolitan port city, nor yet to the crossroads courthouse. Large amounts of money, if and when made in the Northwest, had to come from commerce, from industrial activity, and from real estate whose value depended greatly on its nearness to or location in a town. It was unquestionably the town from which the tone of life in Ohio, Indiana and Illinois came to be taken, rather than from the agriculture in which an undoubted majority of the population was engaged. It is no exaggeration to say that there were five to six times as many such towns per capita here as in Alabama or Mississippi.[42]

The town, becoming the natural focus of exchange for goods and services in the Northwest, must thus inexorably be the focus of politics

---

change by which the bourgeoisie reshaped, and from its own point of view rationalized, the social and political structure that preceded its ascendancy: the democratic method was the political tool of that reconstruction." Joseph Schumpeter, *Capitalism, Socialism, and Democracy* (New York, 1947), pp. 296–97.

[42] The very gaps in available statistics are dramatic. We have no early figures for the Southwest, but by 1853 there were in Alabama only thirty towns with a population of over 200 and only twenty-nine in Mississippi. On the other hand as early as 1833 Indiana, with less than one-half Alabama's 1853 population, had seventy-seven such towns, and Illinois, with one-fifth the 1853 population of Alabama, had thirty-four. By 1847, when Indiana's population had reached the 1853 level of Alabama, it had 156 towns whose population exceeded 200. If complete figures were available for towns of over 500 population the difference would be even more striking: while towns of this size were quite common in the Northwest, they were, aside from the port cities and state capitals, very rare in Alabama and Mississippi. As early as 1821 Ohio, with a population of 581,434, had sixty-one towns with a population of over 200, twenty-nine of 500 or more, and *twenty-two* of over a thousand. J. D. B. DeBow, *Statistical View of the United States . . . being a Compendium of the Seventh Census . . .* (Washington, 1854); John Scott, *Indiana Gazetteer* (Indianapolis, 1833); J. M. Peck, *A Gazetteer of Illinois* (Jacksonville, 1834); E. Chamberlain, *Indiana Gazetteer* (Indianapolis, 1850); John Kilbourn, *Ohio Gazetteer* (Columbus, 1821).

as well; this fact on the very face of it would mean a faster tempo of political life than on the rural countryside. Things were less simple in the town; the organizational needs were more involved; there were more functions to perform, more offices to fill. But what was it that so energized the Northwest town, what sustained this tempo, what made its democracy *real?* It was the fact that every town was a promotion.

The bright young man of talent and enterprise in the Northwest— unlike his opposite number in Alabama—naturally gravitated to the town; it was there that his future lay; rôles in politics or business were enacted from there rather than from rural strongholds. In the Northwest the typical success story of the young man with wits or money, or both, does not show him accumulating baronial acres for the cultivation of profitable staple crops. Instead, if it shows him buying up choice lands—and oftener than not it does—it is with quite different designs in view, designs centering on the development of town sites. It was estimated that during the boom years 1835, 1836 and 1837 over 500 new towns were laid out in Illinois alone.[43] The energetic Wesley Park, first settler at Auburn, Indiana, besides filling many local offices, besides using his cabin as hotel, jail, church and courthouse, had as a matter of course personally platted the town. He had done so, as had all Northwest town planners, to increase the value of his real estate and future business prospects.[44] But there was an essential difference in type between this petty-urban speculator and the speculator who engrossed vast cotton lands and held them for a price rise. The distinction was between the monopolist and the promoter.[45]

It was the promotion which gave the tone to the entire life of the town,

[43] William V. Pooley, *The Settlement of Illinois from 1830 to 1850* (Madison, 1908), p. 564.

[44] In 1836, lots in Peoria sold as high as $100 per front foot while good neighboring farm land was still to be had at the standard price of $1.25 an acre. R. Carlyle Buley, *The Old Northwest: Pioneer Period* (Indianapolis, 1950), II, 116.

[45] This is very clear from an illuminating survey made by James W. Silver of land operations in Tate and Tippah counties, Mississippi, between 1836 and 1861. Most impressive in his findings are (1) the huge amounts of land in which the successful speculator had to deal, and (2) the lengths of time that these men customarily held their land before selling it. In these two counties alone, 337,000 acres were held by single investors, eight of whom held between 3,000 and 4,000 acres, six holding from 4,000 to 5,000 acres, four from 5,000 to 6,000, and three between 6,000 and 7,000; one owned between 10,000 and 15,000 acres, two between 15,000 and 20,000, and one over 25,000. Averages were struck for thirty-one individual speculators owning a total of 197,376.5 acres at an investment of $267,382.19 with profits of $244,824.24. But the average length of time held was *18.6 years;* the profit must thus be figured in terms not of quick killings but of average annual return. For a majority this came to less than 5 per cent. James W. Silver, "Land Speculation Profits in the Chickasaw Cession," *Jour. of South. Hist.,* X, 84–92 (Feb. 1944). This may be called "speculation," but it was speculation on an order quite different from that typically occurring in the Old Northwest.

and most particularly to its politics, which meant that the placation and "cajolery" so displeasing to Baynard Rush Hall in the New Purchase would become, so to speak, universal in the town. Everyone understood that success must depend upon the town's prosperity, that it must be advertised, its virtues broadcast. The town must grow—it was vital to get people there and keep them there. Capital must be attracted—it was of the essence to allure the man with money.

The result was, naturally, a torrent of problems centering in the advancement of business. It was important for the town to obtain for itself the location of the county seat. Here the promoter donated land and made large promises to the county commissioners; in Mississippi the commissioners typically had to *buy* the land for a courthouse site.[46] The population must be increased, for this meant automatic benefits, more customers; in the cotton country it might mean greater competition and a drop in cotton prices. Capital must be brought in; expansion of plant was easier and less risky in an Indiana town than it would be on an Alabama cotton plantation. The town must be made attractive; it must be a suitable place to live in; it must have stable government; lapses of law and order would be a reflection upon its peace. Schools and seminaries must be established (no general public school system would exist in Alabama or Mississippi until after the Civil War);[47] roads, bridges, canals and banks were crucial for the nourishment of the town's enterprise. Civic services, churches, facilities of every sort, were urgently demanded. And the keynote, the watchword, the trumpet call, must be Opportunity.

Without a ready-made structure of leadership, how would such a

---

[46] Here are two typical cases: Wesley Park, who in 1836 laid out the town of Auburn, Indiana, gave one third of the lots to the county, "receiving no compensation," as he piquantly admits, "but the assurance that it would be permanently the county seat." Widney, *loc. cit.,* p. 128. In that very same year, Bolivar County, one of the rich counties of the Delta, was being organized in Mississippi. The proceedings of the Board of Police (a year later) "show the acceptance of the offer of William Vick to sell five acres of land, including the overseer's residence, for the Seat of Justice," at a price of $100 an acre and $300 for the improvements. Florence Warfield Sillers and others, *History of Bolivar County, Mississippi* (Jackson, 1948), p. 12.

[47] A comparison of the two sections in 1840 with respect to primary and common schools is as follows:

	Alabama	Miss.	Ohio	Indiana	Illinois
Population	590,756	375,651	1,519,467	685,866	476,183
No. primary & common schools	659	382	5,186	1,521	1,241
Scholars in common schools	16,243	8,236	218,609	48,189	34,876

Abstracted from *Sixth Census,* U. S. Census Office (Washington, 1841).

myriad of problems be met and who would meet them? "In no country in the world," wrote Tocqueville, "has the principle of association been more successfully used, or more unsparingly applied to a multitude of different objects, than in America."[48] How familiarly do the county chronicles dwell upon mass meetings for worthy objects, upon committees for the advancement of this or that; how appropriate that John Henry and Murray McConnel should trouble themselves for the Jacksonville Lunatic Asylum, for the College, for the Female Academy. Here was a society in which the setting up of institutions was a common experience; indeed, Tocqueville thought that the typical American addressed him "as if he were addressing a meeting," and would infallibly say, "Gentlemen."[49] Everything on the balance line between politics and civic consciousness was directly related to the prosperity of the town's citizens. There was an acute general awareness of this. For instance, the business prospects of a town were much enhanced by its becoming the county seat, and a perennial feature in the history of each Northwest state was the "county seat war" in which entire communities took part. The efforts of towns to make the legislature locate or relocate the seat in their favor typically occasioned great lengths of maneuvering and often actual violence. Scarcely a county in all of Indiana failed to see one or more such "wars."[50]

The very factor of success—an accelerating population—created new enterprises and new opportunities in the Northwest town: an index might be found in the sheer numbers of small business men there in contrast to those in the Southwest.[51] It also created new problems, all of which

[48] Democracy in America, p. 109.

[49] Ibid., p. 152.

[50] In Crawford County, when the seat was first relocated, tradition says that the citizens of Fredonia went in a body to Mount Sterling and forcibly removed the records. "If the records were carried away by force," notes a chronicler, "it was only the first time; they have been carried away from each of the later county seats by force." What more excellent instance of democracy could be found than this ardent and universal participation in the concerns of the community? H. H. Pleasant, "Crawford County," Ind. Mag. of Hist., XVIII, 146 (June 1922). See also Ernest V. Shockley, "County Seats and County Seat Wars in Indiana," Ind. Mag. of Hist., X, 26 (Mar. 1914).

[51] The story is best told by the Census figures.

	Alabama	Miss.	Ohio	Indiana	Illinois
Population	590,756	375,651	1,519,467	685,866	476,183
No. persons in commerce	2,212	1,303	9,201	3,076	2,506
No. persons in mfg. & trade	7,195	4,151	66,265	20,590	13,185

Abstracted from Sixth Census (1840).

meant that talent was at the highest premium. Consider the variety of rôles, commercial and political, to be filled. There would be a rôle for the man with money looking for a place to invest it, a rôle for the business man with a heavy stake in the community (the natural organizer, the booster); there would be one for the early settler-business man who knew the scene and who knew everyone (he would be the mediator of interests, the grand master placator). And a rôle would exist for the bright young lawyer who could make connections, who could manipulate the legislature: he must get a charter for the bank, a charter for the academy; he must press for the county seat, the highway, the canal. Directly to his rear would be the entire town, pressing *him*. This dependence for success upon growth and development, this need for aggressive political representation, forced the community to seize upon whatever talent it could find and watch it closely. Those who rose in politics must continue to placate; the relation between economic welfare and politics was direct and continuing. Such a society would reward its adroitest politicians, not so much with awe and veneration[52] (their activities were too much a matter of general concern), but by reëlecting them to office: they were too badly needed to be dispensed with. Responsibility, here, meant the art of returning home with whatever a politically sensitive electorate might demand.

There is no better illustration of this complexity of political life on the local level, this intimate connection between business and politics, this variety of demand, diffusion of power, and diffusion of pressure than in the promotion of the internal improvement systems of the 1830s. Enthusiasm for improvements found expression all over the country, but the energy of the Northwest states was unmatched for subtle haggling, deep maneuvering, and grandiose objects. The "System" in each of them was like a tract of jungle, lush, overgrown, unplanned, extravagant, magnificent. In Ohio a public works program involving roads and canals at an estimated cost of $8,577,300 was coupled in 1837 with a general law for state aid in credit and subscriptions to private improvement schemes, an act variously known as the "Loan Law," the "General Improvement Law," and the "Plunder Law." The most relentless pressures from all counties lay behind the fashioning of the bill.[53] The Indiana

---

[52] Max Weber was much impressed by the later counterpart of the master placator, the American urban political boss. The boss was thoroughly responsible but not quite respectable. See *From Max Weber: Essays in Sociology,* trans. and ed. by H. H. Gerth and C. Wright Mills (New York, 1946), pp. 109–110.

[53] The Board of Public Works advised in its report "that nothing short of the extension of the canal navigation to every considerable district in the state will satisfy that public will, which justly claims that benefits conferred shall be co-

system, even more spectacular, was in 1836 embodied in a mammoth law of forty-four sections which provided for a network of roads, canals and railroads, omitting virtually no community in the state. It reflected the grand aggregate of many local pressures; the entire movement was of local rather than metropolitan origins,[54] and the interested assemblymen were involved in endless deals and logrollings.[55] The growth of the Illinois Internal Improvement Act of 1837, an imperial scheme of canals and railroads, was the result of a monster bargain. It was kindled by illuminations, bonfires and conventions of the citizenry everywhere, it was energized by the hopes of real estate speculators up and down the state, complicated by the rivalries of Springfield, Alton, Vandalia and Jacksonville over the location of the capital, and compounded by prodigious scheming and haggling in the legislature. Two master Illinois politicians, Stephen Douglas and Abraham Lincoln, were in the very midst of it.[56]

Nothing of any resemblance to this occurred in Alabama or Mississippi, though they too were seized by the internal improvements enthusiasm of the 1830s. Allowing for the probability that the river systems of these states to some extent relieved the need for wide-scale transportation schemes, it is at the same time true that political machinery there was not organized in such a way that local pressures could be anticipated and reacted to with the sensitivity so characteristic in the Northwest. Little or nothing was done there.[57]

---

extensive with the burthens imposed; and that, in those districts, where canals cannot be made, an approximation to equality should be obtained by aid in constructing roads." The warning, in short, was that there must be something for everyone. Ernest L. Bogart, *Internal Improvements and State Debt in Ohio* (New York, 1924), p. 55.

[54] "The role of local government was typically not the planning of a great system of transportation. It was an attempt to gain a favorable competitive position for the particular community...." Carter Goodrich, "Local Government Planning of Internal Improvements," *Polit. Sci. Q.*, LXVI, 442 (Sept. 1951).

[55] Esarey, *History of Indiana*, pp. 352–73.

[56] Theodore C. Pease, *The Frontier State, 1818–1848* (Springfield, 1918), pp. 194–219. Interesting unpublished material on the Illinois system exists: Alan Heimert, "The Internal Improvement Act of 1837: An Introduction to the Study of Illinois Politics in the 1830s" (M.A. thesis, Columbia University, 1950), and John Henry Krenkel, "Internal Improvements in Illinois, 1818–1848" (Ph.D. thesis, University of Illinois, 1937).

[57] The state of Mississippi sought in vain to make a modest loan of $200,000 for internal improvements, backed by its 3 per cent fund, future land grants, and the faith of the state. Dunbar Rowland, *History of Mississippi* (Chicago-Jackson, 1935), I, 553–54. Alabama likewise did next to nothing, and when the Northwest's improvement systems collapsed with the panic of 1837, the governor even congratu-

Now what was it in the Northwest that made these activities so classically democratic? It was dependence on the favor of large numbers of people in market communities where manipulation was a daily habit, dependence on a favor which must be constantly renewed. This was the process by which the "equal rights" attitude, so symbolic of the Jacksonian period, was developed: room for the aggressive young man on the make. This was the setting in which intolerance of cultural and religious differences could not be permitted to interfere with the promotion: the organizer must be free to boast of schools and churches for all.[58] And this fundamental tolerance,[59] this built-in attitude of placation, had its other side. The booster would adjust to his neighbors but would adjust to no one who tried to limit *his* activities; he would instruct his representatives but would not tolerate their instructing *him*. The balance was a delicate one and easily upset by the vicissitudes of business.

Under such conditions a prior structure of leadership, a self-perpetuating planter oligarchy, an aristocracy of money and birth, would simply have melted away. A burgeoning capitalism recognizes no prior structures, is impatient of élites, tolerates few restraints. Expressed in classical

---

lated his state for having remained inactive. As late as 1851 Alabama's Committee on Internal Improvements noted bitterly that there had been "not one serious effort on the part of the Legislature to advance the great interests of agriculture, commerce, or manufactures.... Other states are rich because they are old, but our destiny seems to be to grow old and poor together." William E. Martin, "Internal Improvements in Alabama", *Johns Hopkins Studies in Hist. and Polit. Sci.*, XX, No. 4 (1902), 40, 73.

[58] Baynard Rush Hall, the first professor at Indiana University, was unpleasantly aware of this. "With our own eyes we saw Cash! handled it with our fingers: heard it jingle with our ears! and all at once 'high larning' became as popular as common schools.... Only show that a school, an academy, a college, or, *a church,* will advance the value of town lots—bring in more customers—create a demand for beef, cloth, pepper and salt, powder and shot; then, from vulgar plebeian dealing in shoe leather, up to the American *nobleman* dealing in shops, and who retails butter and eggs, we shall hear one spontaneous voice in favour!" *New Purchase,* p. 400.

[59] This connection between *practical* tolerance and business (ceremonial "tolerance" comes later) can hardly be too much emphasized. In 1849 there was a remarkable act of cultural assimilation in Jacksonville, Illinois. In that year 130 Portuguese exiles from the island of Madeira were brought there, civic committees having undertaken to find accommodations and situations for them, and urged that in coming the exiles "would thus learn our manners, our habits (we hope our good ones only), and our way of doing business of all kinds—and become useful to themselves, and in time amalgamated with us." It was a transaction managed with great efficiency by local groups, including the ladies of Jacksonville, and was highly beneficial to all. George R. Poage, "The Coming of the Portuguese," *Ill. State Hist. Soc. Jour.*, XVIII, 100–135 (Apr. 1925).

theory this is *laissez faire;* acted out on the Illinois frontier it meant unfettered opportunity for all, careers open to talent, and a gleeful willingness to manipulate the government, starting at the local level, in any and all ways that might advance business. The principle whereby a small-town culture such as this accomplished its political needs was typically not that of *noblesse oblige,* but of the bargain. The agents were numerous, the demands constant, the haggling intense. The parallel, then, cannot be that of an élite holding sway, but rather of tradesmen maintaining a clientele.[60]

It is possible to compress virtually everything we have said about political democracy in the Old Northwest into the experience of a single county in Ohio. Let Stark County, organized in 1809, furnish that profile. There, the "primitive" level of pioneer democracy, forcing upon the settlers the burden of organizing communities and fashioning institutions, was to be seen in every township. There, the lack of seasoned leadership in Sandy township did not absolve the Hewitts, the Downings, the Van Meters, from serving as constables, sheriffs, justices of the peace, or from organizing themselves against the Indians. Nor was it possible to be fastidious in Plain township, where the uncouth Henry Friday, a paroled Hessian soldier, was the only man available for constable. (Once during a plague of locusts he had a locust pie made, "which he ate.") Rudy Bair, whose wife once threw firebrands at the wolves to protect her baby, was the first settler in Paris township; he was the first justice of the peace, a delegate to Ohio's constitutional convention, and a member of the first legislature.[61] The very profusion of public rôles during the first few years should give a key to the energy of the people who would shortly organize Canton, Massillon, Alliance and Louisville. The very first election in Lawrence township involved the naming of two justices of the peace, a clerk, a school examiner, three trustees, two overseers of the poor, two fence viewers, two appraisers of property, three supervisors, two constables, and a lister of taxables. This, multiplied by the number of townships (there were fourteen in Stark County by 1816) and added to

[60] Max Weber insisted that this was still true at a much later stage of development. "Industrial monopolies and trusts are institutions of limited duration; the conditions of production undergo changes, and the market does not know any everlasting valuation. Their power also lacks the authoritative character and the political mark of aristocracies. But monopolies of the land always create a political aristocracy." Gerth and Mills, eds. *From Max Weber,* p. 383.

[61] Edward Thornton Heald, *The Stark County Story* (Canton, 1949), I, 42–50, 52–55; John Danner, *Old Landmarks of Canton and Stark County* (Logansport, 1904), pp. 43, 470.

the county officers,[62] is in striking contrast to the relatively simple organization of the Mississippi county court.

Stark County did have one landed baron, Bezaleel Wells, who had all the attributes which would seem to make for influence, leadership and power. Wells's career there, however, so similar in some respects to that of John Cleves Symmes, may typify the vulnerability of the great speculator to the aggressions of small operators in the early Northwest. Brought up in surroundings of refinement, Bezaleel Wells had become a staunch Federalist in the 1790s and had excellent political connections which included Arthur St. Clair and George Washington. His own public activity in Ohio included service as judge of probate, prothonotary to the Court of Common Pleas, clerk to the court of general quarter sessions of the peace of Jefferson County, member of the Ohio constitutional convention, and state senator. Having realized substantial profits from purchases of over 15,000 acres in the Steubenville area, he shifted his activities in 1805 to the present Canton township, undoubtedly with foreknowledge of the Indian treaty of Fort Industry. Though the tax laws and the Harrison Land Act had meanwhile made large-scale operations less feasible than they had been at Steubenville, his holdings of 6,500 acres in Osnaburg, Plain and Canton townships still put him in a class by himself.

Since competition had become greatly enlarged, with new towns being platted everywhere, it was clear to Wells that at Canton he must become a promoter. His inducements for attracting settlers were of the most royal sort: wide streets were laid out, whole blocks were donated for schools and churches, and special terms were offered for the purchase of town lots. He even sponsored a horse race at the south end of town to stimulate interest in sales. He made princely offers to the county commissioners to induce them to fix the county seat at Canton; sizable gifts of land and proceeds of sales were to be turned over to the county should Canton be chosen. The seat was, in fact, located there in 1808, but the artful commissioners—themselves small business men and petty speculators—seized upon the vague and contradictory wording of the proposals to exploit Wells in the most callous fashion. They accused him of fraud; by means of court action and merciless pressure they finally made him disgorge 150 unsold lots and a choice courthouse location. Meanwhile Wells, attempting to set up another town in Wayne County,

[62] Heald, *op. cit.*, p. 66. County organization at that time called for three or more justices of the peace, tax commissioners, a sheriff, a coroner, a recorder, a treasurer, a license commissioner, and justices and clerks of the various courts. Ohio Historical Records Survey Project, Inventory of the County Archives of Ohio, No. 76, *Stark County* (Columbus, 1940), p. 23.

was forced to liquidate the venture when his town failed to be chosen as county seat, and after the disastrous fray with the Stark commissioners his name virtually disappears from Canton history. By 1829 we see Bezaleel Wells—the only man in Stark County's early annals who might possibly have qualified, by virtue of wealth, experience, and extent of landholdings, for anything like a position of privilege—taking the pauper's oath in a debtor's prison. He had failed as a placator.[63]

What of the "secondary" level of democracy in Stark County, that of small-town enterprise? The county's first eleven permanent towns were established between 1805 and 1816—an average of one a year—which was different from the way it was in Alabama: there, even by 1850, only twenty-eight towns of over 200 inhabitants could be found in the whole state.[64] For the success of any of these eleven towns the factor of growth was crucial, and the promoter's art was at a premium. It involved the immediate setting up of services; schoolhouses were built before there were children enough to fill them. It called for toleration, since business always came before religious particularism; it called for placation, and, especially, for the instinct of manipulation; James Leeper's failure to donate lots for churches and schools cost Osnaburg the county seat.[65] The initial problems of settlement were thus carried over into those of promotion, and rôles for the politician and manipulator went hand in hand with rôles for the business man and promoter.

That these rôles, both commercial and political, were not only profuse but interchangeable is seen in the careers of Canton's earliest leading citizens. One result of Bezaleel Wells' disappearance from Canton's town life "was the growth of a democratic, self-reliant, enterprising group of town leaders, who took matters into their own hands." Among the foremost of these, as might be expected, was the chief man on the board of commissioners which had ravished Wells of his holdings, the tavern-keeper Samuel Coulter. Besides entertaining the public, Coulter practiced law, speculated in land, was one of the first trustees of the Farmers' Bank, and served as Judge of the Court of Common Pleas. William Fogle, who kept a general store, was also a county commissioner and later became trustee, director and cashier of the Farmers' Bank, from which he resigned in 1816 to accept the county treasurership. John Shorb, Canton's first

---

[63] Edward T. Heald, *Bezaleel Wells, Founder of Canton and Steubenville, Ohio* (Canton, 1948).

[64] "All of them except Tuscaloosa were situated in agricultural communities; and Tuscaloosa was not really an exception, inasmuch as the mineral resources in the vicinity had not then been·developed." Thomas H. Owen, *A History of Alabama and Dictionary of Alabama Biography* (Chicago, 1921), II, 265.

[65] Heald, *Stark County Story*, pp. 12, 94–96, 217.

storekeeper, became the Bank's first president, was instrumental in founding the first Catholic church, and was highly active in public affairs at large. James Lathrop, a young Connecticut Yankee brimming with talent and ambition, having been admitted to the bar the year of his arrival, plunged instantly into public life, organizing Canton's first library, becoming its librarian, and leading the movement for an Academy. Lathrop was appointed receiver for the Bank when it failed in 1818; he helped get the town incorporated in 1822 and became the first town president; he was elected county auditor the same year and went to the legislature two years later, serving several terms and heading the committee which wrote Ohio's first compulsory school tax law. His name is preserved in Canton legend. The hatter, George Stidger, arriving from Baltimore in 1807, organized and commanded his own company in the War of 1812 and rose to the rank of general. Upon his return, having accumulated considerable real estate before the war, he built a tin and copper shop, set up a tanyard, and ultimately amassed a veritable chain system of such enterprises. He served as Judge of the Court of Common Pleas.[66]

These were the men who headed Canton's "first families." They and their descendants became the only "aristocracy" that Canton could ever have.

[66] Heald, *Bezaleel Wells*, pp. 113–14, 118–19, 122, 126; Damner, *Old Landmarks*, p. 451; Heald, *Stark County Story*, pp. 6, 94–114, 119–23, 126–33, 135.

Suffrage Classes and Party Alignments:
A Study in Voter Behavior

RICHARD P. McCORMICK

THE TRADITIONAL INGREDIENTS OF AMERICAN POLITICAL HISTORY have been personalities, classes, sections, parties, and issues. The voter, except in so far as he has been regarded as an element of a class or a section, has received relatively little attention. More recently, because

Reprinted from the *Mississippi Valley Historical Review* (now the *Journal of American History*) XLVI, December 1959, by permission of the Managing Editor.

of dwindling confidence in the efficacy of the hypotheses of Beard and Turner, we are less sure of our ability to conceive of the electorate in terms of classes and sections. Consequently, we are impelled to re-examine the entire field of voter behavior in order to obtain new understandings of the role of the electorate in the democratic process. In attacking one aspect of this large problem, this study deals with certain limited but critical questions related to the composition and behavior of the electorate in the early national period. More specifically, it is an analysis of the degree to which certain types of property qualifications restricted the size of the electorate and of the relationship of the economic status of voters to their party affiliation.[1]

It is generally understood that in the decades before the Civil War property qualifications for voting existed in most states.[2] What is not known with any degree of precision is the extent to which these barriers excluded adult males from the polls. Neither is it clear what effect extensions of the franchise to lower economic segments of the population had on the relative strength of competing political parties. Equally clouded is the larger question of whether the electorate tended to divide between the major parties along lines of economic cleavage. It is doubtful whether these questions can be answered with assurance for most states, because the nature of the evidence is often such as to preclude methodical inquiry. There are, however, two states that provide highly favorable conditions for analyses of the type proposed, and for that reason they have been selected as the basis for this study.

These states—North Carolina and New York—have been chosen, then, not because they are necessarily typical, but because they afford more reliable and relevant data than can be secured for other states. Both states were unusual in that they had, for varying periods, dual property qualifications for voting. That is, voters having the minimum qualifications could vote for limited categories of officials, whereas those meeting higher qualifications were eligible to vote for all elective officials. This feature, together with others that will be considered, makes it possible to measure not only the restrictive effect of certain property qualifications but also the party affiliations of the different classes of electors.

It is convenient to examine first the experience of North Carolina.

[1] Grateful acknowledgment is made to the Social Science Research Council for a grant that made possible an investigation of early American political behavior, of which this study is one product.

[2] Despite its many inaccuracies, the standard work on the subject is Kirk H. Porter, *A History of Suffrage in the United States* (Chicago, 1918). For an adequate brief summary, see Charles O. Paullin, *Atlas of the Historical Geography of the United States* (Washington, 1932), 126–27.

Its constitution of 1776 created a dual suffrage system. Only adult freemen possessed of fifty acres of land within the county in which they voted could vote for a member of the state senate. But all freemen—including the fifty-acre freeholders—who had paid county or state taxes were eligible to vote for members of the house of commons. After 1835, when the office of governor became elective by popular vote, the lesser franchise requirement was extended to apply also in gubernatorial elections. Not until 1856 was this dual arrangement replaced by general taxpayer suffrage.[3] For eighty years, then, the fifty-acre freeholders can be distinguished as a separate electoral class in North Carolina. In any state election within that period it is possible to analyze the ratio of fifty-acre electors to those voters meeting only the taxpayer qualification. The party preferences of the two suffrage groups can also be determined. For the most reliable results, however, it is desirable to select a period when party lines were distinct and strong and when something approaching a maximum vote was registered.[4] These conditions maintained between 1836 and 1856.[5]

During those years the Whig and Democratic parties contested on a nearly even basis in North Carolina, with the Whigs dominant by a slight margin down to 1848. Voter participation was high, averaging 77 per

[3] Francis N. Thorpe (comp.), *The Federal and State Constitutions, Colonial Charters, and Other Organic Laws of the States, Territories, and Colonies* (7 vols., Washington, 1909), V, 2790, 2796–97, 2799. Neither of the two standard histories of the suffrage in North Carolina makes any attempt to examine the actual restrictive effect of the dual qualifications. John S. Bassett, "Suffrage in the State of North Carolina (1776–1861)," *Annual Report of the American Historical Association, 1895* (Washington, 1896), 271–85; John W. Carr, "The Manhood Suffrage Movement in North Carolina," *Historical Papers of the Trinity College Historical Society* (Durham), XI (1915), 47–78. See also J. G. de Roulhac Hamilton, *Party Politics in North Carolina, 1835–1860* (Chapel Hill, 1916), 77, 84, 117–21. Bassett, Carr, and Hamilton all agree that prior to 1848, when the Democratic candidate for governor unveiled the suffrage issue in the campaign, there was no indication of a popular demand for the elimination of the freehold requirement.

[4] If there were no discernible party lines, or if such lines were indistinct, it would obviously be impossible to relate parties to definable groups within the electorate. If voter turnout was extremely low, the vote might not represent accurately the dimensions of each class of electors. Connecticut provides an illustration of both points. Almost simultaneously with the liberalization of the suffrage in 1818, the Federalist party collapsed, political activity declined, and the percentage of adult white males participating in elections fell off sharply. Such conditions would not be ideal for analyzing the effects of a liberalized franchise. For an excellent study of early Connecticut politics, see Norman L. Stamps, "Political Parties in Connecticut, 1789–1818" (Ph.D. dissertation, Yale University, 1952).

[5] General guides to the political history of North Carolina in this era are Hamilton, *Party Politics in North Carolina,* and Clarence C. Norton, *The Democratic Party in Ante-Bellum North Carolina, 1835–1861* (Chapel Hill, 1930).

cent of the adult white male population. By comparing the size of the vote cast county-by-county for governor with the comparable vote for state senators, it is possible to measure the proportion of the total electorate that could not meet the fifty-acre requirement (See Table I). Then, by examining the distribution of each class of the electorate between the two major parties it can be determined whether economic status influenced party affiliation.

TABLE I. SIZE OF ELECTORAL CLASSES IN NORTH CAROLINA, 1835–1856[a]

Year	Number of Counties in Sample	Vote for Senators	Vote for Governor	Senate Vote as % of Vote for Governor	Governor Vote as % of Adult White Males
1835–36	26 of 64	18,532	33,066	56.0	67.1
1840	46 of 68	31,241	57,460	54.4	83.0
1844	22 of 73	15,209	31,481	48.3	78.7
1856	46 of 82	30,205	62,915	48.0	79.3

[a] The only available source of returns of elections of members of the state senate are the contemporary newspapers, and their coverage was not complete. The elections that I cite were chosen mainly because returns were found for a fairly large number of counties in various parts of the state. Because the returns for the 1836 senatorial elections were inadequate, I have used the returns for the 1835 election and have compared them with the 1836 gubernatorial returns. For the other three elections, the voting for governor and senators took place at the same time. Voting was by paper ballot and elections were held biennially in August. All returns are from the Raleigh *North Carolina Standard,* and can be found in the several issues following each election.

Table I indicates that approximately one-half of the total electorate lacked the amount of property required to vote for state senators. In 1840, for example, 57,460 votes were cast for governor and 31,241 for senator in the forty-six counties for which returns were available. Thus 45.6 per cent of the voters lacked the fifty-acre freehold required of senatorial electors. The fact that a vote equivalent to 83 per cent of the total adult white male population of the state was polled for governor in 1840 would suggest that the requirement that voters must have paid a state or county tax was not a serious limitation on the franchise.[6] Even in states where unrestricted manhood suffrage existed, voter participation did not ordinarily exceed the 80 per cent level.[7] The conclusions regarding

[6] One factor that explains the high proportion of taxpayers to adult white males was the imposition of a poll tax on every free male between the ages of twenty-one and forty-five. Thorpe (comp.), *Federal and State Constitutions,* V, 2799.

[7] Vermont, Indiana, and Georgia, for example, all had no property or taxpaying qualifications, but they never—prior to 1840—registered votes in excess of 80 per

the proportion of taxpayers excluded from voting for senator is based on a sample ranging from 38.3 per cent to 71.7 per cent of the total state vote, and some degree of error could result from this lack of a complete enumeration. But the proportions are sufficiently consistent from election to election to indicate that the true figure would not be far from 50 per cent. This reasoning is confirmed by the observations of the editor of the Raleigh *Standard* in 1848 that there were "between thirty and forty thousand freehold voters" in the state, and that the total electorate was "about eighty thousand."[8]

TABLE II. SIZE OF ELECTORAL CLASSES IN WAKE COUNTY, NORTH CAROLINA[a]

Year	Vote for Senator	Vote for Governor	Senate Vote as % of Vote for Governor
1838	946	1,857	50.9
1840	1,006	2,187	46.0
1842	1,020	2,138	47.7
1844	1,083	2,344	46.2
1846	992	2,161	45.9
1848	1,023	2,284	44.8

[a] The vote figures are from the Raleigh *North Carolina Standard* in August of each election year.

The precise relationship of fifty-acre freeholders to taxpayers varied somewhat from county to county, although a one-to-one ratio prevailed in a remarkably high number of instances. Detailed studies could readily be made to determine whether the proportion of freehold voters was greater in some sections than in others, and such an analysis would be relevant to any intensive investigation of the North Carolina political

cent of their adult white males. Delaware, on the other hand, had taxpayer suffrage but polled 81.9 per cent of its adult white males as early as 1804. These and subsequent references to the percentages of adult white males participating in elections are based on a compilation that I have made of state-wide votes for governor, president, and, in some states, congressmen. This collection, which is being prepared for publication, includes the voting records down to 1860 of those states admitted to the Union by 1836, except South Carolina. I have computed for each election the percentage of adult white males voting.

[8] Raleigh *North Carolina Standard*, July 5, 1848. Similar conclusions are set forth in John C. Vinson, "Electioneering in North Carolina, 1800–1835," *North Carolina Historical Review* (Raleigh), XXIX (April, 1952), 171–88. Although it might be suggested that the low vote for senators was attributable to voter apathy toward that office, this does not seem to have been the case, for after 1856 the senatorial vote was equal to the vote for governor. See, for example, the returns for the state election of 1860 in the Raleigh *Weekly Standard*, August 15, 22, 1860.

environment. Table II indicates the pattern in Wake County, in which Raleigh was situated. The ratio between the two electorates was quite stable, and it was fairly close to the state-wide average.

Because of the dual suffrage system, it is an easy matter to compare the party affiliations of the fifty-acre freeholders with those of the lower electoral class. How wide an economic margin separated the two politico-economic classes is a matter for conjecture—or further research—but it would seem reasonable to assume that there was an appreciable distinction in status. The question, then, is whether the fifty-acre freeholders, as an upper-level economic group, differed markedly in their party affiliations from the remainder of the electorate.

Table III presents the results of a study of three state elections. In the first two columns are given the party distribution of votes cast for senator and for governor in the counties that comprised the sample. Column three gives the assumed vote of the non-freehold electors for governor and has been obtained by subtracting the senatorial vote of each

TABLE III. DISTRIBUTION OF PARTY AFFILIATION BY
ELECTORAL CLASSES IN NORTH CAROLINA[a]

Year	Party	Vote for Senators	Vote for Governor	Non-freehold Voters	% by Party Senators Vote	% by Party Governors Vote	% by Party Non-freehold Vote
1840	Whig	16,760	30,594	13,834	53.7	53.2	52.7
	Dem.	14,481	26,866	12,385	46.3	46.8	47.3
1844	Whig	8,053	16,430	8,377	52.9	52.2	51.4
	Dem.	7,156	15,051	7,895	47.1	47.8	48.6
1856	Whig	13,231	27,035	13,804	43.8	43.0	42.2
	Dem.	16,974	35,880	18,906	56.2	57.0	57.8

[a] The votes have been compiled from the returns in the Raleigh *North Carolina Standard.*

party from the gubernatorial vote.[9] The next three columns show the percentage distribution of the party vote cast by the senatorial electors, by the total electorate, and by the non-freeholders, respectively.

[9] This calculation is necessarily based on the assumption that the freehold voters cast their ballots for the same party candidate for senator and governor. This assumption would seem to be a valid one, for there is little evidence of split-ticket voting. Relying on this assumption, it can be calculated that if in 1840 there were 16,760 freehold votes for the Whig gubernatorial candidate out of the total of 30,594 Whig votes cast, then the remainder—13,834—would have come from those who lacked fifty-acre freeholds.

In each of the three elections the fifty-acre freehold voters were divided between Whigs and Democrats in almost exactly the same proportions as those who met only the taxpaying qualification. In 1840, for example, 53.7 per cent of the freehold electors were Whigs, as were 52.7 per cent of the less qualified electors. In none of the elections was there as much as a two per cent difference in the party distribution of the two classes of voters. Indeed, the similarity of the party affiliations of the two groups was so nearly identical as to be astonishing. The fifty-acre freeholder class was from one to two percentage points more strongly Whig than the less privileged voters, a differential so small as to be inconsiderable. Thus, whether or not a man owned fifty acres or more of land seemingly had little or no influence on his party affiliation. Or, to express it differently, the economic distinction implicit in the dual suffrage system had no substantial significance as a factor in determining party alignments in these North Carolina elections.

The similarity of party distribution within the two classes of electors existed in almost every county; it is not the fabrication of an averaging process. In the 1840 election the same party that obtained a majority of votes in the senatorial election also received a majority in the gubernatorial contest in forty-three of the forty-six counties.[10] In each of the three exceptional cases the vote was extremely close, and local circumstances may well have produced a majority for one party in the election of a senator and for the other in the gubernatorial election. What this means, of course, is that if the election of a governor had been determined by the fifty-acre freeholders alone, the same candidate would have been elected with almost precisely the same percentage of the total vote.

The implications of this analysis are both intriguing and suggestive. If it was true that in North Carolina the restriction of the suffrage to fifty-acre freeholders would have produced the same results as extending the franchise to all taxpayers, what happened in other states when the suffrage was broadened? Is there convincing evidence that when lower economic strata of the population were given the vote there resulted some measurable change in party alignments? Did the new voters, presumably homogeneous in their economic status, tend to move as a group into one of the two major parties?

Certain more or less ideal conditions must exist before this question can be answered with assurance for any state. There should be a marked reduction in suffrage qualifications occurring at a time when party lines

---

[10] It is pertinent to mention that the parties in North Carolina were not highly sectionalized; both parties had strength in all sections of the state. See William S. Hoffmann, *Andrew Jackson and North Carolina Politics* (Chapel Hill, 1958); Hamilton, *Party Politics in North Carolina*, 40, 66.

were distinct and stable and when voter participation was at a sufficiently high level that the effect of the change in suffrage could be measured. The first condition is found in a number of states, but not usually in association with the two others. Most of the lowering of suffrage barriers in the United States took place before 1824 in a period when party alignments were unstable, weak, or non-existent.[11] After 1824 Rhode Island, Louisiana, Mississippi, and Virginia broadened the franchise, but in the first three states the increase in the proportion of adult white males voting was so small as to be inconsiderable. In Virginia the liberalization was accomplished in two steps, in 1830 and 1850, which rather lessened the impact of the change.[12]

Probably the state which most nearly fulfills the specified conditions is New York. Moreover, because that state also had a dual suffrage system, it lends itself to analyses similar to those made for North Carolina. Under the New York constitution of 1777, only those men who owned freeholds valued at £100 were eligible to vote for governor, lieutenant-governor, and state senator. Those who had freeholds worth

[11] I have particular reference to the changes that were made between 1800 and 1824, most notably in Maryland in 1802, in New Jersey in 1807, in Connecticut in 1818, and in Massachusetts in 1821. It would be difficult, I believe, to demonstrate that the reduction of suffrage barriers in the last three states resulted in any marked expansion of the electorate.

[12] Rhode Island altered its suffrage requirements in 1842, and there was a marked temporary rise in the percentage of adult white males voting, but even with the increase there was only one occasion (1843) prior to 1860 when as many as half of the adult white males voted. In Louisiana, similarly, voter participation normally remained below the 50 per cent level despite suffrage changes in 1845 and 1852. In 1832, Mississippi, which had previously required militia service or the payment of a state or county tax, conferred the franchise on free white male citizens. Not until 1839, however, was there any significant upward surge in voter participation. With respect to Virginia, there was a considerable jump in voter participation between the presidential elections of 1836 (35.1 per cent) and 1840 (54.6 per cent), several years after the redefinition of suffrage qualifications in 1830. Voter participation in the 1848 presidential election was 47.9 per cent of the adult white males. This figure rose to 61 per cent in the 1851 gubernatorial election, which followed the suffrage liberalization of 1850. The Democrats received 50.8 per cent of the total vote in 1848 and 52.3 per cent in 1851. Many other factors would have to be considered, but on the basis of these figures it is not apparent that the increase in the size of the electorate had much effect on party alignments. Detailed studies of votes by counties in the state elections might produce sounder evidence for evaluating the effect of suffrage changes than do these state-wide figures. For a recent analysis of the suffrage in Virginia see J. R. Pole, "Representation and Authority in Virginia from the Revolution to Reform," *Journal of Southern History* (Lexington, Ky.), XXIV (February, 1958), 16–50. Pole does not attempt to estimate the extent to which the electorate was increased by the suffrage changes of 1830 and 1850.

£20, or who rented tenements with a yearly value of forty shillings and paid public taxes, could vote for assemblymen and members of Congress. This dual system ended when a new constitution, effective February 28, 1822, conferred franchise privileges on all adult male citizens who paid county or state taxes, performed (or were exempted from) militia duty, or labored on the public highways. In 1826 all property and taxpaying requirements for voting in New York were eliminated.[13]

There is no difficulty in determining how many electors were in each of the two suffrage classes. New York conducted censuses of electors at least once in every seven years between 1790 and 1821, and from these records the restrictive effect of the various suffrage qualifications can be computed and tabulated.

TABLE IV. SIZE OF ELECTORAL CLASSES IN NEW YORK, 1801–1835[a]

Year	Adult White Males	Total Electors	Total Electors as % of Adult White Males	£100 Electors	£100 Electors as % of Adult White Males	Electors Other	Other Electors as % of Adult White Males
1801	125,000	85,907	68.7	52,058	41.6	33,849	27.1
1807	170,000	121,289	71.3	71,159	41.8	50,130	29.5
1814	239,000	151,846	63.5	87,491	36.6	64,355	26.9
1821	299,500	202,510	67.6	100,490	33.5	102,020	34.1
1822	312,700	259,387	82.9	–		–	
1825	352,300	296,132	84.0	–		–	
1835	467,000	422,034	90.3	–		–	

[a] New York (State), Secretary of State, *Census of the State of New York for 1855* (Albany, 1857), ix-x, xli-xliii. The 1855 census contains a compendium of all preceding electoral censuses, giving the number of electors in each category by counties. This remarkably detailed information has been surprisingly neglected by students of voter behavior. Several other states, among them Ohio, Louisiana, Kentucky, and Tennessee, also conducted censuses of electors, but none was comparable in excellence to those of New York.

The data in this table indicate that prior to 1822 roughly two-thirds of the adult white male population could vote. The £100 freeholders averaged about 38 per cent of the adult white male population. Between one-quarter and one-third of the adult white males possessed only the

[13] Thorpe (comp.), *Federal and State Constitutions*, V, 2630–33, 2642, 2652. The 1822 constitution made a distinction between white and colored voters. The latter had to be citizens of the state for three years and possess a freehold of $250, upon which taxes were paid, in order to vote. *Ibid.*, 2642–43.

lower of the two suffrage qualifications and were therefore unable to vote for governor, lieutenant-governor, and senator. Approximately one-third of the adult males lacked the qualifications to vote in any elections before 1822. As a result of the constitutional change in the suffrage in 1822, the total electorate rose sharply to include 83 per cent of the adult white males. Most important is the fact that the number of those eligible to vote for governor rose from 100,490 to 259,387, an increase of almost 160 per cent. The elimination of the taxpaying requirement after 1825 had a relatively slight effect on the size of the electorate. In general terms, the economic-electoral classes within the population of New York in 1821 can be described as follows: the top third enjoyed full franchise privileges; the middle third had limited privileges; and the bottom third was disfranchised.

We can, as in the case of North Carolina, inquire whether the two suffrage classes in New York differed in party alignment. The election held in April, 1816, at which time a governor and members of Congress —as well as legislators—were chosen, saw the Federalists making their final full-scale effort against the Republicans.[14] Because complete returns by counties for both the gubernatorial and congressional contests are available, it is possible to use these votes to determine the party alignments within the two suffrage classes (See Table V). The governor was elected by the £100 freeholders alone; the total electorate was eligible to vote for members of Congress.

TABLE V. DISTRIBUTION OF PARTY AFFILIATION BY
ELECTORAL CLASSES IN NEW YORK, 1816[a]

Party	Vote for Governor	% by Party	Vote for Congress	% by Party	Non-freehold Voters Congress	% by Party
Republican	45,412	54.0	67,757	54.9	22,345	57.0
Federalist	38,647	46.0	55,514	45.1	16,867	43.0

[a] The returns for both the gubernatorial and congressional elections, which were held at the same time, are from the Albany *Advertiser,* June 15, 1816. The results of the congressional election were used because those returns were complete and those for the assembly districts were not. The estimates of the numbers of non-freehold voters participating in the congressional elections has been computed with the same procedure that was used in the North Carolina analysis.

Table V would seem to show that the non-freehold voters were only slightly more biased toward the Republican party than were the elite

[14] Dixon Ryan Fox, *The Decline of Aristocracy in the Politics of New York* (New York, 1919), 188–93.

electors. Two circumstances, however, make interpretations of these data hazardous. If the voting figures are taken at face value, they indicate that 93 per cent of those eligible to vote for governor actually went to the polls. This percentage is so suspiciously high as to suggest that many who lacked the £100 freehold may have voted in the gubernatorial election. Again, the figures imply that only 48 per cent of the eligible non-freehold electors cast their ballots. If this was indeed the case, the question arises as to whether such a low turnout constitutes a realistic sample.[15] The safest conclusion to be drawn is that the presence at the polls of the non-freehold electors—as evidenced in the congressional vote—did not significantly alter the party alignments manifested in the gubernatorial election.

The final problem to be examined is the effect of a marked broadening of the electorate on party alignments in New York. The liberalization of the suffrage in 1822 increased the number of those eligible to vote for governor from approximately 33 per cent of the adult white males to 84 per cent. The two parties in New York at this period were the Republicans and the Clintonians—the candidate of the latter for the governorship in 1820, 1824, and 1826 being De Witt Clinton. In 1820, prior to the expansion of the electorate, Clinton received 50.9 per cent of the total gubernatorial vote of 93,437. In 1824, when lowered suffrage requirements resulted in a total vote of 190,545, his percentage was 54.3. In 1826 he polled 50.9 per cent of the 195,920 votes cast.[16] There is every reason to assume that the increased vote came from those electoral classes that previously had either lacked the vote entirely or had been ineligible to vote for governor.[17]

[15] It can be calculated from the electoral census that approximately 172,300 men were eligible to participate in the election of members of Congress and 90,440 in the election of the governor, leaving 81,860 electors who lacked the £100 freehold requirement. It is from these base figures that the proportions of each electoral class participating in the 1816 elections have been computed. The question that should be resolved before the New York returns can be used with confidence is whether the suffrage qualifications were rigorously enforced. It would seem doubtful that they were.

[16] The gubernatorial vote figures are from Edgar A. Werner (comp.), *Civil List and Constitutional History of the Colony and State of New York* (2nd ed., Albany, 1886), 164.

[17] It is pertinent to note that the newly enfranchised voters were slow to exercise their privilege. Approximately 84 per cent of the adult white males were eligible to vote for governor in 1824, as indicated in Table IV. But the actual voter turn-out was only 56.1 per cent of the adult white males. This was a considerably higher proportion than had ever voted in the state before, but it implies that nearly one-third of the eligibles did not vote. In view of this manifest apathy on the part of the new voter, it is relevant to raise the question of how eager the disenfranchised class was to obtain the vote.

According to the most recent authoritative survey of New York history, Clinton was regarded by the conservative forces as their champion; and the "liberal elements, whose strength was augmented by the widened suffrage, followed the leadership of the Albany Regency."[18] Yet the foregoing analysis of the voting in New York demonstrates that the only observable effect of the extension of the suffrage was a very slight increase in Clinton's majority. Certainly the New York experience offers no support for the belief that even a drastic enlargement of the electorate resulted in any measurable change in party alignments.[19] On the contrary, it gives added weight to the view that economic status as defined in suffrage restrictions had little or no influence on the party affiliations of voters. The new voters, drawn from an economic level that had previously been barred from the polls, apparently divided fairly evenly in party preferences between the Republicans and the Clintonians.

Perhaps Erastus Root was right when, speaking in the New York constitutional convention in 1821 in defense of manhood suffrage, he rejected the notion that the propertyless must be held in check because their interests were antagonistic to those of men of substance. "We have," declared Root, "no different estates, having different interests, necessary to be guarded from encroachments by the watchful eye of jealousy. We are all of the same estate—all commoners."[20]

This analysis of suffrage conditions and voter behavior in North Carolina and New York suggests several conclusions and raises some questions that merit further investigation. It is quite clear that in both of these states property qualifications effectively limited the size of the electorate. In North Carolina nearly one-half of those who went to the polls to vote for governor were unable to vote for state senators because they lacked the requisite fifty-acre freehold. In New York prior to 1821 approximately one-third of the adult white males were totally excluded from voting and another third was not qualified to vote for governor.

In both states the abandonment of property tests led to a sharp and immediate rise in the number of votes cast for those offices that had previously been elective by voters possessed of special qualifications. In New York, however, it seems quite probable that the constitutional restrictions were not rigidly enforced, with the result that a sizable number

[18] David M. Ellis, James A. Frost, Harold C. Syrett, and Harry J. Carman, *A Short History of New York State* (Ithaca, 1957), 148.

[19] It is recognized that party alignments in this era exhibited the confusion that was typical of New York politics and that voter participation was well below the maximum potential level. Consequently, the conditions stipulated for an ideal situation were not completely fulfilled. However, the general attributes of the New York situation are relatively satisfactory when compared with those of other states.

[20] Quoted in Ellis *et al., Short History of New York,* 147.

of inadequately qualified voters participated in gubernatorial elections. Moreover, when the suffrage was liberalized, the newly enfranchised voters manifested considerable apathy toward the exercise of their newly gained privilege.

Studies of other states—most notably New Jersey and Massachusetts— have tended to minimize the importance of property requirements as a factor limiting the size of the electorate.[21] Obviously, for the period studied, this was not the case in New York or North Carolina. The point is that the experience of each state must be carefully investigated before any sweeping generalizations are made. The particular definitions of the suffrage qualifications must be examined, as well as the practical arrangements that existed for enforcement of the legal or constitutional requirements.

Although North Carolina and New York are not cited as "typical," they were two important—and even representative—states. Consequently, the conclusion that the upper economic-electoral class in each state divided between the major parties in almost the same proportions as the lower economic-electoral class raises significant questions about the general validity of economic-class interpretations of political behavior. Of course, the fact that parties did not reflect lines of economic cleavage in the periods under investigation does not necessarily imply that in other periods the same condition maintained. Here, again, is a field for further study.

It does not appear that the liberalization of the franchise had any measurable effect on the relative strength of the contending parties in either of the states investigated. To put it even more bluntly, when the common man was enfranchised in New York after 1821, he did not upset the political balance by throwing his weight heavily on the side of one party. Either he did not vote, or he showed as much preference for one party as for the other. If the broadening of the franchise did result in a major realignment of parties in any other state, that fact, I believe, has yet to be demonstrated.

The behavior of the voters of the lower electoral class in both North Carolina and New York indicates that there was little reason for the more substantial voters to fear the consequences of entrusting the masses with the franchise.[22] How important was this fear factor, actually, in

[21] See Richard P. McCormick, *The History of Voting in New Jersey, 1664– 1911* (New Brunswick, 1953); Robert E. Brown, *Middle-Class Democracy and the Revolution in Massachusetts, 1691–1780* (Ithaca, 1955); and J. R. Pole, "Suffrage and Representation in Massachusetts: A Statistical Note," *William and Mary Quarterly* (Williamsburg), 3rd Series, XIV (October, 1957), 560–92.

[22] This point is most ably developed in Louis Hartz, *The Liberal Tradition in America* (New York, 1955), 106–10.

delaying the general movement toward white manhood suffrage in other states? Conversely, how vociferous were those who lacked the franchise in demanding voting privileges? Neither of these questions has been studied sufficiently in individual states to permit any firm general conclusions.

Finally, preoccupation with such matters as franchise restrictions and the influences shaping a voter's party preference should not result in neglect of the equally relevant problem of what stimulated voters to go to the polls. In North Carolina nearly all of the eligibles participated in elections. In New York a considerable fraction—around one-third in 1824—did not choose to vote. Such large variations in the rate of voter participation from state to state require explanation. It may well be that the factor most responsible for increasing the size of the actual electorate after 1824, for example, was not the elimination of suffrage barriers but rather the surge to the polls of voters who previously had not been sufficiently stimulated to cast their ballots. The voter, then, must be added to the traditional ingredients of American political history. Studies of his behavior hold some promise of adding a new dimension to our perception of the nature of our democracy.

Jackson Men with Feet of Clay

CHARLES GRIER SELLERS, JR.

THE CONTAGIOUS ENTHUSIASM FOR GENERAL ANDREW JACKSON that in 1824 swept thousands of voters for the first time out of their accustomed tutelage to the established leaders demands careful study as a major phenomenon in the history of political democracy. It demands study also as an example of the frequently neglected influence of local political maneuvers on national developments. Though a few historians have intimated that Old Hickory's popularity could not have been converted into an electoral plurality without the aid of disgruntled politicians pursuing conventional factional and personal advantages in the various

Reprinted from the *American Historical Review* LXII, April 1957, by permission of the Executive Secretary.

states,[1] little attention has been paid to the Tennessee politicians who brought him before the country in the first place.

The accepted interpretation assumes that the men behind Jackson's candidacy—principally Judge John Overton, Senator John H. Eaton, Felix Grundy, and Major William B. Lewis—were moved by sincere admiration and affection for their friend. They are also credited with a shrewd perception that the ground swell of democratic discontent building up beneath the surface of American politics might be mobilized to make the popular general President.[2] A close scrutiny of the events of 1821-1823 in Tennessee reveals, however, that the objectives of Judge Overton and most of his associates were by no means so large and disinterested. There is evidence to show that Jackson was nominated for the presidency only in order that specific local political advantages could be achieved and that "the original Jackson men" actually favored other nominees.

When General Jackson retired to private life in the winter of 1821-1822, seven years had elapsed since his victory over the British at New Orleans had made him a national hero. The sporadic talk that he might be a presidential possibility had never been entertained seriously in any responsible quarter, and Jackson himself had never taken it seriously. President-making was still left exclusively to the political leaders, and they were already grooming more than enough entries for the presidential sweepstakes of 1824. Already in the field, or soon to be there, were the major contenders: President Monroe's Secretary of State, John Quincy Adams of Massachusetts; the Secretary of the Treasury, William H. Crawford of Georgia; the Secretary of War, John C. Calhoun of South Carolina; and the Speaker of the national House of Representatives, Henry Clay of Kentucky. Among the long shots being mentioned were Congressman William Lowndes of South Carolina, soon to be removed by death, and Governor DeWitt Clinton, leader of the opposition to Martin Van Buren's pro-Crawford Bucktail faction in New York.

Jackson's attitude toward these candidates was dictated mainly by personal considerations. Grateful to Adams and Calhoun for their defense of his violent incursion into Spanish Florida in 1818, he was hostile to Crawford and Clay, whose friends had attacked the Florida expedition in Congress. Crawford was slated by the old-line Republican leaders to receive the nomination of the regular congressional caucus, but Jackson

---

[1] See especially Philip S. Klein, *Pennsylvania Politics 1817–1832: A Game without Rules* (Philadelphia, 1940), pp. 117–24.

[2] Cf. James Parton, *Life of Andrew Jackson* (New York, 1861), III, 11–23; John Spencer Bassett, *The Life of Andrew Jackson* (New York, 1911), I, 326–29; Marquis James, *The Life of Andrew Jackson* (Indianapolis, 1938), pp. 335–53.

declared that he "would support the Devil first."[3] The Georgian had earlier impugned some of Jackson's Indian treaties, and he was being supported by the general's personal and political enemies in Tennessee.

The exigencies of factional politics largely controlled the attitudes of Tennesseans generally toward the presidential candidates. Overton, Eaton, and Lewis were associated with a faction that had dominated Tennessee for most of its history. Founded by William Blount, the architect of a fabulous land speculation involving most of the acreage in the state, this faction had been concerned primarily with making good its land claims and later with exploiting the possibilities of the banking business. Jackson had worked with this loosely knit group in his early days of political activity, and he was still personally intimate with Overton, now its unofficial leader, Eaton, Lewis, and their principal allies in East Tennessee, Overton's brother-in-law, Hugh Lawson White, and Pleasant M. Miller, a son-in-law of William Blount.

John Sevier had led the opposition to the Blount-Overton faction in the state's first years; more recently his mantle had fallen on a group of vigorous men who were all deadly personal enemies of Andrew Jackson. They included Senator John Williams and several congressmen, while their principal strategist was a Middle Tennessee planter and land speculator, Colonel Andrew Erwin, with whom Jackson was, in 1822, engaged in a bitter litigation that brought Erwin to the brink of financial ruin.[4]

Since Erwin and his friends were solidly in the Crawford camp, the Blount-Overton men were certain to be anti-Crawford, and Jackson undoubtedly hoped to line them up behind Adams or Calhoun. This hope was threatened, however, when Henry Clay entered the presidential competition as the first western candidate in the history of the office, attracting strong support that cut across factional lines in Tennessee. Judge Overton had visited Clay in the summer of 1821, and as soon as the Kentuckian became a candidate, the judge promised him Tennessee's electoral votes. Clay got additional support from another important Tennessee politician, Felix Grundy, who a decade before had worked closely with him as one of the congressional War Hawks in precipitating the War of 1812. Grundy, like Overton, had been in communication with Clay during 1821, urging him to become a candidate and assuring him of Tennessee's support. Still another Clay backer was Governor William Carroll.[5]

[3] Jackson to James Gadsden, Dec. 6, 1821, draft copy, Andrew Jackson Papers, Library of Congress.
[4] Charles G. Sellers, Jr. "Banking and Politics in Jackson's Tennessee, 1817–1827," *Mississippi Valley Historical Review,* XLI (June, 1954).
[5] Overton to Clay, Jan. 16, 1822, Henry Clay Papers, Library of Congress; Nashville *Constitutional Advocate,* Sept. 17, 1822.

Overton, Grundy, and Carroll spanned the political spectrum in Tennessee, and a union of their followers for the Kentuckian would have ensured his success in the state. Overton and his faction had been in eclipse since the Panic of 1819, which had generated a storm of public resentment against the banks they operated. Grundy, the only important Tennessee politician not identified with either major faction, had shrewdly capitalized on this popular discontent to become the dominant figure in the legislature, while veering back and forth between the two factions. Carroll was the ultimate beneficiary of the panic-generated discontent. Running as the Erwin faction's candidate for governor in 1821, he won a smashing victory over the Blount-Overton candidate. It was, in fact, the Overton men's desperate efforts to regain their ascendancy that led to Jackson's nomination for President.

The accounts left by Major Lewis and Judge Overton both indicate that the movement to nominate Jackson developed in the winter of 1821-1822, hard on the heels of Carroll's election. According to Lewis, the general's friends around Nashville "began now to speak of him as a candidate and, in *good earnest,* to take the necessary steps to place his name prominently before the country." The first public manifestation of the movement, Lewis continues, was an article in one of the Nashville newspapers in January, 1822, and soon afterward the Nashville *Gazette,* organ of the Blount-Overton faction, "took the field openly and boldly for the General."[6]

Overton's account is similar, but he claims credit for originating the movement. Early in 1822, says the judge, "it forcibly struck me that he [Jackson] ought to be the next President and by proper means might be made so." Overton goes on to recall that he had "praises thrown out" in the Nashville *Gazette.* "They were lightly thought of," he says, "but that made no difference with me."[7]

Contemporary evidence makes it clear, however, that Overton was not the first to envision Jackson as a presidential candidate. Indeed, even after the Jackson talk had started, the judge preferred another. In a letter of January 16, 1822, he assured Clay that "as far as I know the public mind, you will get all the votes in Tennessee in preference to any man whose name has been mentioned." Though Overton reported "some whispering conversation here that Jackson would suffer himself to be run," he was

[6] Lewis to Gov. Lewis Cass, undated letter, probably written in the 1840's, in the Henry L. Huntington Library.

[7] Overton to his nephew, Feb. 23, 1824, quoted in a sketch of Overton by Judge John M. Lea, a newspaper clipping in the Overton Papers on microfilm at the Joint University Library, Nashville. In the letter, Overton dates these events in early 1821, but this is an obvious slip, since he speaks of them as immediately preceding the legislature's nomination of Jackson, which did not occur until 1822.

"almost certain that he will not, and my information is derived from good authority." The judge added that Jackson could probably "beat you himself" in Tennessee, but that the general could not induce the voters to prefer Adams or Calhoun over Clay. Overton particularly requested Clay to keep his remarks confidential. "Inasmuch as I, and our family have always been friendly with Jackson," he wrote, "I should not like him to know of any interposition of mine on this subject."[8]

The apparent conflicts in the foregoing evidence are not irreconcilable. It would seem that the Jackson-for-President talk actually started with a group of politically ineffectual men around the general, most notably Major Lewis, that Overton was converted to the idea shortly after he wrote to Clay, and that Overton then instructed the Gazette's editor to launch the public campaign. If things happened this way, Overton's claim that he initiated the movement is essentially valid, since without his support it would never have gotten beyond the stage of talk. At any rate, the movement was certainly being pushed "in *good earnest*" by February, when Jackson's wife complained that "Major Eaton, General Carroll, the Doctor and even the Parson and I can't tell how many others—all of his friends who come here—talk everlastingly about his being President."[9]

Why did Overton throw his great influence behind the Jackson movement? Much of the answer to this question may be found in a letter he received about the time he must have been making his decision. On January 27, Pleasant M. Miller of Knoxville, leader of the Blount-Overton forces in the lower house of the legislature, wrote to the judge suggesting that Jackson should be run for governor in 1823.[10] Though Miller's epistolary style was highly ambiguous, the most casual reader could hardly miss his reiterated suggestions that Jackson's popularity might be used to effect certain local political objectives. Overton would have had no trouble understanding Miller's intimations that Governor Carroll, whose overwhelming strength was the chief obstacle to a Blount-Overton comeback, might thus be defeated at the state elections of 1823, that a new legislature purged of Jackson's enemies from the Erwin-Carroll faction might be elected at the same time, and that the various legislative purposes of the Blount-Overton men might thus be achieved.[11]

[8] Overton to Clay, Jan. 16, 1822, Clay Papers.

[9] Augustus C. Buell, *History of Andrew Jackson: Pioneer, Patriot, Soldier, Politician, President* (New York, 1904), II, 157–58.

[10] Miller to Overton, Jan. 27, 1822, John Overton Papers, Claybrooke Collection, Tennessee Historical Society, Nashville.

[11] Among the issues to which Miller alluded were the location of the state capital and a proposed penitentiary, land legislation in which the speculators were vitally interested, and revision of the state judiciary. The judicial question was related to the land issue, the state supreme court having recently made a ruling

A single paragraph of Miller's long letter will sufficiently suggest its tone:

1st is there any man whose personal popularity is so likely to assist in fixing the seat of government permanently at any given point as Andrew Jackson, if so why should he not be the next governor, or why should this not be wish[ed] for by those who desire this result. I am satisfied that this cannot be done with the present legislature.

A more reliable legislature could be elected along with Jackson in 1823, Miller was suggesting. Even in Bedford County, Andrew Erwin's stronghold, Miller was confident the Jackson question would be potent enough to ensure the right kind of representation. In addition, Senator John Williams, whose term was expiring, could be replaced by a reliable Blount-Overton man. Miller had himself in mind for this position, as subsequently appeared.

At the time Miller wrote, there was talk of calling a special session of the legislature to meet during the summer. This legislature, having been elected along with Carroll the previous year, was untrustworthy from the Blount-Overton point of view. Hence Miller was anxious to prevent a special session, or if it were called, to keep it from acting on the matters he mentioned.

Miller had got wind of the talk about running Jackson for President, and he was by no means opposed to the idea, his comments implying that the general had no chance to be elected, but that his candidacy might yield certain collateral advantages. Miller was reported to favor Adams for the presidency about this time,[12] and though his meaning is obscure, his letter of January 27 seems to suggest that Tennessee and other southern states cooperate with the smaller northeastern states in electing the New England candidate. Jackson's nomination would actually help Adams in the electoral college by depriving Crawford and Clay of votes from Tennessee, Alabama, Mississippi, and Louisiana, in most of which the New Englander had no chance anyhow. Crawford's defeat would aid in prostrating the Erwin-Carroll faction in Tennessee. Miller knew that Grundy "has different views at the called session," which doubtless meant a plan to nominate Clay. But, he told Overton, "I know that if you fall in with my notions that you will know how to act." He particularly urged the judge to "take time to consider of these matters so far as they concern our local affairs & ascertain how far certain persons will

---

disastrous to the speculators, and Overton was anxious to return to the supreme bench for the purpose of rectifying matters (see Patrick H. Darby to Jackson, July 4, 1821, Jackson Papers).

[12] Statement of Hugh Lawson White, in the Nashville *Union*, Sept. 25, 1835.

act on them," and concluded by promising to visit Nashville in March, when "we can converse more freely."

Overton's desertion of Clay and endorsement of the Jackson movement was substantially a fulfillment of Miller's hope that the judge would "fall in with my notions." The project of running Jackson for governor was found impracticable, but his nomination for President was to serve the same purposes. Although it was Miller who actually conceived the essential strategy first, Overton was doubtless responsible for abandoning the plan to run Jackson for governor and concentrating on his presidential candidacy. Early in the spring, Miller made his promised trip west to concert strategy with Overton. The special session had now been called for July, and it was agreed that this body should nominate Tennessee's hero formally.

Miller's subsequent letters to Overton throw further light on the motives of Jackson's two principal managers. "I have Jackson's interest deeply at heart," he wrote on June 8.[13] "I think I know how bringing him forward is to operate upon the next congressional election &c. &c. I should not have went to the west when I did but with this view, & I think the effects of my visit will shew itself in some shape." The time had come, he thought, "for the papers to come directly forward" and call on the legislature to nominate Jackson at the special session. "Tell Jackson to come up Wednesday of the first week while people are all in a good humour—ask his friends to see him," Miller advised. "He can say he feels proud he has once returned to private life. If he has any redgmental coat were it, put on little milletary dress &c. You know more I need say no more."

Miller did not hesitate to admit that "I have motives for this matter." Jackson's nomination was the best way of frustrating Senator Williams' plan to win reelection at the special session. "There ought not to be an election for Senator at this time," Miller insisted, "—these good people must be held in check & this is all the hold we have—in a state of excitement publick opinion will keep them down unless that election is over." Should Williams be reelected, he predicted, there would be "a prodigious struggle" to realign Tennessee's congressional districts so as to favor Erwinite congressmen who "will in caucus vote for you knowho [sic] [Crawford]. I believe however I understand this matter tolerable well & expect to frustrate these views," Miller continued. "If I fail it will be the first time [.] keep your eye on [the] fidler & work even a head & let me alone for the rest." Almost parenthetically he reported talk "I am a candidate for the Senate, & that my visit to the west was to promote that view."

<hr>

[13] Miller to Overton, June 8, 1822, Overton Papers.

Several weeks later, Miller wrote again,[14] in terms indicating that he and Overton were working closely together toward mutually agreeable objectives. "I have rec[eive]d your two letters," he told the judge, "& things will be attended to to your satisfaction in part or in whole. I am using all my exertions to bring old hickory to view during the approaching session."

Meanwhile Overton and Miller had acquired an important recruit. Felix Grundy had become estranged from the Erwin-Carroll men and, in danger of political isolation, was ready to jump aboard any band wagon that happened along. The Jackson movement offered him a perfect opportunity to reinstate himself in the good graces of the Blount-Overton faction, and he did not hesitate. It was Grundy who on June 27 signed the note asking Jackson whether he had any objection to the proposed nomination.[15] Jackson seems not to have replied, but silence was as good as open assent.

The last possible obstacle removed, Overton, Miller, and Grundy now made their final preparations, and the Nashville newspapers endorsed the plan for a legislative nomination. State pride kept even the Erwin-Carroll men from opposing Jackson publicly,[16] though the editorial of endorsement in their organ, the Nashville *Clarion,* had a sarcastic ring. When the special session assembled on July 22, Miller was able to push his nominating resolutions through the lower house promptly, though the Erwin-Carroll men delayed action in the senate for two weeks.[17]

The reactions to Jackson's nomination by well-informed politicians outside the circle of Jackson managers were significant. All the comments that have been discovered agree in predicting that Jackson would not remain in the race as a serious contender. A month before the nomination, one of Governor Carroll's associates, Colonel Andrew Hynes, had informed Clay that Jackson had no hope of being elected and that he was

[14] Miller to Overton, June 25, 1822, *ibid.*

[15] Grundy to Jackson, June 27, 1822, Jackson Papers. Grundy was probably enlisted during Miller's visit to Nashville in the spring. Miller had even foreseen Grundy's cooperation, having informed Overton in his letter of January 27 that Grundy had "abandoned the head of department at Nashville [Governor Carroll] & said that he would stick to me."

[16] Andrew Hynes (an associate of Carroll) to Henry Clay, June 30, 1822, Clay Papers; James, *Jackson,* p. 351.

[17] James, *Jackson,* pp. 352–53. Though inaccurate in details, Overton's account, cited in fn. 7 above, illuminates the roles of the principals. "The Legislature met," says the judge, "and then I communicated to a leading member my views which he gave into, communicated them to Grundy, who at first seemed a little surprised, but gave into the measure of recommending him by our Legislature which was done unanimously. The resolutions were preceded by a speech which I wrote for a member." Most of these negotiations took place, as we have seen, some time before the legislature met. The "leading member" was unquestionably Miller.

being brought forward "not so much with view of promoting his own elevation, as to subserve an Eastern or Northern interest."[18] The same explanation was advanced as late as the summer of 1823 by that astute politician, Thomas Hart Benton, following a two-month tour of Tennessee in the interest of Clay. "Jackson out of the way the state will go for you," Benton told the Kentuckian, "and there is hardly anyone who thinks he has any chance, and many see in his offering nothing but a diversion in favor of Adams."[19]

During the special session of 1822, Colonel Hynes discovered an additional explanation for the nomination. According to a "secret rumor that is afloat in the air," he informed Clay, Jackson's nomination was designed mainly to affect the senatorial election.[20] This was corroborated by a Colonel McClung, one of the leading citizens of Knoxville, who asserted that Pleasant Miller had "played off this manouvre to bring Jacksons name to bear, & make a point in the election of Senator." McClung was confident that Williams would be reelected by the special session despite the Jackson movement and that "so soon as the election of Senator is over, we shall hear no more of a Tenn. candidate for the office of President."[21] McClung's judgment was wrong, for Miller's strategy succeeded in blocking Williams' reelection at the special session, and the senatorial election was postponed to the regular session of 1823.

Meanwhile, Governor Carroll was spreading reports that Jackson would probably not remain long in the running and telling Clay that he still had a good chance for Tennessee. The governor also informed the Kentuckian that Grundy had promised to support him "if the prospects of Jackson became hopeless . . . and that he would indeavour to have you nominated at the next meeting of our legislature."[22] About the same time, Colonel Hynes was in New Orleans assuring the Louisiana politicians that Tennessee would ultimately go for Clay.[23]

Skepticism about the seriousness of Jackson's candidacy was also expressed by one of his sincere admirers. "Whatever may be the estimate in which he is held by the people of this State (and surely even here he is very differently estimated)," wrote Thomas Claiborne to a friend in Virginia, "I confess that I fear he will not be likely to unite sufficient strength in other States to secure his election. There are too many great

[18] Hynes to Clay, June 30, 1822, Clay Papers.
[19] Benton to Clay, July 23, 1823, *ibid.*
[20] Hynes to Clay, July 31, 1822, *ibid.*
[21] McClung's remarks were reported by one of Clay's correspondents, George C. Thompson, Thompson to Clay, Aug. 12, 1822, *ibid.*
[22] Carroll to Clay, Feb. 1, 1823, *ibid.*
[23] *Ibid.*; Isaac L. Baker to Jackson, Mar. 3, 1823, Jackson Papers.

men in other States to suffer a man from the young & small State of Tennessee at the present day to be made President of the United States."[24]

Whatever their ultimate purposes or expectations, Miller and his allies did everything they could to raise a Jackson excitement in the state campaign of 1823. Meetings to endorse Jackson were organized all over the state; pro-Jackson candidates for Congress and the legislature were put up in most districts; office seekers were called upon to say whether they would vote against Williams for senator and for Jackson in the presidential election; and an unsuccessful effort was made to induce Jackson to aid his supporters by touring East Tennessee.[25]

One of the hottest contests was in the Knoxville district, home of Williams, Miller, and Judge Hugh Lawson White, where Miller had entered a Doctor Wiatt as the pro-Jackson candidate for the legislature against the senator's brother, Thomas L. Williams.[26] This placed Judge White in a particularly embarrassing position. One of Jackson's oldest friends, a brother-in-law of Overton, and long a leader of the Blount-Overton faction, White was also related to Senator Williams and reluctant to oppose him. When he took the Williams' side in the Knoxville legislative campaign, he and his sons became involved in such a bitter personal broil with the Miller-Wiatt party that several duels were barely averted.

"If Genl Jackson has any wishes or prospects of success, I never was more disposed to aid him than now," White explained to Overton; "but I will not, as far as I can prevent it, permit scoundrels by the use of his name, to effect their dishonest or dishonorable purposes." White never doubted that Miller's senatorial aspirations lay at the root of the Jackson-for-President movement. "The whole cry is that Jackson must be President," he complained. "They have no more notion of trying to make him President than of making me. If he had a wish that way, and there was any prospect of success no three persons in this State would aid him more zealously than me and my sons; but I will not consent that scoundrels under a pretense of that kind shall rule, or tyrannize, over me and mine."[27] Recalling these events later, White maintained that Wiatt was in reality for Clay, while Miller wished "to use the name of Gen. Jackson, only

[24] Claiborne to David Campbell, Sept. 9, 1822, David Campbell Papers, Duke University Library.

[25] Samuel Martin to Jackson, June 17, 1823, Jackson Papers; John Williams to Rufus King, Nov. 19, 1823, Rufus King Papers, New York Historical Society; James Campbell to David Campbell, Apr. 3, 1823 [misplaced 1825], Campbell Papers.

[26] J. G. M. Ramsey to Francis P. Blair, Oct. 5, 1835, Blair-Lee Papers, Princeton University Library.

[27] White to Overton, Jan. 30, 1823, Overton Papers. White expressed similar sentiments in a letter to David Campbell, June 19, 1823, in the Campbell Papers.

for the purpose of securing the election of .Mr. Adams, by dividing the western vote."[28]

When the state election finally occurred in August, 1823, the results were inconclusive. The Williamses defeated Miller's pro-Jackson candidate for the legislature in the Knoxville district, but Andrew Erwin lost to a pro-Jackson candidate for Congress, and a pro-Jackson legislator was elected in Erwin's bailiwick, Bedford County.

Meanwhile there had been two important new developments. First, an astonishing and unprecedented upsurge of grass roots support for Jackson had manifested itself in various places outside Tennessee. A veritable "contagion" of Jacksonism was spreading over Alabama, as an alarmed Clay backer had to admit, and it rapidly attained sufficient proportions to block the expected election of a Crawford man as United States senator.[29] Major Lewis had been sounding out North Carolina and Mississippi politicians with surprisingly gratifying results.[30] Most startling of all was the outburst of Jackson sentiment in Pennsylvania, stemming, as one of Calhoun's lieutenants sneered, from "the grog shop politicians of the villages & the rabble of Philadelphia & Pittsburgh."[31] But contempt quickly turned into intense concern when the swelling Jackson enthusiasm prevented the anticipated nomination of Calhoun by the state Republican convention in March.[32] Major Lewis was virtually the only member of Jackson's inner circle who seems to have anticipated anything like this. As early as October, 1822, he had predicted that Jackson's popularity with the masses would give him such states as Pennsylvania and North Carolina, that Calhoun would be forced to withdraw, and that Jackson would fall heir to the South Carolinian's following.[33] At the time it was written, Lewis' estimate had been the wildest optimism, but by the summer of 1823 it was a sober statement of a reality that was daily becoming more apparent.

Simultaneously with these surprising indications of his national strength, Jackson began demonstrating a disturbing independence of the Blount-

[28] Quoted in the Nashville *Union*, Sept. 25, 1835.

[29] James, *Jackson*, p. 370; Charles R. King, ed., *The Life and Correspondence of Rufus King* . . . (New York, 1900), VI, 494.

[30] Albert Ray Newsome, *The Presidential Election of 1824 in North Carolina*, James Sprunt Studies in History and Political Science, XXXIII, No. 1 (Chapel Hill, 1939), 90–91; Lewis to George Poindexter, Oct. 10, 1822, J. F. H. Claiborne Papers, Mississippi Dept. of Archives and History (copy furnished the writer by Dr. Edwin Miles).

[31] George McDuffie to Charles Fisher, Jan. 13, 1823, Charles Fisher Papers, Southern Historical Collection, University of North Carolina Library.

[32] James, *Jackson*, p. 370.

[33] Lewis to George Poindexter, Oct. 10, 1822, Claiborne Papers.

Overton faction on state issues. Entering Tennessee politics many years before under the aegis of William Blount, Jackson had joined the Blount men in land and mercantile speculations based on paper credit and political power. But his business ventures had ended in a bankruptcy that cured him of all sympathies for the speculative system. He was outraged, therefore, when Grundy, Overton, and Miller induced the special session of 1822 to pack the state supreme court with judges who would overturn an earlier ruling adverse to the land speculators and to pass a punitive law aimed at Patrick H. Darby, a self-educated attorney who had been bringing suit against the speculators' doubtful titles. When Darby established a newspaper in self-defense and announced for the legislature against Grundy from the Nashville district, Jackson upheld him warmly, which "put Judge Overton in a great state of fretfulness" and produced a perceptible coolness with Grundy.[34]

Banking was an even more important issue than land speculation in 1823. The banks, which were controlled by Blount-Overton men, had not paid specie on their notes for four years, and the new legislature would finally decide their fate. Here too Jackson's views were inimical to his managers, and he egged Darby on to expose the fraudulent misuse of federal pension funds by the Overton ally who headed one of the principal banks. Jackson was telling all who would listen, in fact, that he opposed all banks on principle.[35]

Thus by the time the new legislature met in 1823, Jackson's conservative managers were in a dilemma. Their candidate had begun to display his dangerous tendencies just at the moment when he unexpectedly became a major contender. Most mortifying of all, they had initiated the whole business. But Jackson's candidacy might still be killed. John Williams' reelection to the Senate would indicate that Jackson did not control his own state and keep worried politicians in states like Pennsylvania from jumping aboard the Jackson band wagon. Even Tennessee might be held for Clay after all.

The crucial importance of the Tennessee senatorial election was appreciated far beyond the borders of the state. Senator Ninian Edwards came down from Illinois to represent Calhoun's interests, while Thomas Hart Benton of Missouri spent several months in Tennessee on a similar mission for Clay.[36] When the legislature assembled at Murfreesborough

---

[34] John Spencer Bassett, ed., *Correspondence of Andrew Jackson* (Washington, D.C., 1926–1935), III, 194.

[35] Sellers, *loc. cit.*

[36] Elihu B. Washburne, ed., *The Edwards Papers* (Chicago, 1884), p. 207; John Williams to Rufus King, Nov. 19, 1823, King Papers; Benton to Clay, July 23, 1823, Clay Papers; Jackson to [Eaton ?], Oct. 4, 1823, draft copy, Jackson Papers.

in September, the little village was crowded with "extra members," who had flocked in from every part of the state to influence the legislators in the senatorial election. Judge White had come from Knoxville to "spread himself against Jackson,"[37] and was frequently seen with Senator Williams "in deep consultation on the woodpiles about the square."[38] The pro-Jackson delegation on hand to ensure Williams' downfall included Senator Eaton, Major Lewis, Thomas Claiborne, fresh from his defeat for the legislature on the anti-Grundy ticket, and Sam Houston, the dashing young lawyer who had just won a seat in Congress as Jackson's protégé.

During the preceding weeks, John Williams had been touring the state to line up his supporters, and despite Miller's active campaign the senator reached Murfreesborough with the assurance of a comfortable majority over the announced opposition. Much of his advantage arose from the fact that Miller was not the only politician hoping to ride into the Senate on Jackson's coattails. William G. Blount, son of the great speculator and a former congressman from East Tennessee, threatened to enter the race, while Jackson's old crony, the veteran East Tennessee politician, John Rhea, had actually abandoned his seat in Congress to offer as a candidate. Neither Miller nor Rhea would withdraw, and the Jackson men were forced into desperate efforts to stave off the election until they could unite on one of their two candidates. The least division would ensure the election of Jackson's notorious enemy and almost certainly destroy his presidential prospects.[39]

There is strong evidence that Overton and Grundy were now working for just this result, with the important assistance of Judge White. Since January, Senator Williams had been writing familiarly to Overton about his chances,[40] and now Thomas L. Williams implored Overton to come to Murfreesborough and help his brother. "As the friends of our opponents assemble to influence members and to promote the views of their favourite I think ours should be permitted an equal liberty," he wrote, betraying not the slightest doubt of Overton's sympathy. "Will you come up next week."[41]

Grundy, meanwhile, was leading the fight to bring on the election at

[37] J. G. M. Ramsey to F. P. Blair, Oct. 5, 1835, Blair-Lee Papers.

[38] Nashville *Union,* Sept. 22, 1836.

[39] John Rhea to Jackson, June 18, 1823, Jackson Papers; R. G. Dunlap to Jackson, July 2, 1823, *ibid.;* John Williams to Rufus King, Nov. 19, 1823, King Papers; *Correspondence of Andrew Jackson,* III, 201n.; Tenn. *House Journal,* 1823, pp. 20, 76–77; Tenn. *Senate Journal,* 1823, pp. 29–30, 37, 59–60.

[40] John Williams to Overton, Jan. 14, 1823, Overton Papers.

[41] Thomas L. Williams to Overton, Sept. 20, 1823, *ibid.*

once. "His vote had been firmly fixed from shortly after his arrival here," a newspaper reported him as saying in debate; "previous to that time a difficulty had existed with him on the subject which but one man [John Williams] could remove; and he now could say that the difficulty had been removed fully and satisfactorily, and he was now ready to give his vote."[42] This was merely part of a concerted effort to convince members that Williams was not unfriendly to Jackson and would not oppose his presidential aspirations. Simultaneously, Grundy introduced resolutions instructing Tennessee's senators to do their best to prevent the congressional nominating caucus. All of this convinced Jackson's friends that Grundy was leading the Williams forces and had introduced his caucus resolutions to obviate the most serious objection to Williams, the expectation that he would attend the caucus and help nominate Crawford.[43]

The suspicious Jackson men now sent a delegation to question Williams on his attitude toward the general, and when he equivocated, they dispatched a messenger urging Jackson to hasten to Murfreesborough and save the situation. Jackson refused to come, but he did insist on Williams' defeat and denounced Grundy and the other "schemers of the opposition."[44] By this time, as Governor Carroll reported to Clay, the situation was extremely "strange and uncertain."[45] When it became clear that Miller had too many personal enemies to overcome the well-organized Williams forces, the Jackson men persuaded the general to endorse Rhea, but even this left them three votes short of a majority. Jackson again refused to come personally to their aid, and the election could be staved off no longer.

Finally, in desperation, Eaton and Lewis had Jackson's name placed before the legislature as Williams' competitor for the Senate. When the messenger bearing this news reached the Hermitage, Jackson mounted up and left post-haste for Murfreesborough, arriving in the middle of the night preceding the election. Even with Jackson as a candidate and present at the election, Williams was beaten and Jackson elected senator by a vote of only thirty-five to twenty-five.

In Washington the following winter, Senator Jackson charmed friend and foe alike. Pennsylvania soon endorsed Tennessee's hero, most of Calhoun's support shifted to Jackson when the South Carolinian was

[42] Nashville *Whig,* Sept. 22, 1823.

[43] William Brady and Thomas Williamson to Jackson, Sept. 20, 1823, Jackson Papers.

[44] Jackson [to William Brady and Thomas Williamson], Sept. 27, 1823, draft copy, *ibid.;* Nashville *Union,* Sept. 22, 1836.

[45] Carroll to Clay, Oct. 1, 1823, Clay Papers.

forced to withdraw, and everywhere the popular enthusiasm for Old Hickory mounted.

Though Grundy, Overton, Miller, and White now joined Lewis and Eaton in the five-year campaign that carried Jackson into the White House, their situation was ironical. A movement started by obscure Tennessee politicians for their own local purposes had unexpectedly been caught up by a deep ground swell of democratic aspiration. The original Jackson promoters found themselves uncomfortably astride a whirlwind of their own devising.

None of these conservative men were fundamentally sympathetic to Jackson's social philosophy, as it began to manifest itself in the 1820's or as it was implemented in the 1830's. Old Hickory was hardly inaugurated before Miller went into opposition. Overton and Eaton evidenced their discomfort by trying to block Van Buren's vice presidential nomination in 1832. Overton died shortly afterward, while Eaton opposed the Jackson party covertly in 1836 and openly in 1840. Major Lewis dissembled from about 1833 on, professing friendship to Jackson but actually aiding his enemies. Judge White ran for President against the Jackson party's candidate in 1836. Only the adaptable Grundy, acutely sensitive to Old Hickory's popularity, managed to remain loyal until his death in 1840.

Since the foregoing account depends at some points on inference from rather ambiguous documents, it has been necessary to present much of the evidence in relatively raw form. This evidence each reader may evaluate for himself; but to the writer the following conclusions are clearly indicated:

1. Major Lewis and a few other politically inconsequential personal friends were the first Tennesseans to think seriously of making Jackson President, and these men could never have initiated the Jackson movement by themselves.

2. Jackson's nomination by the Tennessee legislature in 1822 was the work of Pleasant M. Miller, John Overton, and Felix Grundy, none of whom preferred Jackson personally and none of whom thought he had a chance to be elected, or even to be a major contender. Miller seems to have favored John Quincy Adams, while Overton and Grundy hoped ultimately to carry Tennessee for Henry Clay.

3. The primary motive of these "original Jackson men" was to use Jackson's popularity to achieve certain local political advantages. Miller, who apparently sold this strategy to Overton in January, 1822, was particularly motivated by a desire to succeed John Williams in the United States Senate.

4. Overton and Grundy, surprised by the ground swell of Jackson sentiment outside Tennessee and dismayed by Jackson's increasingly manifest social philosophy, sought to kill his presidential candidacy by securing John Williams' reelection to the Senate in 1823.

American history is full of ironies, but surely few are more striking than the situation of these conservative Tennesseans as they unwittingly launched the movement that carried popular democracy to victory in national politics. The episode in itself is hardly more than a fascinating footnote to the Jackson story, yet for historians it is significantly representative. Scholarly indifference to the local and particular ends that are often the springs of political behavior has shrouded much of our political history in a pervasive unreality. The Jackson movement originated in a curious amalgam of local machinations by obscure politicians and of broad national developments. The political system thus imposed on the country has continued to rest on just such an amalgam. We shall never understand that system and its history adequately so long as able scholars confine themselves to congressional and cabinet level materials, while regarding investigations at the base of political life as work for inferior talents.

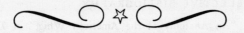

SELECTIVE
BIBLIOGRAPHY

In writing about the advance of Democracy in America historians have tended to accept the inevitable, and although they have their sympathies and preferences, they do not fall easily into new and old, or Federalist and Democratic schools. One helpful distinction to draw is between studies which emphasize constitutional development (mainly in the states) and those which pay most of their attention to the primary social and economic material of political life. American historians had always been aware of these elements; but the explicit search for material motives behind the democratic movement broke the surface in Charles A. Beard's *Economic Origins of Jeffersonian Democracy* (New York, 1915). Older studies which emphasize constitutional development but which attribute it, in varying degrees, to economic and social forces, still offer useful guidance, each on a state or regional basis: they include Fletcher M. Green, *Constitutional Development in the South Atlantic States, 1776–1860* (Chapel Hill, N.C., 1930); J. A. C. Chandler, *History of Suffrage in Virginia* (Baltimore, 1901) and his *Representation in Virginia* (Baltimore, 1896); William A. Robinson, *Jeffersonian Democracy in New England* (New Haven, Conn., 1916). More recent work tends to rely on more exhaustive research, though it is not always as clearly written as the older books used to be. There is much solid information in Paul Goodman, *The Democratic-Republicans of Massachusetts* (Cambridge, Mass., 1964) which contains an excellent bibliography.

The American Revolution had many bearings on internal democratic development. A soundly researched exposition of the American Whig position is in John C. Miller, *Origins of the American Revolution,* 2nd ed., with bibliography (Stanford, Calif., 1959); R. G. Adams, *Political Ideas of the American Revolution* (New York, 1920) remains a stimulus to thought. For the English and Scottish antecedents of American Whig principles, Caroline Robbins, *The Eighteenth Century Commonwealthman* (Cambridge, Mass., 1959) is essential; Clinton Rossiter, *Seedtime of the Republic* (New York, 1953) is a useful companion. Bernard Bailyn's Introduction, "The Transforming Radicalism of the American Revolution," to his edition of *Pamphlets of the American Revolution,* Vol. I (Cambridge, Mass., 1965) is a brilliantly written essay, which may be read in conjunction with a review article, "An Anatomy of the American Whig," in *The Historical Journal*, IX, 2 (1966). A revised form of Bailyn's essay has appeared as *The Ideological Origins of the American Revolution* (Cambridge, Mass., 1967).

Louis Hartz in *The Liberal Tradition in America* (New York, 1955) expounds a general thesis about American political ideas; for another absorbing analysis, see Yehoshua Arieli, *Individualism and Nationalism in American Ideology* (Cambridge, Mass., 1964). Representative institutions are traced in J. R. Pole, *Political Representation in England and the Origins of the American Republic* (London and New York, 1966). Chilton Williamson's *American Suffrage from Property to Democracy* (Princeton, N.J., 1960) supersedes previous works on this fundamental institution. A very good example of the value of work on suffrage and elections at the state level is Richard P. McCormick, *The History of Voting in New Jersey, 1664–1911* (New Brunswick, N.J., 1953).

Eighteenth-century Americans believed that political parties corrupted the freedom of elections. An unfavorable account of the influence of political parties on the democratic process, after a century's experience, appeared in M. Ostrogorski, *Democracy and the Party System in the United States: A Study in Extra-Constitutional Government* (New York, 1910). But the great majority of constitutional as well as political historians would subscribe to the view that parties help to make the Constitution work and have been vehicles of the advance of more democratic ways. A standard work is W. E. Binkley, *American Political Parties, their Natural History*, new ed., (New York, 1961). The formation of parties in the Federalist era, which forms an important part of the theme of this book, can be followed in: Noble E. Cunningham, *The Jeffersonian Republicans: the Formation of Party Organisation, 1789–1801*, (Chapel Hill, N.C.; 1957); Joseph Charles, *The Origins of the American Party System*, (Williamsburg, Va., 1956); a useful synthesis is William Nisbet Chambers, *Political Parties in a New Nation: The American Experience, 1776–1809*, (New York, 1962). To these must be added Richard P. McCormick, *The Second American Party System: Party Formation in the Jacksonian Era* (Chapel Hill, N.C., 1966).

The emergence of democracy is implicit in much of the political history of the first half of the nineteenth century, though it often seems to emerge through greed and intrigue as much as through ideological pressure. See, for example, Thomas P. Abernethy, *From Frontier to Plantation in Tennessee: A Study in Frontier Democracy* (Chapel Hill, N.C., 1932) for one aspect of the frontier; and for older states, Arthur B. Darling, *Political Changes in Massachusetts, 1824–1848* (New Haven, Conn., 1925), and Philip S. Klein, *Pennsylvania Politics, 1817–1832: A Game Without Rules* (Philadelphia, 1940).

An impressive brief interpretation of what Jacksonian Democracy was all about appears in Richard Hofstadter, *The American Political Tradition and the Men Who Made It* (New York, 1948); the view that class and ideological issues were involved is developed by a distinguished older study, Dixon Ryan Fox, *The Decline of Aristocracy in the Politics of New York* (New York, 1919); and again in Charles Grier Sellers' notable biography, *James K. Polk, Jacksonian* (Princeton, N.J., 1957). A strongly "committed" interpretation of the Jacksonian cause is in Arthur M. Schlesinger, Jr., *The Age of Jackson* (Boston, 1945); but this type of approach has been subjected to a searching challenge in Lee Benson's *The Concept of Jacksonian Democracy: New York as a Test Case* (Princeton, N.J., 1961).

The study of the frontier thesis begins with Frederick Jackson Turner, *The Frontier in American History* (New York, 1921). After a long period of severe handling (see, for example, Richard Hofstadter, "Turner and the Frontier Myth," *American Scholar*, XVIII [October, 1949]) it is finding some support, in forms that acknowledge the validity of some of the criticism; for this tendency, see Stanley M. Elkins and Eric McKitrick, "A Meaning for Turner's Frontier: I, Democracy in the Old Northwest; II, The Southwest Frontier and New England," *Political Science Quarterly*, LXIX (1954). And for a recent favorable reinterpretation, see Ray Allen Billington, *The Frontier Thesis: Valid Interpretation of American History* (New York, 1966). For the urban aspects of frontier development, Richard C. Wade's *The Urban Frontier* (Cambridge, Mass., 1959) rejects much of Turner.

There are many city histories and the most important general treatment is Carl Bridenbaugh, *Cities in the Wilderness* (New York, 1948) and *Cities in Revolt . . . 1743–1776* (New York, 1955); Carl and Jessica Bridenbaugh, *Rebels and Gentlemen: Philadelphia in the Age of Franklin* (New York, 1942) shows the growth of democratic politics; but we have no specific study of the connection between the rise of the city and the growth of democratic forms of government.

Collections of original materials tend to be grouped around specific problems or events. Bernard Bailyn (ed.) *Pamphlets of the American Revolution*, Vol. I (Cambridge, Mass., 1965) contains extremely good pamphlet evidence of the development of the democratic side of the American argument, and is to run to four volumes. The ideas of democracy and local rule entertained by opponents of the Constitution are gathered (not without criticism) in Cecelia M. Kenyon (ed.) *The Antifederalists*, (Indianapolis, 1966). *The Federalist*, of which many editions are available, contains much that is relevant to democracy. A good collection dealing with a critical phase of state constitution-making is Robert J. Taylor (ed.) *Massachusetts, Colony to Commonwealth: Documents on the Formation of Its Constitution, 1775–1780* (Chapel Hill, N.C., 1961). On constitutional reform in the states preceding the election of Jackson, see Merrill D. Petersen, *Democracy, Liberty and Property: The State Constitutional Conventions of the 1820s* (Indianapolis, 1966). Useful collections on Jacksonian ideas are Joseph L. Blau (ed.) *Social Theories of Jacksonian Democracy* (Indianapolis, 1954) and Edwin Rozwenc, *Ideology and Power in the Age of Jackson* (New York, 1964). Of the many published accounts by travellers, two are fundamental: Alexis de Tocqueville, *Democracy in America,* of which there are many editions, including a convenient abbreviation edited by Henry Steele Commager (London, 1961); and Michel Chevalier, in John W. Ward (ed.) *Society, Manners and Politics in the United States* (New York, 1961).

The development of an advancing subject tends to be registered in articles rather than books. Other than those printed in this volume, see: George D. Langdon, Jr. "The Franchise and Political Democracy in Plymouth Colony," *William and Mary Quarterly,* XX, 4 (October, 1963). James A. Henretta, "Economic Development and Social Structure in Colonial Boston," *W.M.Q.,* XXII, 1 (January, 1966). Roy N. Lokken, "The Concept of Democracy in Colonial Political Thought," *W.M.Q.,* XVI, 4 (October, 1959); Thad. W. Tate, "The Social Contract in America, 1774–1787: Revolutionary Theory as a Conservative Instrument," *W.M.Q.,* XXII, 3 (July, 1965). Fletcher M. Green, "Democracy in the Old South," *Journal of Southern History,* XII (1946); also, "Cycles of American Democracy," *Mississippi Valley Historical Review,* 48 (June, 1961). B. Katherine Brown, "Puritan Democracy: A Case Study," *M.V.H.R.,* 50 (December, 1963). Cecelia M. Kenyon, "Republicanism and Radicalism in the American Revolution: An Old-Fashioned Interpretation," *W.M.Q.,* XIX, 1 (April, 1962); also, "Men of Little Faith: The Antifederalists on the Nature of Representative Government," *W.M.Q.,* XII, 1 (January, 1955). J. R. Pole, "Suffrage Reform and the American Revolution in New Jersey," *Proceedings of the New Jersey Historical Society,* LXXIV, 3 (July, 1956); also, "Representation and Authority in Virginia from the Revolution to Reform," *Journal of Southern History,* XXIV, 1 (February, 1958); "Constitutional Reform and Election Statistics in Maryland, 1790–1812," *Maryland Historical Magazine* (December, 1960); "Historians and the Problem of Early American Democracy," *American Historical Review,* LXVII, 3 (April, 1962). Staughton Lynd, "Who Should Rule at Home? Dutchess County, New York, in the American Revolution," *W.M.Q.,* XVIII, 3 (July, 1961). Jackson T. Main, "The Origins of a Political Elite: The Upper Houses in the Revolutionary Era," *Huntington Library Quarterly* XXVII, 2 (February, 1964); Clarence L. Ver Steeg, "The American Revolution Considered as an Economic Movement," *Huntington Library Quarterly,* XX, 4 (1956–1957). J. Merton England, "The Democratic Faith in American School Textbooks, 1783–1860," *American Quarterly,* XV, 2, Part I (Summer, 1963); Hugo A. Meier, "Technology and Democracy, 1800–1860," *M.V.H.R.,* 43 (1956–1957). Paul C. Nagel, "The Election of 1824: A Reconsideration Based on Newspaper Opinion," *J.S.H.,* XXVI, 3 (August, 1960).

67 68 69 70   7 6 5 4 3 2 1